Meath East Co-Operative S

PRESENT

FROM THE NANNY TO THE BOYNE

A local history of the villages and townlands on the East Coast of Meath.

Compiled
By
Margaret Downey

Edited
By
John McCullen

Research by M.E.C.O.S./ FAS Participants

Published by Meath East Co-Operative Society Ltd., Bettystown, Co. Meath.
Printed by North East Printers Ltd., Industrial Estate, Donore Road, Drogheda.

Dedicated to the memory of Joe Kieran (1942-1998)

CONTENTS

Preface / Acknowledgements   4.
Foreward   5.

Chapter 1   "Distant Origins of East Meath"   6.
Chapter 2   "The Invaders"   17.
Chapter 3   "Monastries Dissolved"   33.
Chapter 4   "Rebellion, Drogheda, Years of Violence"   37.
Chapter 5   "Penal Times and More Rebellion   43.
Chapter 6   "A Turning of the Tide?"   58.
Chapter 7   "Famine and Disease"   67.
Chapter 8   "A Flavour of Mornington"   86.
Chapter 9   "Open for the Season"   101.
Chapter 10   "Good Sports"   114.
Chapter 11   "Railway People"   125.
Chapter 12   "The Murder at Coney Hall"   132.
Chapter 13   "New Century, New State, New Churches"   148.
Chapter 14   "Education and Care"   172.
Chapter 15   "The Stormy Sea`   181.
Chapter 16   "A Threat from the Sky"   186.
Chapter 17   "Modern Times"   191.
Chapter 18   "Cherished Memories and Changing Times"   197.

References   208.
Sponsors   216.

Preface / Acknowledgements

The creation of this book has involved many people and the completion of it became an important milestone in Margaret Downey's life. We have dedicated the work to Joe Kieran, who initiated the original idea. Joe died on the 7th February 1998, just as we entered the final stage of the work. May he rest in peace.

We wish to record our sincere gratitude and appreciation to the following people:
John McCullen, for his valuable time, energy and professional advice given freely and with great generosity. His wisdom and guidance remained consistent from the beginning to the ultimate completion of the book.

Jim Garry, Editor, of the Old Drogheda Society Journal, for a fund of support and assistance in obtaining references and research pieces.

Denise McDonough, Jackie Lynch and Caroline Hageman, for research work.
Mary McGee for her research on Ninch.

The Drogheda and Navan Libraries.
Especially - Andy Bennett and Frances Tallon, Meath County Library, Navan, Co. Meath.

The many local people who provided anecdotes, memories and oral history, and those who kindly lent us their cherished photographs and original material:

Sean and Tillie Faulkner,
Willow Kenehan,
Ted and Evelyn McCormack,
Dorothy McQuillan,
Marie Callan,
Brigid Weir and Tommy Weir,
Maurice Daly,
Paddy Monahan,
Bawn Drew,
Des Taaffe,
Patrick and May Reynolds,
Christy Reynolds,
Peadar McQuillan,
Maureen Taylor,
Dessie and Betty Lynch,
Frances Moran,
Mary Stafford
Leo Boyle,
Vincie Mullen,
Margaret Gordon,
Kevin Somers,
Pat Rooney,
Frank Johnson,
Pauline Lally,
Ann Kieran

And in conclusion Martin Hampshire (Supervisor). Anne Somers (Assistant Supervisor) for her assistance in the layout and preparation of the book for the printers.
Margaret Downey our final compiler whose dedication ensured the completion of the work.

We also wish to remember Michael Ward, a well respected local historian, who died 31st August 1998.

Foreword

Countless books and essays have been written and published detailing various aspects of the history of Meath from earliest times. Valuable research work has been completed over the years by dedicated local historians, but this is in fragmented form. A local history of our area has yet to be compiled.

This book has been compiled as a FAS Community Employment project under the direction of Meath East Co-Operative Society Ltd. While the project is not a complete account, it draws together for the first time an overview of the history of the area and reflects the diligence and enthusiasm of the researchers. This is but a compilation of such work to portray the area "From the Nanny to the Boyne", read and enjoy.

****

CHAPTER 1
"Distant origins of East Meath".

The village and townlands of Laytown, Bettystown and Mornington line the fringe of the County Meath coastline south of the Boyne Estuary. This small area of land has played a significant and unique part in the formation of Irish history since the arrival of the earliest settlers around 7,500 BC.

These Mesolithic (Middle Stone Age) people were primitive hunters and fishermen who probably sailed the short sea crossing from Scotland and settled along the coast and major river valleys of the North East of Ireland. At that time Ireland was extensively covered by forests, interrupted only by rivers and lakes, which gave access into the interior of the country. The location of the river Boyne as a navigable waterway probably drew the earliest colonists to populate the land at the entrance to its estuary.

The continuing importance of the Boyne in the making of Irish history is underlined by the construction of the distinctive megalithic monuments along its banks at New Grange, Knowth and Dowth, dating back to 4,000 BC, (the Neolithic or New Stone Age period). The Neolithic settlers brought with them the skills of agriculture. Their ability to cultivate land enabled them to establish permanent settlements, which marked the arrival of civilisation here.

The Boyne monuments, built around 2500 BC as passage graves and sites of ritual cremation are the first and most striking examples of about 1,250 similar tombs built north of a line from Mayo to Louth. Their use through pagan times and into the early Christian era (400-500 AD) as ceremonial centres of worship is confirmed by archaeologists dating of finds of rings, beads, brooches and bracelets.

By the beginning of the Bronze Age (2,000 BC) the Atlantic coast seaways from Scandinavia to the Mediterranean were busy trade routes and the North East became increasingly prominent. Irish bronzesmiths exported axes, spearheads, daggers and swords to Britain and the Continent. There is no doubt that the Boyne played its part in this trade and the tradition of seafaring has lived on in our locality through the ages.

The three most important historic intrusions into Ireland over the centuries which radically changed and influenced the course of Irish History, were the coming of the Celts about 600 BC, the coming of St. Patrick 432/3 AD and the conversion to Christianity, and the Norman Invasion 1169 AD.
The Tain is our earliest known chronicle of historical events. It dates from the seventh century AD and gives a picture of Ireland at the start of the Christian era. However, this is not to say that no events of pre-historic importance took place, but for obvious reasons, the long list of Milesian kings coming down in unbroken succession from about the tenth century before the Christian era, must be taken as legendary, and cannot be considered as historic truth.[1]
With the enormous contribution to history by archaeologists using a radiocarbon dating method, we are given a clear insight into ancient pre-Christian times which enables historians to piece together the pre-historic events of Ireland dating back as far as 7,500 BC.

By 600 BC, towards the end of the Bronze Age, Iron-using tribes led by wealthy chiefs, were establishing themselves in central Europe. These warriors were brave and fearless, made up of different peoples linked by a common language, dress, and way of life. They were known to the Greeks as Keltoi or Celts. Because of their superior weapons, they spread west to Spain, east to Asia Minor and north to England and Ireland.

The Celts entered Ireland at two points, west from the Continent, and north east from Britain.[1a] By the middle of the fourth century BC the Celts were established in Ireland. The changes they brought about in Irish native life were revolutionary and their influence has continued to be felt even to the present day. The use and manufacture of Iron, the concept of Druidism, the Celtic art form called La Tene. (Celtic art was divided into two periods: called Hallstadt and La Tene, from two towns, the former in Austria the latter in Switzerland, where the remains of Celtic settlements were found in the last century).

The Hallstadt period lasted from 1000-500 BC La Tene, from 500-Christian period, the latter (La Tene) is distinguished by its intricate delicacy and graceful symmetry), a language from which Gaelic is derived, the Clan system, and the rule of Kings, are all trade marks of Celtic culture. [2]

Apart from the great legacy of monuments and stone structures mostly in ruin, little remains of the Stone Age - hunters, farmers, herdsmen and bronze age metal workers, who had lived and died in Ireland for many hundreds of years. Their beliefs and traditions have all now disappeared. [3]

By 150 BC, well before the Christian era, Ireland was a Celtic country. Not much is known about the long line of Monarchs reigning in Ireland in the pre-Christian era.

However, there are some exceptions. According to O'Flaherty, Ollamh Fodhla, fortieth on the list of kings, was a conscientious ruler. He is remembered for establishing the first Feis at Royal Tara. Princes, Druids and Bards collectively assembled every three years to discuss old laws and their function, also to enact new ones. Records of these assemblies were kept, and duly updated at each Feis at Tara. The book in which these facts of history were carefully recorded was the Psalter of Tara, and was handed down to posterity as authentic History.[4]

Tuathal of Connaught, towards the end of the 1st.century AD crossed the Shannon and seized land around Mullingar, making Uisneach his Royal seat, during his reign as King of Ireland in the early second century, he imposed the Boro Tribute on the kings of Leinster. It was demanded of the succeeding kings of Leinster, which caused endless disputes and petty internal wars.[5]

Cormac Mac Airt, was the first king of Ireland to have his royal seat at Tara. He ruled Ireland from 226 to 266 AD, and was considered " a most illustrious monarch" and a man of great prudence. He was in a constant state of alert against a possible invasion from the Romans, who were holding Britain in bondage. But his fame is altogether surpassed by that of his son-in-law Fionn Mac Cumhail, leader of the Fianna. The exploits of Fionn and the Fianna have been illustrated by the genius of Oisin, the son of Fionn, who was a poet as well as a warrior.
However, King Cormac Mac Airt is described as Irelands first lawmaker, and as conqueror of Alba (Scotland) and of most of Ireland itself. In the words of the unbiased chronicler of Clonmacnoise, he was:
Absolutely the best king that ever reigned in Ireland before himself... wise, learned, valiant and mild, not given causelessly to be bloody as many of his ancestors were; he reigned majestically and magnificently. (Trans: C.Mageoghagan)

Myths and Legend
Christianity embraced many aspects of pagan Ireland; whatever was loved and respected of the old order was assimilated into the new ways. The stories of Fionn and his Fianna were no exception. Oisin, (son of Fionn) on his return from the Other-world of pagan Ireland (Tir-na-nOg) in search of the Fianna, found himself in the newly Christian land of Patrick's conversion and enabled these stories to be widely transcribed.[6]

Long, long ago, beyond the misty space,
Of twice a thousand years.
In Erin old there lived a might race,
Taller than Roman. [7]

The following is one such story, chosen from the many, because of its association with the Boyne.
After Fionn's father Cumhail was killed by the sons of Morna, his mother took him to Sleive Bladhma where he was raised by Bodhmall, the Druidess and Liath Luachra.
Fionn was taught wisdom and strength, by his two guardians, and only saw his mother once again when he was six years old.
When he reached young manhood, Fionn set off in search of Crimhall, his father's brother whom he believed lived in Connacht. When Fionn found Crimhall and the Fianna they were very glad to see him and hoped he would remain with them as their leader.

But Fionn had a thirst for more knowledge, and became a servant to a poet and seer named Finegas, who lived by the side of the Boyne River.

Taking the name of Deimne, he remained with Finegas for seven years, learning all he had to teach. Finegas waited by the side of the Boyne to catch the Salmon of Knowledge, for there was a prophecy fortelling that he would eat of it. At last, Finegas caught the salmon, and gave it to his young student to cook, instructing him on no account to eat any of the flesh. When the salmon was cooked Fionn took it to the old poet, who said, 'Have you eaten any of the fish'? Fionn shook his head. 'No, but as I was cooking it, I burnt my thumb, I put my thumb in my mouth to ease the pain'.

Finegas, then gave him the whole fish to eat, 'Your name is not Deimne, it is Fionn, and it was of you that the prophecy spoke'. Thereafter Fionn had only to put his thumb into his mouth to know whatever he wished, because of which he became known throughout Ireland - not only for his strength, but also for his wisdom.[8]

Cuchulain, (The champion of Ulster).

Cuchulain was another legendary Celtic warrior with strong connections to the Boyne and Nanny rivers. Cuchulain was renamed when he was a boy, he was originally called Setanta. He accompanied King Conor of Eamhain Macha, on a visit to Culann, as it was customary in those days for a 'man of means' to invite the King to a great feast in his house. Setanta arrived late and managed to over-power Culann's mighty watchdog. Culann lamented the loss of his great watchdog. Setanta said "I'll be your watch-dog". And so it was, they renamed Setanta CuChulain, which means Hound of Culann.

Legend tells us that Cuchulain's lady love Eimear came from a place called the Garden of the Sun God Lugh, which is known to-day as Lusk in Co. Dublin. Cuchulain was totally smitten by this beautiful maiden and vowed to marry her. On his many visits to her, Cuchulain and his Prince of Charioteers, Leag, had to cross the Boyne and Nanny rivers, and so, a strong association with this noble Celtic warrior from Ulster was established many centuries ago. The legend of the 'Battle of the two Bulls', Queen Maeve's white bull from Connacht and the brown bull from Cooley, with its many heroic deeds, glorious battles fought and won. The romantic adventures, which spilled over into Louth and East Meath, still lives strongly in the minds and hearts of the people from the Boyne and Nanny (Nemnech) river valleys.[9]

The sparkling river Nanny rises east of Tara at a place called Curragha and winds its way through the beautiful plains of Meath and enters the sea at Laytown (An Inis, the Inch of Holm). This beautiful river is associated through song and poetry with many legendary stories of this area: It was by this river that legend tells us King Cormac Mac Airt watched one of his "concubines", who was in an advanced stage of pregnancy, grinding corn in a quern along the river bank. She was called Cairnat, the daughter of the king of the Picts, and was very beautiful, and one of Cormac Mac Airt's favourites. He was moved to compassion as he watched Cairnat grind the corn, and to spare her labours, he ordered a mill to be built on the river. Thus, the first water-powered corn mill in Ireland was built at Sandyhall, Julianstown, on the river Nanny.[10]

The Mote:

About one mile from Laytown, on the north bank of the river, there is a large burial mound, known as the 'mote' (the meaning of the word 'mote' is either earth or dust), tradition says that this mound is the burial place of Laogh, who was the charioteer of Cuchulain.

Iron Age burial mound at Ninch, Co. Meath.

Laogh's Tomb:
In "The Triumph and Passing of Cuchulain" by Standish O' Grady, the charioteer says:-
"My mound of burial will be on the north bank of the river, hard by this ford, and my name will be on this place forever"

"Sleep lays his heavy thumbs upon my eyes,
shuts out all sounds and shakes me at the wrists.
By Nanny water where the salty mists weep over Riangabra,
let me stand deep, beside my father.

Sleep lays heavy thumbs upon my eyebrows,
and I hear sighs of far loud waters, and a troop,
that comes with boughs of bells............" by... Francis Ledwidge[11]

In 1973, the owner of this historic monument (Iron Age Burial Mound) at Ninch, Co Meath, having been granted planning permission to build a house on the site, commenced demolishing the mound. A preservation and guardianship order was placed on it, and in 1979 the National Parks and Monuments Branch of the Office of Public Works undertook limited archaeological excavation and conservation work on the monument. During the course of this work two inhumations were discovered near the base of the mound. A charcoal sample taken from immediately above the first burial gave a radiocarbon date of 1820±115 BP (UB No. 2425) and a sample of the bones from this burial gave a radiocarbon date of 1510±65 BP (GU No. 1453), which calibrates (using Clark 1975) to 460±85 AD.

The Burials:

The skeleton was orientated east-west with its head to the west and had an overall length of c.1.65m. The chin was leaning on the right shoulder giving it a slightly crouched look. The elbows were bent slightly outwards, the right hand rested on the lower pelvis and the left hand on the lower thoracic vertebrae. The skull had collapsed along the sutures in antiquity, probably due to the pressure of the mound. The right patella was missing and the distal end of the right tibia was broken both ends of right fibula and the right foot was missing. The broken and missing bones from the right leg are attributed to the bulldozing activity and this is demonstrated by the freshness of the breaks on the remaining fragments. Further examination of the skeleton indicated it was the remains of a mature male between twenty-five and thirty years.

The second burial is located immediately to the west of the first burial, and was partially exposed by persons unknown outside working hours. The exact morphology of this burial was not determined since the director of the project had no brief to excavate undisturbed areas of the mound. But the mode of the burials are very similar, and are almost certainly contemporary. A date for the burial and the charcoal deposit at the end of the Earlier Iron Age or the beginning of the Later Iron Age seems very probable. On completion of the excavation of the destroyed area of the mound and the recording of the burials, the site was reconstructed.[12]

The River Nanny

The river was also known by another name, Nemnech, which Laogh the charioteer called it. Nemnech meaning pearly, and according to Dinnseanachus, pearls were found on the riverbed, hence, the name.

St. Patrick was also associated with the Nanny River, and we are told he put a curse on it, and as a result, no salmon have been caught in it to this day. There are many versions of this story. The most popular one is that Patrick was in a hurry to cross the river at high tide, the salmon fishermen refused him passage because they had caught no salmon that day and were very disappointed with their days work. Patrick struck a bargain with them, that if they caught salmon, they would take him across, the fishermen agreed. On their next draft they landed the largest amount of salmon ever caught on a single draft. The fishermen became very greedy and broke their promise to Patrick. He was outraged and said, "there will never be another salmon caught in this river". Although the Nanny river is large enough to house salmon, no salmon has been caught in it since.[13]

The Nanny River and Ballygarth Castle in the distance.

The Nanny Water Stream..........by James McCullen (1848).[14]

Young men and maids, I crave your aids, assist my slender quill.
Until I relate the praises great along this purling rill.
There is Ballygarth, with skill and art, which proves on every side,
where the waves doth flo, both to and 'fro, by the rolling of the Tide.
Where young men and maids do walk and talk their evening joys to crown,
And the Colonel he and his fair lady in their small boat up and down.
I must away, I cannot stay, I have another view.
Within one mile of this grand pile on the North and South side too,
down by a brook my way I took where there by chance I espied.
A spacious building fine and new along the river side,
I heard the blackbird and the thrush as I did rove along.
The Chapel banks of Rogerstown it was their constant song-
that your stately walls may never fall, that was built in '32,
until longlost sheep return and seek salvation there it is true.
As I passed by I cast my eye upon that holy frame,
there I knelt down upon the ground for to respect the same.
Erected high, I did espie the cross in public view,
where longlost sheep whose wounds are deep, will be healed by the Heavenly dew.
There is Dardistown of high renown, which does much pleasure yield,
where the bleating lambs beside the dams adorns every field,
where I seen held in esteem that gentlemen to ride,
on a comely steed of the greatest speed along the river side.
There is Cooperhill in splendour still stands on the other side,
where the hunting lads are neatly clad in their scarlet coats dost ride.
Where the huntsman he does sound right free his bugle loud and shrill,
calling on the dogs to chase the fox to show sport their fill.
I moved along determined on these verses for to fill,
where I espied on the North side a blooming bleaching mill.
As white as snow all in a row the linen it was laid,
and on this grass there is no trespass allowed for to be made.
My heart does fill at Beamont mill that place I think upon,
while still remains there in great fame a worthy gentleman.
With praises great I must relate his name is Mr. J. McCann,
when the poor is filled at Beamont Mill, it is their next retreat,
and what they creave they shall receive at Mount Hanover gate.
I looked up then, that long white glen, I had Hilltown in my view,
where the primrose and the daisy spring beneath the morning dew.
Where you would meet in pairs, the fox and hares, askipping o'er the plain,
where the fleecy flocks and well fed ox spreads o'er the whole demesne.
I have to state of that ancient seat where splendour once did glow.
And nobles great rolled in pomp and state at Duleek here below.
But now that place is in disgrace which fills me with surprise,
that building wide is occupied by a minister of lies.
To Annesbrook fair I did repair where the streams do gently glide,
and cupid works most cunningly down by the river side.
Where the milking maids and Duleek blades together they do go,
with hand in hand along the banks in ranks to and fro.
But my joys were crowned when I looked around, and beheld the Castle Wall,
where Harry's breed did long succeed butmark what did befall.
A gentleman with gold in hand from Drogheda he came there,
And bought that place which does disgrace and leaves me in despair.

On returning to the time of the Celts we find that the Romans never conquered Ireland, which remained a separate identity from Europe. For many centuries Ireland enjoyed freedom from invasion, but internal feuds and battles for supremacy continued unbroken.

Ireland was divided into seven Kingdoms - Munster, Connacht, North west Ulster, North east Ulster, Meath, North Leinster and South Leinster. Each of these over-kingdoms was sub-divided into smaller kingdoms called tuaths, and, depending on its size, it could appoint a chief or over-lord. Each tuath operated a system of rank depending on status and material wealth.

Brehon Law

The law of the land in pre-Christian Celtic Ireland was called Brehon Law, and part of that law was the structure of society into tribes, tuaths or clans. Brehon Law derives its origin from Judge-made laws. Before one could attain to the rank of Brehon he must have had legal training of twenty years. The Brehons were men learned in traditional law. They were considered to be of the same status as Druids and Bards. The law was respected and strictly upheld. Transactions were completed by exchange and barter.[15]

In the fourth century AD, the men of Connacht, (The Connachta or Dal Cuinn), crossed the Shannon and destroyed the Ulster kingdom with its capital at Emain Macha. The greatest leader of the Connachta was Niall of the Nine Hostages. From two of his brothers descended the ruling families of Connacht and his own sons, the Ui Neill, founded kingdoms in North west Ulster and in Meath. The people who had formerly ruled from Emain Macha put themselves under the protection of the Ui Neill and formed nine little kingdoms known as the Airgialla (hostage-givers), hence the name Niall of the Nine Hostages. The capital of the southern Ui Neill was fixed at the old pre-historic site on the Hill at Tara, which was seized from the king of Leinster.

The occupation of Tara was followed by the migration of the inhabitants of the surrounding lands to south Leinster and Wales. They were replaced by the Connachta. Hostility existed between the inhabitants of the new kingdom of Meath and the Leinstermen until the beginning of the 6th century when the Leinstermen lost control of southern Meath.[16,17]

Around the period, early fifth century, St. Patrick, then a youth of sixteen years, was captured near Boulogne, by the kinsmen of Niall of the Nine Hostages and taken to Ireland with thousands of others. Patrick was sold as a slave to Milchu an Antrim farmer, where he spent the next six years of his life as a shepherd on Slemish mountain.
It is said, that Niall of the Nine Hostages met his death in the same area, where Patrick was captured.[18]

St.Patrick
To begin the story of St. Patrick, the following are two interesting passages taken from *'his Confession'*.

THE CONFESSION

Citizen of the Roman Empire 400 AD

'I am Patrick, a sinner, the most unlearned of men, the lowliest of all the faithful, utterly worthless in the eyes of many. My father was Calpornius who was a deacon and a son of the priest Potitus. He ministered in a suburb of Bannaven Taberniae where he had a country residence nearby'.

Joseph Duffy tells us in his introduction, that St Patrick wrote his Confession for the benefit, not only, for his friends but also his critics. He wanted them to know the truth about himself, when he had departed from their midst and was no longer around to defend himself against the charges of arrogance and incompetence which were raised against him.

> 'Let you be astonished, you great and small men who revere God! Let you, learned clergymen, heed and consider this! Who was it who called me, fool that I am, from among those who are considered wise, expert in law, powerful in speech and general affairs? He passed over these for me, a mere outcast. He inspired me with fear, reverence and patience to be the one who would if possible serve the people faithfully to whom the love of Christ brought me. The love of Christ indeed gave me to them to serve them humbly and sincerely for my entire lifetime if I am found worthy'.

There has always been difference of opinion as to the exact date and birth place of St. Patrick.
Joseph Duffy's *Behind the Legend,* account of the life of our patron Saint, is somewhat different to the popular romantic version which most of us learnt at school or read during our lives. However, the following includes some details of Patrick's life, which put an interesting slant on this old familiar much-loved story.

Patrick was born about 400 AD into an upper-class family of the diminishing Roman colony of southern Britain. The family left southern Britain and settled in the port of Bononia, (now Boulogne-sur-mer on the French side of the English Channel) where Patrick's father worked as a church and civil official. Patrick's boyhood language was the unpolished coarse Latin of northern Gaul, which was only slightly different from the dialect of Britain where he later lived.
At the age of sixteen he was captured with thousands of others, who were brought to Ireland as slaves. After six years he escaped and returned to Gaul, where there was widespread desolation from the raging civil war (420s) between the Roman Gauls and Visigoths. After many unrecorded adventures, Patrick reached his wrecked home at Boulogne, from there he continued on to his relatives in Britain, who welcomed him as one of their own.
During the following years Patrick made known his vocation, and studied at Auxerre the island monastery on the Yonne river. He was ordained deacon, and shortly after the death of Palladius (the first Bishop to Ireland) Patrick was consecrated Bishop of Ireland.
Patrick set off from Auxerre in 432 AD to return to the land where he spent his youth in captivity. But his mission to convert the Irish was far from being the instant triumphal success imagined by later biographers. He was a very young Bishop at a little over thirty years of age, and much younger than his counterparts in Britain, which caused unease. He lacked basic education, (secondary education in to-days world) he had no formal training in theology, and was constantly embarrassed, because he had made no arrangements for financial backing.
Patrick's mission to come back and walk among the Irish, was a vision and a direct calling from God, and it was likely that his enthusiasm and love of God did not allow him consider anything else with any great importance. But the constant barrage of ridicule about his lack of learning sowed doubts in his mind regarding his own competence and, sadly, he succumbed to his critics, temporarily losing sight of his dream.
After a lapse of seven/eight uneventful years in southern England, Patrick eventually found the courage to follow the call from the Irish, and so, with his helpers he sailed for Ireland. Five years into his mission in Ireland Patrick was once more called upon to defend himself. It appears his wayward past had come back to haunt him. Patrick was not without enemies, people remained jealous of his power and position in Ireland.
Germanus, (Patrick's mentor in Auxerre) on his deathbed, 'let slip' a confession made by Patrick many years before in Auxerre, about his boyhood days. This unexpected ordeal almost succeeded in destroying the saint's morale. When all seemed lost, he was vindicated in a dream. Patrick continued his work in Ireland with renewed peace of mind and heart.[19]

It would be difficult to conclude the story of St. Patrick without making reference to Muirchu and Bishop Tirechan's account, which describes the triumph of Patrick at Tara and his labours in Meath. Since the basis of this account is largely based on local traditions, and compiled nearly two hundred and fifty years after Patrick's death, we do not know if the events were set down in the order in which they happened.

Bishop Patrick landed with his companions at the mouth of the Boyne, and proceeded on foot to the hill of Slane. It was Holy Saturday and in accordance with the Christian practices, they proceeded to light the Paschal Fire. Laeghaire, son of Niall was King of Ireland, and the pagan festival was about to be celebrated at the Royal palace at Tara. There was a standing law forbidding any fire to be lit for a considerable distance around, until the great fire should be visible from the heights of Tara. King Laeghaire, his Druids and Nobles were outraged at the sight of the Paschal fire at Slane. The King demanded that the culprit be brought to him, and so it was that the first part of the remarkable conversion of the Irish people to Christianity took place on the plains of Meath. At the time of the Paschal fire it was remarked by one of the King's Druids that "unless that fire, which we behold be extinguished this night, it will live forever".

St. Cianan was born in 442 AD and is said to have been baptised by Patrick. Saint Patrick and his disciples founded many monasteries in Meath. We are told that the first stone church built in Ireland was erected at Duleek, founded by St Cianan, whose name is still celebrated in the locality.[20] The influence and authority of this great church and abbey would have extended the short distance to coastal Meath. Its importance as a centre of learning and worship continued through to Norman time.

In the years that followed, Patrick identified fully with his Irish flock, sharing in their lives and feeling for their problems. His life was long and active, there is no reliable date for his death, but it is considered 480 AD a reasonable assumption.[21]

St. Patrick's Well:
St. Patrick's Well is a small natural spring just east of the Dublin/Belfast railway line, and one hundred yards south of Mosney station. According to legend, St. Patrick baptised his first convert Benen at this well, who later became St. Benignus.[22]

St. Columba

Columba was born at Gratan (Little Field), Donegal, of noble birth with royal lineage by both parents. Christianity was well established in Ireland at that time, and Columba was born and baptized Christian. He became a pupil at Moville, Co. Down, (the Ecclesiastical School founded by St. Finnian in 540 AD) and there he was ordained deacon.

After leaving Moville, he went to Master Gemman, an aged Bard of Leinster, where he became confirmed in his love for the old poetic tales of Ireland, which, according to Irish tradition he retained throughout his life. From Master Gemman, Columba went to the monastic school of the abbot St. Finnian, the Wise Tutor of Erin's Saints, the most famous in Ireland at Clonard, which was founded about the year 520 AD.

(Columba got the name 'Colum-Kill'-'Colum of the Kill or cell'-because of the amount of time he spent reading his psalms in the cell (Tir-Lughdech) while he was still under the care of the good priest Cruithnechan, his foster parent).

Columba was ordained priest during his time spent at Clonard by Bishop Etchen, of Clonfad.

During the years 545 AD to 562 AD Columba founded many churches and monastic societies.

One of the most famous of ancient Irish manuscripts, the 'Book of Durrow', the Gospels of the Vulgate, still preserved in Trinity College, Dublin, is attributed to Columba's own hand.

Another of Columba's foundations was the monastery of Kells, in Meath, and from this monastery is named another famous and beautiful manuscript, the 'Book of Kells'.

Other Columban foundations were as follows: Arran, Boyle, Swords, Tory Island and Drumcliff. The most remote of his monasteries was that of Glen Columcille, in the most western part of Ulster.

Such were the foundations of a single holy man in that astonishing age of piety in Ireland.

However, Columba's greatest work was to be done among people, sunk in paganism, the Picts of Alban, who dwelt beyond the Grampians, in the eastern parts of what is now known as Scotland.

In 563 AD, Columba left Ireland, two years after a great battle between Diarmait, King of Ireland and Columba's kinsmen, the Clan Neill fought at Culdreimhne (now Cooladrummon), six miles north of Sligo.

According to tradition, Columba himself was the instigator of this battle between Diarmait and his own kinsmen, for the purpose of avenging two grievances he had against the King. And, also according to tradition, because of this battle and the bloodshed, Columba left Ireland forever, and made Iona *'his everlasting rest'*.

One grievance was that Diarmait had slain Columba's clansman, young Prince Curnan, who had taken sanctuary with him (Columba), after having caused the death of a playfellow during sports at Tara. The second grievance was a decision given against him by Diarmait, regarding the ownership of a book, which Columba considered very unjust. On a visit to Clonard, St. Columba secretly made a copy of the beautiful book of the Psalms, kept by the Abbot Finnian in the church. When the abbot found out, he demanded the copy as his right, Columba refused to hand it over. The dispute was brought before Dairmait, King of Ireland. The King's ruling was 'To every cow its calf, and to every book its copy', Columba was obliged to surrender the copy to his old master. Sorely grieved at his loss, he exclaimed, 'This is an unjust decision, O' Diarmait, and I will be avenged!'

In 563 Columba sailed north from his beloved Derry to Iona and his new life. He spent the next thirty four years in Iona, until his death in 597 AD. Many books have been written about his great work on Iona, and his passion and love for Ireland his homeland. These can be obtained from the Meath County Library, in Navan.[23]

Of course St. Columba was associated with east Meath and around the Boyne valley. We have two churches named after the saint, St. Columba's in Colpe, and St. Columba's in Mornington, (the latter, possibly built in thirteenth/fourteenth centuries had a belfry, the ruins of which are still standing in Mornington cemetery today).

The following gives a brief description of 'holy wells' in the area, dedicated to Saint Columba or Columcille.

St. Columcille's Wells:
One is situated in the townland of Shallon, and tradition tells us this well has the cure of warts and sores. There is a small statue surmounting the well (it is unlikely that it represents Saint Columcille, as the statue dates from the fourteenth century) carved from oolite stone brought in from England. The second well dedicated to St. Columcille is at Minnistown, and is reputed to have the cure for toothache.[24]

Tara (the end of the glorious days, but the music lives on)
'Oh, to think of it, oh, to dream of it'.
Stand at the foot of Tara hill, this great and historic monument of our past, and imagine for a moment or two, what it was like in those days, many centuries ago, when life was so much different to what it is today. To the passing stranger they see a hill. It is just another hill with no important significance for them. But to the Irish, it is 'Tara' and the very word makes music, just to stand there in the peaceful tranquillity, and with a strong sense of pride in one"s past. One can very easily drift back in time and get a glimpse of the pomp and pageantry of those illustrious days.

We are told that King Diarmuid, (the 'eventual' successor to Tuathal 527-544 AD) was for certain, the last monarch to sit at 'Tara'. His arrogance and disrespect towards the monks and their kinsfolk, brought about his downfall. St. Ruadhan and other monks outraged at his bad behaviour went to Tara and cursed both Diarmuid, and Tara.

That ancient palace gradually fell into decay, its halls fell silent, and the lament of a modern poet is well known that the harp of Tara hung silent upon the palace walls. On the rare occasion on which its chords were touched it was only to sing of the ruin of Tara.[25]

The Harp That Once Through Tara's Halls

The harp that once thro' Tara's halls,
The soul of Music shed,
Now hangs as mute on Tara's walls
As if that soul were fled:

So sleeps the pride of former days,
So glory's thrill is o'er;
And hearts, that once beat high for praise,
Now feel that pulse no more!

No more to chiefs and ladies bright
The harp of Tara swells;
The chord, alone, that breaks at night,
Its tale of ruin tells:

Thus Freedom now so seldom wakes,
The only throb she gives
Is when some heart indignant breaks,
To show that still she lives!

Thomas Moore[26]

In the diocese of Meath there were eight Episcopal sees in ancient Christian times. Clonard, Duleek, Kells, Trim, Ardbraccan, Dunshaughlin, Slane and Fore. All of the above monastic settlements, with the exception of Duleek and Kells, were consolidated, and their common see fixed at Clonard before 1152 AD. The monastery at Duleek was founded by St.Cianan, who became its first Bishop and later the patron Saint.

For six hundred years an uninterrupted succession of bishops ruled here. Duleek is also a district of ancient crosses, churches and monasteries. The relics of St.Cianan and other saints were preserved here up to a couple of centuries ago. There are no records as to the whereabouts of these relics now, or as to when they were removed.
The Book of Gospels, which belonged to St.Patrick was committed to the care of this church.[27] Ireland adopted Christianity with great ease - the tendency of the Irish temperament towards a self disciplined way of life must have contributed to it.
Teachers in the new Christian schools worked extremely hard during the fifth and sixth century, boys learned Latin and became fluent in the language. The best of them could enjoy reading classical authors and writing excellent Latin verse.
There were also the Celtic schools of poets and lawyers in Ireland well established from pre-Christian times. For a considerable time these schools remained completely separate from the learning brought by the church.
One of the most exciting and historical facts of the seventh century is that these two quite separate worlds, of Latin and Irish, began to borrow ideas and techniques from each other, but the old method of learning by memory did not cease.
The seventh and eight centuries became known as the golden age of Ireland, a land, which had not been invaded since pre-historic times and was Christian for more than three centuries. However, at the end of the eight century disaster struck, and the Irish golden age was suddenly brought to an end.[28]

CHAPTER 2
"The Invaders"

In 795 AD long low ships with multi coloured sails became visible on the ocean. The Viking warriors armed with heavy swords and iron spears, raided and ransacked the monastic village of Iona, taking away valuables and slaves. These raiders returned in 802 AD, and again in 806A.D, at which time they murdered many of the monks. During this period, other monastic settlements around the Irish coast, which were easily accessible, were also being looted and plundered. This pagan tribe of invaders came from Norway and parts of Scandinavia, they were commonly known as the Vikings, in their homeland they were farmers and seamen, skilled in many crafts.

By 837 AD the voyagers and invaders from Norway and Scandinavia became more organised on a much larger scale. There were sixty ships in the mouth of the Boyne and sixty more on the Liffy. They continued to plunder and raid the monasteries, murder and slaughter the monks throughout Ireland, but the chief Viking effort became apparent and was directed at the seizure of land for settlement. The Scandinavian populations were growing too big for the amount of farmland available at home.[1]

The abbey of Duleek, was plundered by the Viking/Danes in the years 830 AD and 878 AD and also in the following years 1023,1033 and 1037 AD.[2]
We are told that in 1032 AD, Sitric the Danish Chief landed at Colpe (the mouth of the Boyne), and proceeded from there to Mornington, where he defeated the local inhabitants in the "battle of Mornington" with the loss of nearly three hundred men.[3]

This must have been an isolated incident because Brian Boirimhe (Boru), the then self imposed king of Ireland, defeated the Danes at the battle of Clontarf in 1014A.D. This great victory for the Irish marked the end of the Viking era, also the deaths of Brian and his son. The annals of Duleek tell us their bodies were brought by the monks of Swords to the abbey of Duleek, where they stayed overnight, the bodies were then moved to Louth and from there to Armagh, their final resting place.[4]

Ireland's encounter with the pagan warriors from the sea lasted a little over two hundred years. Nevertheless, they stamped their faces on Irish History, as fearless ruthless heathens who cared nothing for holy people, sanctuaries or sacred objects. This was mainly because the source which historians had access to was limited and came mostly from the records kept by the monasteries. The Norse left many permanent marks on the Irish apart from plundering and murdering. Some of them became Christian while more of them inter-married with the Irish. Even before the battle of Clontarf, Dublin had begun to mint silver coins, the first ever in Ireland, which continued to the time of the Normans. Words from their language were borrowed into Irish, especially in connection with ships and trade, also in our place names, (i.e. Stadr: homestead, Ulster, Stabannon, Stameen, Stamullen. Holm: an island, Holmpatrick, Skerries. Ey: island, Dalkey, Lambey).[5]

After the death of Brian Boirimhe (Boru) at the battle of Clontarf 1014 AD, the high kingship of Ireland returned to Mealseachlainn, until his death in 1022 AD.

There is some confusion as to who held the high kingship position during the following one hundred and forty years, however many kings claimed supremacy. It was not until Ruaidri Ua Conchobair (O'Connor) son of Toirdelbach Ua Conchobair of Connacht took the high kingship in 1166 that it looked like some kind of law and order would be restored in Ireland at last, similar to that existing in other countries in Europe. However, this last great hope for Ireland was short lived. The quarrels and rivalry between kings and chieftains continued.[6]

The Normans
The origin of the Normans is not certain, but it is possible they came from a similar background to that of the Vikings. They settled in northern France (Normandy) and became Christian. In 1066 AD they invaded England and gradually, over a few decades, most of England came under their control.
Unrest and violent bloody battles continued in Ireland, King against King, chieftain against chieftain, unwittingly paving the way for an inevitable Norman invasion of Ireland.

By 1155 AD, Henry 11 of England had already discussed Ireland with the Pope, regarding the religious and Christian disposition of the Gaelic Irish, and obtained the permission he needed to invade Ireland, so it was only a matter of time before it happened.

In 1166 AD, after the defeat and overthrow of Diarmuid Mac Murrough king of Leinster by his arch rival Tiernan O'Rourke of Breifne, Diarmuid sought the help of King Henry 11, in regaining his throne. Henry gave Diarmuid the permission he required to enlist the support of the Norman lords of Wales. Under the leadership of Richard de Clare, (Strongbow) the Norman forces landed at Wexford and through their military superiority quickly defeated the defending Irish in the south east of the country. They conquered vast areas of land and placed their leaders as lords over these territories.

In 1171 AD, Henry 11, worried at Strongbow's huge success in Ireland, came to Ireland to secure the submission of the Norman colonists. Most of Leinster was held by Strongbow as a vassal of the king.

Hugh de Lacy/ Establishment of the Monasteries/ Feudal System.

In 1172, the 'Kingdom of Meath' was given to Hugh de Lacy as a counter-balance to Strongbow. The organising of the 'Kingdom of Meath' was one of the notable achievements of the Normans and its success was largely due to the masterly talents of Hugh de Lacy. He sub-divided Meath amongst his followers and fellow knights, but retained most of the " Kingdom of Meath" for himself as seignorial manors. These large areas of land were further sub-divided into manors by the grantees. These manorial lords and the settlers who colonised Meath and other regions of Norman Ireland had to construct their own settlements. Hugh de Lacy also encouraged the Gaelic Irish to till the land and herd the cattle.[7]

In pre- Christian Celtic times the lands of Ireland were divided into petty kingdoms and tuaths. In Norman times the petty kingdoms became Baronies, and the tuaths became parishes, (subsequently subdivided again into manorial villages and hamlets) and have remained so to this day.

Settlements

The primary rural settlement form in medieval times was the manorial village (e.g. Marinerstown now known as Mornington) which would generally have contained a castle, a manorial house and a number of dwellings. From this settlement the lands of the manor, which held no open field, would have been formed.

In these medieval settlements, the castle, manor house and church were the most likely to survive because they were generally built of stone, while ordinary dwellings were constructed of mud and wattles. Associated with the manorial villages were a number of small hamlets which consisted only of dwellings with no church (e.g. Betaghstown now Bettystown and An Inis, the Inch of Holm, now Laytown). A number of these hamlets also contained a tower house or a large stone house, often with a bawne, which is a group of small dwellings. Virtually all these "hamlets" were located at a short distance from the manorial village and some were Betagh settlements. The betaghs (who were the servile tenants) occupied a separate area to the manor, and it is likely that on these lands they lived in small nucleated settlements, separate from the free farmers who lived in the manorial villages. However, the inhabitants of both these communities were concerned with cultivating the land.[8]

The diagram below taken from: Settment and Society in Medieval Ireland, gives some idea how these 'settlements' were laid out.

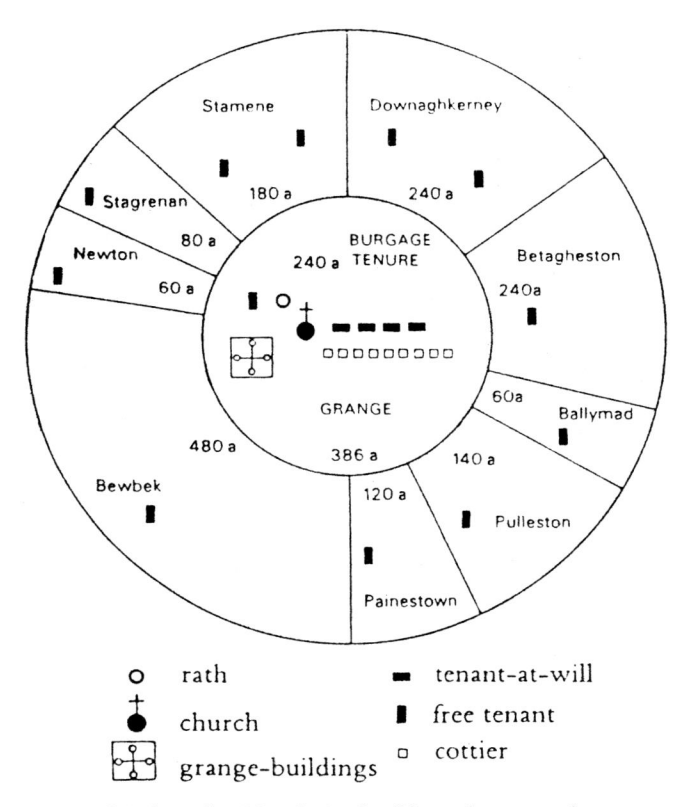

Spatial model of the manor of Colpe, Co. Meath, in the fifteenth century.[9]

Ninch (Nynche): - An Inse ('river meadow' or 'flood plain')

According to the Civil Survey of 1654 Ninch/Laytown (which is one townland, 'An Inse', but this name has varied in spelling and meaning down through the centuries!), is listed as one of the townlands of the parish of Julianstown/Stamullen, and bordering the parish of Colpe.

The following is only a very brief account of the history associated with this extraordinary place.

A typical Ring Fort/Rath in these areas would normally measure 30m or 60m in width. The Ring Fort/Rath on the hill at Ninch is approximately 25m wide and, according to the experts, the walls are too high. However, the little blue beads found there, signify some early Christian activity.[10]

Nynche, now known as 'Ninch', is in the barony of Lower Duleek. It covers the area from St. Mary's Church of Ireland, Julianstown to the sea at Laytown. The introduction of the Railway line 1838/1844 brought about a new boundary line to the parish of Julianstown/Stamullen. On the sea side of the railway line, we assume, that Ninch became part of the Laytown/Bettystown parish, formerly St. Mary's parish, Drogheda. The history and legend surrounding Ninch (Nynche) goes back to the time of Cuchulain and the Celtic period.

With the Nanny River flowing through this area, and its associations with legend and history, the contribution Ninch has made in the formation of our illustrious past is tremendous. Ninch, we are told, was the territory of the Cianachta, natives of east Meath, around the time of the Norse/Viking invasions in the ninth century. An entry in the annals of Ulster, dated 852, states- that there had been a slaughter of the 'foreigners' at the Inse on the East of Brega, Brega being the Irish for that portion of East Meath bordering the sea. History tells us Inse was the original name for Ninch at the mouth of the Nanny River.[11]

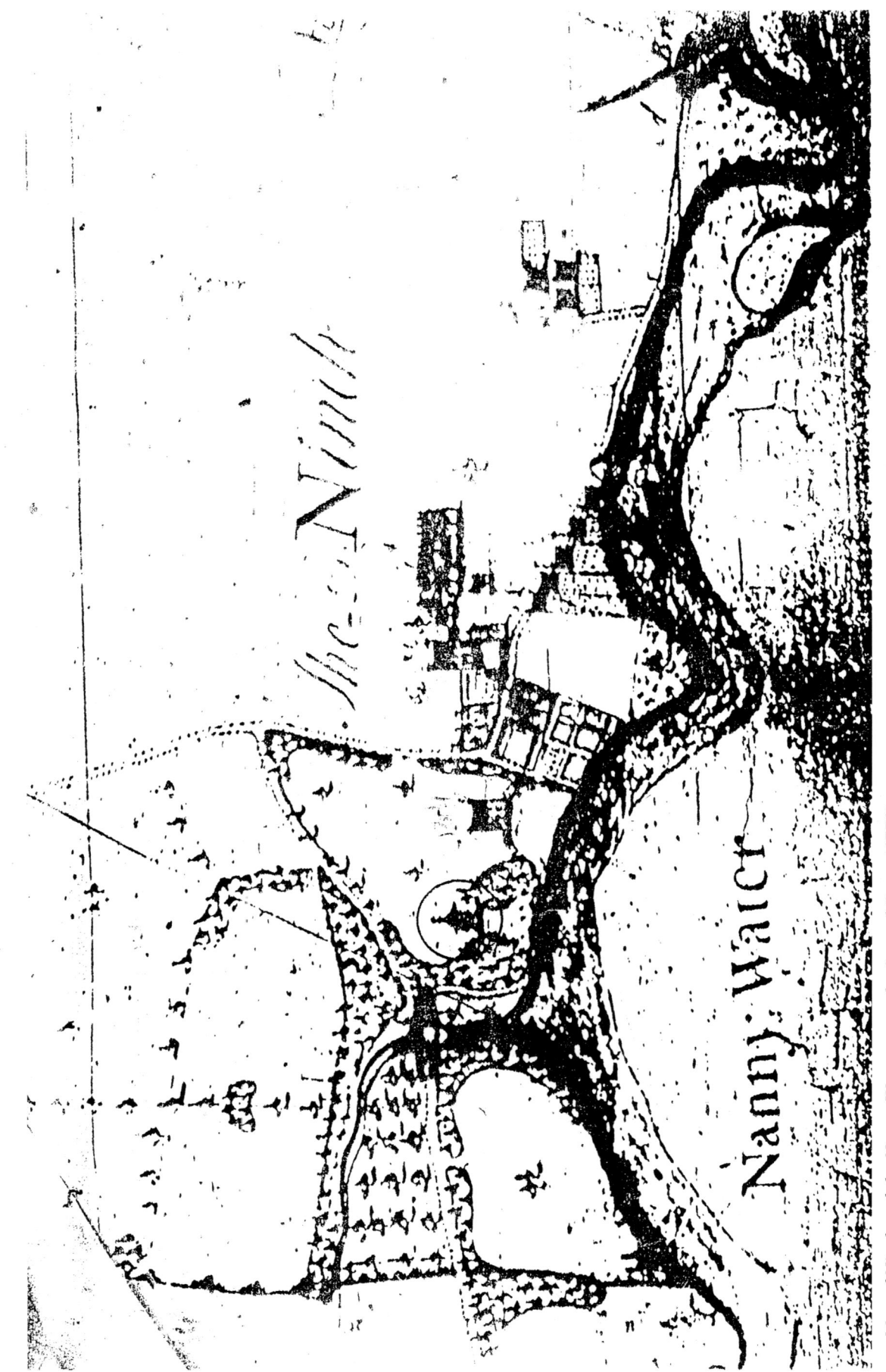

Map of Ninch and the Nanny Water.........by Samuel Bowe (1771).

The following passage is taken from the Gormanston Register (1175-1397).

Charter: In 1314, Johanna de Say, granted to her son, Henry Fitz Lenys, a messuage, one carucate of land, all her rent, and a fishery, with the lordship and services of her free tenants, in the Nynche, near Baligarre,(Ballygarth) in the tenement of Deuelek. To hold to Henry, his heirs and assigns for ever, of the chief lords of that fee, by the services due thereout; as in mills, waters, pools, streams, wells, weirs, fisheries, dovecotes, woods, moors, marshes, meadows, feedings, pastures, ways, paths, tollbolls, and other liberties and free customs. Johanna and her heirs will warrant.

Letter to be intentive: Johanna de Say to her free tenants and farmers in the Nynche, near Baligarre,(Ballygarth) in the tenement of Deuelek. She has given to her son Henry all her land, together with the rent, demesnes and services of her free tenants and farmers in the Nynche aforesaid, as in her charter is contained. She commands them to be intentive and respondent to him in everything concerning the said land, rent, and appurtenances. Dated 19th June 1314.

In 1388, Mariota, widow of Robert Fitz Leones (Lenys) son of Henry, released to Robert de Preston, all her right and claim to the lands, tenements, rents and services, in the manor of the Nynche, which formerly belonged to Robert.

In 1389, Nicholas, son and heir of Robert Fitz Leones and grandson of Henry Fitz Lenys, has forever released to Robert de Preston, knight, all his right and claim to all the lands, rents, services etc. in the manor of the Nynche. Nicholas and his heirs will warrant.[12]

Nynche (Ninch) became an important manor of the de Preston property, during the fourteenth and fifteenth centuries.

At the suppression of the monasteries by Henry VIII, the monastic possessions of Llanthony passed into lay hands.

In 1569, Francis Agard of Grangegorman, received a twenty one year lease on the lands of Julianstown, Dimanistown, Rogerstown, Nynche (Ninch), Laytown and Minnistown.

In 1640, the Civil Survey lists the proprietors of Nynche (Ninch) and Leatown (Laytown), as Lord Netterville, Hollywood of Arglagore and Roger Preston of Rogerstown.

In 1666, one hundred and thirty three acres in Laytown, were granted to the Duke of York, and later James II.[13]

In 1690, Gerald Peppard and Rory Oge (foster brother) from Swords were also associated with the manor of Nynche (Ninch) around this period. Ninch was part of the Preston estate well into the seventeenth century. Some local opinion suggests that Ninch became part of the Ballygarth estate during the last three hundred years, although retaining separate farms, perhaps, because of the river Nanny running through the lands.

The Ninch House is from the Queen Anne period and, according to Griffith's Valuation of 1856, Mr. Edmund Doran was the owner/occupier of the above manor house and estate, consisting of over one hundred and seventy eight acres. An update of Griffith's Valuation was conducted in 1922, and an Edith Dobbyn Pepper is listed as the owner of Ninch House and estate, while the previous owner is listed as Charles Pepper.[14] So it appears this part of the Ninch lands did belong to the Pepper family and was part of the Ballygarth estate for some years before Colonel Pepper died in 1927.

In the late 1940's Ninch west was taken over by the Land Commission, for division, but was sold instead to the Stafford family, resulting in a boycott by locals interested in getting part of the Ninch farm. However, due to great generosity shown by the Stafford family, the boycott died away quietly and this part of the Ninch farm remained with the Stafford family until 1977, when it was sold to Mr. Luke Van Doorslaer.

In the orchard of the now unoccupied Ninch House there is a dovecote (five sides) red brick structure, with three hundred and fifty pigeon nesting boxes. It is now roofless, but up to a few years ago, the roof was intact and was surmounted by a copper weathercock. Pigeon houses played a significant part in medieval domestic economy in Europe. Their importance as appurtenances of monasteries and manor houses is seen in the frequent reference to them in legal records and in the care, which was exercised in their design and construction.

Before the introduction of root crops to these islands in the early eighteenth century it was extremely difficult to winter sheep or cattle. It was realised that pigeons, especially the Mondain and Carneaux breeds, because of their exceptionally short breeding cycle, could provide an almost constant supply of fresh meat. Until 1800, the pigeon was a protected bird, detested by the small farmer on whose corn they freely fed until fit for the lord's table. Despite their legal protection it is likely that many privileged birds ended up in the farmer's stew pot.[15]

Ninch east and west, according to the present owner Mr. Luke Van Doorslaer, consists of around four hundred statute acres, not including the land on the sea side of the railway line. In the Down Survey 1655/58, Ninch is recorded, as consisting of three hundred and forty four acres, probably Irish acres. However, the last 'update', in 1922, of Griffith's Valuation, shows the total area of the townland of Ninch as consisting of approximately seven hundred and seven acres. In 1856, Griffith Valuation states: the registered land-owner of Ninch east as John Hammel and James Walsh as the tenant.

In 1913, the registered owner was Mr Owen Walshe, who died in 1914. Probate of his will made in July 1913, left the property to his widow Alice and his daughter Emily Mary.

In 1914, the property was sold to Mr. Bartholomew Grimes. In 1922, the property passed to his son Joseph, (Joe Grimes) who lived there for thirty eight years. In March 1960 it came on the market again, and was bought by a Mr. John Purfield, who was related to the Purfield's of Gormanston. In 1961 the Develter family from Belgium bought Ninch east, Mia Develter married Luke Van Doorslaer also from Belgium, and they are now the present owners of the entire Ninch farm. The house occupied by the Van Doorslaer family, was built around eighteen hundred and is also called Ninch House.
Before 1836, Ninch east consisted of nearly four hundred acres.[16]

Sonairte, The National Ecology Centre, Laytown, Co. Meath, is a small part of the 'the Ninch farm', situated on the lush grassy banks of the River Nanny. In 1989 approximately 7 acres was acquired by a few dedicated environmentalists on a long term leasing agreement with the owner Mr. Luke Van Doorslaer for the purpose of transforming this derelict eighteenth century farm centre into a twenty first century ecology centre, designed to demonstrate how best we can adapt our lifestyles to live in harmony with other life on this finite and precious Earth.
A visit to Sonairte on a Sunday afternoon brings to mind how people in the past worked with nature. This historical site containing the 6th century 'Rath', strategically commands a view of the river mouth and sea, also contains a Queen Anne period manor house in ruins, a sunny south facing walled organic orchard and garden of 1.8 acres, four old courtyards and a large windmill.
ìSonairte is the Irish for 'Positive strength', and seeks to show, practically, the actions that can be taken to safeguard the future of our children on this Earth.[17]

Nearby the Nanny meanders quietly to the sea. The name 'Nanny' would suggest a benign and caring body of water, but in fact the origin of this name is an Anglicised version of its original name Ainge, which comes from the word Aingidhe (Aingiall) meaning 'furious' or 'the irrational one'. This reveals the true character of the river, which has often unexpectedly flooded in the past.

*Our mountain brooks flow fierce and fast
O'er fell and rocks cascading,
The Shannon tide our land divides
Its beauty rare unfading,
There are rivers fine, like Nore and Boyne
Lakes and bays we've many,
But none so fair that can compare
With the winding river Nanny.*

by.... Tom Wiseman[17a]

Ninch Farm in 1948 - James Stafford and his two sons, Francis and Miuchael

The history of Ballygarth Castle has been well documented in many history books, a recent one being "The History of Julianstown", from which some of the following passages have been taken.

This ancient, mystical castle, overlooking the river for many centuries, remains a constant reminder of our history and our past. Not only is Ballygarth Castle very historic, it is also steeped in legend and folklore. The townland of Ballygarth was originally known as Beal-atha-Gairt, meaning-Fort of the enclosed field. The date of the erection of Ballygarth Castle is not known and the earliest documentary reference to it is in 1372. The West Wing and Tower being the oldest part, the rest of the current structure is a fortified or castellated mansion much of which dates from the eighteenth century. The castellation is mainly for decorative purposes and the building was domed until a great windstorm in 1839. The Castle and estate belonged to the Netterville family until it was confiscated as a result of the Cromwellian Plantation. In 1660, the Peppard family were confirmed in their ownership of Ballygarth Castle and estate by Charles 11. The Peppard family were large landowners from Ardee, whose ancestors came to Ireland with the Normans in the twelfth century. They were also prominent in the affairs of Drogheda. In the seventeenth century the Ballygarth estate was again confiscated, as a result of the Peppard family supporting James 11, in the Battle of the Boyne. However, this was only a temporary setback and they managed to retain ownership, which continued in direct line until the death of Colonel Charles Pepper in 1927.

Samuel Lover immortalised the Legend of " *The White Horse of the Peppers*" in story and, later, in a play, which tells of how the confiscated lands were recovered largely through the saga of a white horse belonging to Ballygarth Castle. Up to the present century a white horse was kept on the estate in memory of the original horse. The ruins of a church, which are in the castle grounds, enclose Peppard family graves from 1719. When the graveyard adjoining St. Thomas' church, Dublin, was demolished to make way for street widening, the remains of several members of the family were exhumed and interned in a communal grave in the grounds of Ballygarth Castle.

Along with the many major alterations made to the original Castle of Ballygarth the Peppers also acquired the lands and house of Moymurthy (Mosney) which remained in their possession until 1927. The last place in Ireland where oxen were used for ploughing was on the Ballygarth estate where they were working up to 1907. The oxen were imported from France. In 1979, Miss Wintle-Pepper died the last in the line of the Pepper family who lived at Ballygarth Castle for over three hundred years. Ownership of the lands returned to the English branch of the Barnwall family for a short period of time. In 1979/80 Frank and Ena Delaney from Co. Dublin bought Ballygarth Castle and estate. In September 1980 an auction was held on the premises to sell the contents of the Castle. Ministown in the east of Co. Meath became the Delaney's home for the following eighteen years. On the 13th December 1997 Frank Delaney died. After her husband's death Ena left Ministown, and returned to live in Donnybrook, Co. Dublin. Their son Brian is now managing the business of Ballygarth Castle and the estate.

Magh Muireadha -Millmurdery-Moymurthy- Mosney:
Mosney is a comparatively modern name, and the origin of this name comes from the famous printing-yard at a place called Mesney near Preston, Lancashire, England.
In 1798 Thomas Pepper introduced calico printing to Meath, when a cornmill at Moymurthy was converted into a printing mill. Smith & Co., a firm of calico printers, moved their business from Islandbridge, Dublin, to the new site beside the Bradan river.
One lasting result from that industry was the old townland name of Moymurthy replaced by the English name of Mesney (Mosney). This was not unusual in Ireland with many old Irish placenames, especially along the east coast, already replaced by an Anglicised version.
It states in the Gormanston Register records that Moymurthy was part of the Preston estate. In 1584, Moymurthy belonged to Sir Peter Barnwall. The Barnwall family was one of the most powerful and distinguished families in Ireland at that time. In 1598 a Castle there was considered amongst the most stately in Co. Meath. By 1641, forty three years later this elegant mansion or castle had disappeared almost without trace.
Mosney House, which is now part of Mosney Holiday Centre, was built on the site of the old castle. [18]

Mosney House, 1948

Butlin's Holiday Village, Mosney, officially opened to the public in July 1948. I was born and raised in Mosney. I can recall the general unease, when the quietude of Mosney was disrupted, when the trucks trundled in to build Butlin's Holiday Village. Before then it was mainly a farming community, with only three private dwelling houses in the actual townland of Mosney. Mr. John Oram was the owner of Mosney House and estate, the gate lodge, which was later occupied by Mr. John (Johnny) Byrne and his wife. Sean Lynch farmed the land adjoining Mr. Oram's land, he lived with his family in the farmhouse built on the land, which extended to the sea and included St. Patrick's Well just east of the railway embankment.

At the very beginning the small community of Mosney and the surrounding areas looked on the Butlin's Holiday Village with great fear and suspicion. The building of the Catholic Church at the entrance of the village made a huge difference and gradually local attitudes changed. Fr. John Brady (Meath Diocesan Historian) was the Roman Catholic chaplain in the 'Village' for many years. The beautiful painting of the 'Last Supper' by Bonifazio Veronese, placed over the main entrance inside the church, was very much admired by all who visited the church.

Butlin's Holiday Village was well and truly here to stay and with the early teething problems ebbing away, it brought with it, new life, employment and an air of prosperity to the area. It won the hearts of the Irish people and soon became one of the most exciting holiday venues in Ireland, especially if you were a child.

Management of the 'Village' in the fifties, were mainly of English stock. Major Noel E.E. Roper, was general manager, Mr. Kenneth M Newington was controller of the 'Village', while Mary Hebhilwhite was Major Roper's secretary. Mary Hebhilwhite took a great interest in the history of Mosney and could tell of many 'strange happenings' in Mosney House during her time there. According to legend many 'white' monks were slaughtered in the nearby woods trying to escape at the time of the Dissolution of the Monasteries. The Braden river we are told, ran red with their blood for days. Also, according to folklore, the imprint of a monk's foot was found on one of the stones in this same area, (near Shaffrey's bridge). Nothing further is known about this stone, or, if it ever did exist. Mary became Roman Catholic and eventually entered the Poor Clare Convent in Newry.

I remember Butlin's in those early years, not without a touch of nostalgia. One of my earliest memories was before the Butlin/Mosney road was built. All the visitors going to Butlins had to take the Richardstown road, which passes my house: buses and cars in those early years were just unbelievable, the constant stream of traffic by the gate was a regular Sunday occurrence. The Butlin road (now Mosney road) was built in 1950/51.

Sunday was the most popular for the day visitors, and many times we were able to by-pass the long queue by presenting Mrs Smithwick (who was a member of the Smithwick's brewery family) with a large punnet of freshly picked raspberries. This tiny lady would thank us graciously and let us pass through!
During the week we had to help on the farm picking raspberries and potatoes. We could hear everything that went on in the Holiday Village through Radio Butlin, from announcements like - this is Radio Butlin speaking - *there is a baby crying in chalet no. 5. or, Good morning campers, its five minutes to eight and breakfast will be served in five minutes time in the dinning-room, etc.*. But most of all it was the music which brought a great holiday atmosphere about the place. The gardens and lily ponds were exquisite. There was also the teams, Slane and Tara, and the rally call for each team went as follows: 2,4,6,8, who do we appreciate S.L.A.N.E. or, 1.2.3.4. who are we for T.A.R.A.

Every Friday evening, a Variety Concert was held in the 'Holiday' Theatre. It is very difficult to describe this show from all those years ago, but to young teenagers then, it was truly magnificent. The theatre auditorium could seat one thousand four hundred people and was always packed. A full orchestra seated just in front of the stage would play the opening melodies and suddenly the curtains went up for variety concert 'spectacular'. The following are just a few of the celebrities who honoured us with their presence during those early years - Danny Cummins, Jack Cruise, Phyllis Power, Eamonn Andrews, Cecil Sheridan and Austin Gaffney.

There was also Ursula and Noel Doyle who sang and danced together to a ditty called - 'Me and my Shadow', and so on.

After the show we would make our way to the Ballroom, just in time to hear 'Good night sweetheart, prayers and super over' for all the small children, before they retired for the night. When the ballroom was cleared, and not a child in sight, the resident orchestra would take over. Then the fun started, especially for us young teenagers, (we had to be home by nine o'clock!) so, we had just about an hour, to get a glimpse at the adult world in action, and the ballroom of romance in the making, those were wonderful times.

Other memories I have, were the interesting and unusual names on the different rendezvous, 'The Pig and Whistle', and the 'Wishing Well' lounge. The skating rink was a great attraction, as was the swimming pool with its high diving board, the weather was very agreeable, and for most of the Summer season it was sunny and warm, and many of the holiday competitions were conducted around the pool. Motor bike racing and Gymkhanas held in the sport's field were also very exciting events. These have long since gone, replaced by other interesting and exciting activities.

Butlins Holiday Village was sold to The Rank Organisation in 1973. Mr. Desmond Scaife was the then managing director. In 1981/82, Mr. Phelim McCloskey, a local man from nearby Drogheda, bought Butlin's Holiday Village and took over in December 1982. Under his new management the village was changed to - Mosney Holiday Centre. Since then great changes and major improvements have taken place.

The painting of the 'Last Supper' was sold at an auction in Christies, London, in 1983.

To-day we have a modern holiday venue providing all kinds of facilities, catering for thousands of holiday-makers, but geared especially towards the family, who come in their droves from all over Ireland and abroad, with special weeks during the season allocated to the handicapped, under-privileged and senior citizens. With the All Ireland Community Games held there in May and September, and the Classic and Vintage Car Rally/Show held in mid-June, and many more exciting events, we can safely say Mosney Holiday Centre has changed radically since the swinging 'fifties and sixties'. However it has managed to retain that special 'something' while catering for over two hundred thousand visitors during the holiday season, that makes them return over and over again.

In 1998 Mosney Holiday Centre celebrated fifty years in the holiday business, 'with fun for all the family', and are now well and truly part of these ever changing ancient and historic lands on the east coast of Meath. With the present owners Phelim and Betty McCloskey at the helm, backed up by people, some of whom are there since almost the beginning, families from all parts of Ireland can, no doubt, look forward to many more years of enjoyable holidays.

Mosney did not begin with Butlin's Holiday Village or the Barnwall family, or the calico printing mill, the name may have changed, but the place, is as old as the rivers, as old as history itself:

There are countless epics, historic and otherwise, many of which are related through legendary stories and folklore, associated with this place, that could keep one writing for weeks, but, for the present we will have to be content with the following:
The greatest warrior legends of this land, the introduction of Christianity by Patrick, the beach-head of the Pale and its retention for centuries through patronage and slaughter, have all a direct bearing on this one coastal townland, possible more intense than anywhere else in Ireland.
The culmination in our time of a Holiday Centre, unrivalled in scale and diversity in any other part of the country, begs the question that this can be no ordinary place. That here, there is something older than legend and tradition itself, something in the nature of the place, something that is the very mystery itself. To unravel it one has to fight a dragon, but, as in the quest for the Grail, the reward is simple, beautiful and enchanting.[19]

A woman out of here once offered Dunlugh O'Hartigan, two hundred years of life and joy, and an existence without death, cold, thirst, hunger or decay, if he'd only stop fighting for a single day. But Dunlugh joined the battle and 'foremost, fighting fell', which one supposes, is why he's remembered. This is sidhe country, and all must beware, but that being said:

"All is game, joy and glee,
Well is him that there may be". [20]

The Bradan river/stream.

Colpe Monastery

The medieval parish of Colpe in the barony of lower Duleek comprises of several thousand acres of land, sub-divided into twelve townlands, grouped together in south east Meath. They are as follows; Ballymad, Beabeg (Beaubeg), Beamore, Bettystown (Betaghstown), Colpe, Donnycarney, Mornington (Marinerstown) Newtown, Painstown, Pilltown (Pilton) Stagrennan and Stameen.

Colpe, which includes the Ecclesiastical Division of Marinerstown (Mornington) is situated on the south bank at the mouth of the River Boyne. In 1182, ten years after Hugh de Lacy 'Palatine of Meath' arrived in Ireland, he founded an abbey at Colpe, for canon regulars of St. Augustine, dedicated to St.Columba, and was made a cell of the Priory of St. Mary of Llanthony in Monmouthshire, Wales. Extensive areas of land were granted by Norman landowners to the various monastic houses established in Meath. Hugh de Lacy endowed the abbey at Colpe with the tithes of the lands at Coungerie and Donnacarney, the church of Marinerstown, also the church of Aney (Julianstown on the Nanny) including the tithes and fishing rights associated with the above areas mentioned and much more besides. Some of the Monastic houses in Meath (principally the Cistercian and the Augustinian) divided their lands into granges, (e.g. the grange of Colpe). A grange may be defined as an independent monastic farm, each unit being worked on by a team of lay people.

The lives of the native Irish in the parish of Colpe evolved around the Monastery, but the rules laid down by Hugh de Lacy were not all of religious fervour. One of his rules was that no native Irish person could be admitted into these religious houses, which at time we are told only served the gentry. This led to unrest and retaliation by the Irish chieftans by keeping Normans out of their establishments, which were very poor in comparison to the enormous wealth accumulated by the Abbeys. This did not work and the Normans took control of the local parish churches, which was part of their conquest. The Abbeys at Colpe and Duleek continued to flourish during the twelfth and thirteenth centuries and became exceedingly wealthy, holding many properties and hoards of gold and silver, not to mention the tithes due to them from the thousands of acres of lands in their possession.

The Normans can also be credited with the introduction of urban life to Ireland, and in Meath, they formed a number of Boroughs. The most important towns in Meath today originated from early Norman times. The earliest medieval borough in Ireland was Drogheda-on-the-side-of-Meath, granted by Walter de Lacy in 1194. Other Medieval Meath settlements, which obtained borough status included Colpe (1408) and Marinerstown (Mornington) (1235); described then as follows -

"the settlement consisted of a church, a stone tower, a mill and some messuages (dwelling places) makes it clear that despite its borough status, Marinerstown is no more than a manorial village".

The Normans established in Meath a system of settlement and agriculture, which revolutionised the landscape of the area.[21]

Hugh de Lacy

The Normans not only came to Ireland to conquer and transform, but also to adapt themselves to the country. They looked on the Gaelic chiefs as their social equals. Hugh de Lacy married Rose, daughter of Rory O'Connor, High King of Ireland, much to the displeasure of Henry 11 of England who was already deeply concerned about the rapid pace with which the Norman Lords were becoming exceedingly powerful in Ireland. Hugh de Lacy was killed on the site of the castle at Durrow in 1186 by a native Irish worker. In a short fourteen years, this man's power unequalled success and influence on the County of Meath (which consisted at the time of Meath, Westmeath, Longford, with parts of Laois, Offaly and Cavan) was to last for more than seven hundred years.[22]

Mornington, Co. Meath, at one time gave the titles of Earl and Baron to the Wellesley family of Dangan Castle near Trim.[23] The Castle was burned down in 1748, and in 1793, the lands and castle were sold to Captain Thomas Burrows.

St. Columba's Church of Ireland, which was erected in 1809, occupies a portion of the origional Abbey site. Archdall, writing in the last century, remarks of the ruins then existing: "The walls of the church in ruin are still to be seen here. The arches of which are both in the Gothic and Saxon style, and the east window appears much older than the other part of the building, and maybe, we suppose a part of the Abbey. On the north side is a small chapel, and to the south are two other chapels, one of which is at present the burial place of the family of Bellew".[24]

Colpe

The history of Colpe on the banks of the Boyne estuary did not begin with the monastery founded there by Hugh de Lacy. Colpe had already been a place of worship before the Normans: (one remnant of an earlier church lies in the porch of the St. Columba Church, it is a small high cross of the tenth century).

Small sandstone High Cross and base (Colpe, Co. Meath).

The cross discovered by Canon Ellison, formerly stood embedded upright in the ground about 8m to the south of the centre of the south wall of the Church of Ireland church at Colpe. It was excavated and described by Kieran Campbell, (Archaeologist), Laytown, shortly before Christmas 1981, when it was removed at the behest of the rector, Canon A. J. Nelson, to its present position in the church porch.

Description of the cross:

It is an imperforate sandstone cross 64cm high, 62cm across the arms and 20cm thick. There is a roll moulding on the edge of the cross-shaft and arms, with a narrower moulding inside it, but the ring bears only scant traces of mouldings. The moulding runs along the bottom of each face, which might suggest that the cross formed an entity in itself, but a tenon, now almost completely hacked away, on the bottom of the shaft suggests that it was supported beneath. There is a mortise hole on top, getting wider as it rises. The ends of the arms rise inwards at a slight angle.

A small sandstone High Cross and base, found in the grounds of Church of Ireland church, Colpe, Co. Meath. From the tenth century.

The directions (east/ west) given below are notional.

Fig. 176 East Face

At the centre of the head there is a slightly domed boss, surrounded by two circular ribs. The surface of the boss seems to have been somewhat damaged, but it was probably decorated originally, perhaps with interlace or fretwork. The arms are decorated with interlace, that on the left seeming to have a thicker ribbon than that on the right. The shaft bears an irregular, angular interlace.

Fig. 177 West Face

The centre of the head is occupied by the figure of the crucified Christ, clad in a short garment. His arms are long and emaciated, and they slope slightly upward towards the hands, stressing that the body is hanging on the cross. His legs are probably bound by a rope Flanking him are Stephaton and Longinus, though neither of the figures have clear attributes which could help to identify them. It is not clear if there is anything above Christ's head, but there would appear to be an unidentifiable figure at the end of the arm in a similar position to those on the cross at Duleek to which this cross is stylistically related. Beneath each of Christ's feet there is a spiral, out of which two serpents unroll themselves. One of the serpents from each of these spirals crosses a serpent from the other spiral and runs out along the bottom of the cross. The other two serpents respectively curl outwards and upwards in a semi-circle, terminating near the outer side of Christ's leg.

Discription of cross at Duleek
To the north of the modern church in Duleek stands a squat high cross, probably of the ninth century date. On the west face are the crucifixion and some scenes perhaps illustrating the early life of the virgin Mary. The cross is decorated with bosses, interlacing with two Evangelists symbols the eagle and the ox.[25/26]

COLPE is also well extablished in local folklore and legends.
The name Colpe (Cope), we are told derived its origin from Colpa the Swordsman, one of the legendary heroes of Milesian mythology in 1700 BC. Colpa, a son of Milesius, was drowned in attempting to land at the mouth of the river Boyne, resulting in the estuary of the river being called 'Inbhear Colpa'. This name was later transferred to the district south of the mouth of the Boyne river, which is known to-day as Colpe.

Rath-Colpa, is a flat topped circular mound about one 120ft in diameter and 15ft in height, situated north of the nineteenth century church, and is, according to legend, the burial place of Colpa the Swordsman.[27] The church of Rath-Colpa is referred to in ancient Irish records. The original church was supposed to have been founded by St.Patrick, but this is by no means certain, because of the confusion that still exists as to which river St.Patrick and his companions entered when they first arrived in Ireland, Inver Boinde (Boyne) or Inver Ailbine (Delvin). But the significant historical find made at Colpe in 1987 shows beyond any doubt, that soon after the time of St.Patrick there was a monastic settlement at Colpe. Over a hundred burials were discovered in a big enclosed church site. The Archaeologists have dated this monastic enclosure as "early Christian period", possibly sixth /seventh century. Items found with the burials have been dated as seventh century. This finding, in addition to the sandstone Cross shows evidence of a major Christian site.[28]

Prominent Anglo-Norman families
The following are some of the more prominent Anglo-Norman families, descendants of Hugh de Lacy, who retained large estates on the east coast of Meath (originally parcelled out at the time of the Norman invasion) through marriage and inheritances.

The manorial rights of Mornington passed from the **de Geneville** family to the **Cusack** ownership in the fourteenth century. The **Cusack** family arrived in Ireland with King John in 1210. **Sir Simon Cusack's** niece Catherine, was married to **Nicholas de Castlemartin**. **Nicholas** was seized of the castle and manor of Mornington, and other manors. There were two daughters of this marriage, **Joan** and **Anne.**

In 1386, **Sir Richard de Wellesley,** sheriff of Kildare (1416- 1418) married **Joan de Castlemartin,** (second marriage). In 1423, **Joan** with her husband **Sir Richard** received general pardon for the obvious errors of her father **Nicholas de Castlemartin.** And in her right added to her husband **Sir Richard de Wellesley's already very large estate the** manors of Kilskyre, Coulatyn etc., including the lands of Marinerstown (Mornington) Donacarney, Pilotstown (now Piltown) and Colpe.

They had five sons but **Christopher** was the only one to leave descendants.

Mornington was one of the earliest seats of the **Wellesleys** and remained in the possession of the family until the estate was broken up and sold in 1816.[29]

Arthur Wellesley, Duke of Wellington was born in 1769, he was nicknamed the "Iron Duke". Local belief is that **Arthur** was born in Mornington, Co. Meath, but there is no real proof of this. According to Canon Ellison in his article in Riocht na Midhe, there are eleven possible birth places, which include Mornington, Co. Meath the other places mentioned are as follows: Mornington House, 6 Merrion Street, Dublin (now 24 Upper Merrion Street) 114, Grafton Street, Molesworth Street, Dublin, Dangan Castle, Co. Meath, Trim in Co. Meath is listed twice.

The 11th, and last birth place mentioned is the most interesting of all, 'between Dangan and Dublin' now that could mean in a coach travelling along the highway between either place!, or it could mean in a 'stable'. The latter and most popular, being associated with one of the Duke's best remembered sayings, *"because a man is born in a stable does not make him a horse"*. The 'stable' story appealed to the romantic side of the Irish, something perhaps, they could identify with at that time! But the Duke of Wellington was probably making another statement in a very subtle way: the fact that he was born in Ireland did not make him an Irishman!

It is well documented that the Duke of Wellington was one of the greatest military men of all time, crowning a successful career by victory at the battle of Waterloo against Napoleon.

One of Ireland's most important encounter with the 'Iron Duke' was his handling of Catholic Emancipation, while he was Prime Minister in 1829.

He was appointed Chief Secretary of Ireland in 1807. At that time he 'mildly' opposed Catholic Emancipation, but was on the other hand very sympathetic to the Irish situation. He spoke out against absentee landlords and forbade triumphalist celebrations on the anniversary of the defeat of the United Irishmen at Vinegar Hill 1798. He expressed his concern many times about the ongoing deplorable poverty in Ireland. In 1814 he was created as first Duke of Wellington for his victory at Waterloo. In 1828 the Duke of Wellington became Prime Minister of England. In the same year Daniel O'Connell won a seat in County Clare, but was not allowed to sit in Parliament because of the remaining 'penal' laws in Ireland. The Duke of Wellington became acutely aware of this chronic situation in Ireland. At that time the King was totally against giving any relief to Catholics as this would reduce Protestant power. As a result of this opposition it was an uphill struggle for the Duke, as Prime Minister, to get support to have his Catholic Relief Bill pass through Parliament. In April 1829 Catholic Emancipation became law. He paid a dear price for supporting Emancipation for the Catholic Irish, his government was defeated in 1830, and a new government was formed.

The Duke of Wellington died in 1852 at the age of eighty three.[30]

In 1816, when Donacarney and Mornington were sold in the **Wellesley** estate auction **James Brabazon** was named as lessor. He was in possession of a "Substantial elegant spacious mansion, seated on a lawn a short distance from the sea, with offices of all descriptions".[31]

CHAPTER 3
"Monastries Dissolved"

This Monastic accumulation of wealth and general progress in Irish Medieval life came to an end in the sixteenth century, with the reign of Henry V111 and the Reformation, leading to the dissolution of the monasteries. The primary strategy of the government of Henry V111 after 1540 was that it sought to purchase the loyalty of gentry families by extending to them the benefits of dissolution. As it continued to be Tudor policy to use former church lands both to encourage and reward loyalty, it is possible to gauge the degree of favour in which a gentry family was held by reference to the number of land leases or grants it obtained. In 1558 the "grange of Colpe", comprising of one hundred and twenty acres, was granted to Henry Draycott (Remembrancer of the Irish Exchequer). The great bulk of the estates of Llanthony and both religious houses in Duleek and Colpe was granted by King James to Sir Gerald Moore.

The Reformation & Dissolution of Monasteries
The Draycott Family in Mornington

Edward & Elizabeth Becke
1514: Edward Becke was a Merchant from Manchester with a licence to trade freely throughout Ireland.
1534: Employed as a courier between the Kings Secretary (Thomas Cromwell) and several Irish people. His job was to advise the Secretary on the division of the spoils of land, i.e. former Monastic lands.
1538: In January, Becke himself got the lands of the abbey of Duleek and Furness Abbey including Mornington.[1] Edward Becke died in 1544 or 1548.

At that time Mornington consisted of about a thousand acres, most of this land was owned by the Wellesley"s of Dangan. Elizabeth wife of Edward Becke inherited the remainder of the land at Mornington, which became part of the marriage settlement between their daughter Mary to Henry Draycott.

Henry Draycott
Henry Draycott of Mornington profited significantly during his life from the dissolution of the monasteries. Considering the vast amount of wealth and property Henry Draycott managed to accumulate as a direct result of Henry V111's (King of Ireland 1541) government plan to *bribe or reward* (with former church lands) *loyal subjects of the 'established church'*. It is difficult to say where his loyalty lay. However, it is well documented that for the most part, his descendants were of Roman Catholic persuasion.

1541: Henry Draycott came from Derbyshire on 21st of April. He began his career in Irish administration, which was to last thirty one years. It is reported that in the same year a convent situated in Donacarney was granted to the Draycott family during the dissolution of the monasteries.[2]

1545: On the 23rd of September Henry Draycott was appointed chief Rembrancer of the Exchequer, he held this office for twenty one years.

1550: He lived in Dublin until his marriage in October to Mary Becke of Mornington. They had five children, John, Mark, Alice, Amy and Ismay. Henry Draycott had at least three more daughters, Elizabeth, Ann and Mary, who were probably married and settled before he made his will. In the course of the next fifteen years, he received title to numerous 'tithes' (i.e. a tenth of the annual produce of land devoted to the support of the clergy before the reformation, now converted into rent charge to be paid to the owner of 'tithes'). These 'tithes' expanded over a wide area of land and included rectories in the counties of Meath, Louth, Westmeath, Dublin, and Kildare.

1553: The accession of Mary 1 to the throne did not, as might have been expected, greatly disturb the security of those Meath families who had benefited from the reforming policies. Henry Draycott was confirmed in all he possessed and indeed, further extended his land holdings.

1558: The "grange of Colpe" described as comprising of eighty acres for tillage and forty acres for grazing, including a large stone house and other appurtenances was, together with two gardens in Marinerstown, devised by Philip and Mary (Mary 1) to Henry Draycott.[3]

1559: In October, Henry had most of the land converted into estate-in-tail which remained in the Draycott family for the most part, until the family died out in the early eighteenth century. From the late Cistercian Abbey in Furness in England, came three hundred acres in Mornington, four hundred acres in Beymore, two hundred and forty acres in Beybeg all in Colpe parish. Furness Inns in Drogheda and the Watermill called Glinnes in Mornington. Christopher Darcy of Platen obtained part of the monastery at Duleek and Colpe at the dissolution.

1562: Under the reign of Elizabeth 1, Draycott continued his steady rise on the 23rd January of that year he was appointed chancellor of the Exchequer. He was commissioned to *'Execute the Queen's ecclesiastical jurisdiction in the province of Meath and Armagh, with power to correct all heresies and ecclesiastical offences therein'*.

1563: In May he was ordered to administer the Oath of Supremacy to all persons 'that are within the words of the statute'. Henry Draycott had a strong antiquarian interest in the collecting and preservation of ancient manuscripts. Among the manuscripts he kept in his personal library in Mornington, acquired following the closing of the monasteries, were the register of St. John's hospital in Dublin and the black book of Llanthony, a fine manuscript missal, once the property of the church at Mornington.

1572: Henry Draycott died on 25th May of that year.
(In October 1568, Henry Draycott had been ordered to surrender Logher, held under a lease (June 1552) to Sir William Brabazon. However, in the inquisition of Draycott's estate, it was found that he still held one hundred and seven acres in Logher). Henry was succeeded at Mornington by his eldest son John who was born 24th August 1558. He does not seem to have had the same role in public life that his father had. His widow Mary re-married Owen Moore, who was granted the wardship of Draycott's son and heir John. He devoted himself to the management of his father's estate and to the care of his Library.[4]

The Death of Alice Draycott

1576, Alice Draycott daughter of Henry died. She was described as "a kind gentle woman whom the Earl of Essex was very fond of". Alice was an innocent victim of the planned poisoning of Walter, Earl of Essex. She was dining one evening with the Earl of Essex at the home of Nicholas Pentony, an Alderman of Dublin, when she drank from the cup intended for the Earl, and was accidentally poisoned. She died in great pain on the 9th September 1576 on her way home to Mornington. When Henry died in 1572 his three daughters whom he mentioned in his will were unmarried, so it maybe presumed that Alice was a very young woman at the time of her death in 1576, while her brother John, the eldest son of was only eighteen years.

A Document connected with Alice's death is of considerable interest. It is a letter of condolence addressed to her mother Mary, at Mornington.

The following is the letter addressed:
> To his lovinge Awnte Mistris Mary Draycott
> geve these at Marynerton

Dated 13th September 1576.

Awent, next unto our commendacons, your and owre late losse is suche as for owre partes we are inwardlie sorry and do knnowe that for your parte you cannot take it in good parte yet. We requiure you as hereto fore you have passed these events and chaunces by losse of as deere and nere friend as she was, that you will nowe take it in good parte and give unto God the praise therefor. She was His not yours. You were by Him Appoynted to be but hir norse and audix to bring hir up as a fytt maid. For Him who now I trust hath hit and must have us all, wherefore we require, sythe the chaunces of deathe be commen as well to princes as meane estates, that yt is the path we all must tread when or what tyme nothinge more uncertan, that you will nowe take unto you that consolacon, which we all hope one daye to see which is, that in the Resurrecon we shalbe gloryfied with our celestall Father in his Kingdome and be felloew heirs with his sonne Jesus our onelie savyoor: To you that are wyse sermoninge nedethe not, nether so wee dowpte, but that you will take all in good parte which God senethe. Desaringe you will pardon us, that we weare not at hir burial for she was buried before we knewe of any deathe neues of which was twsday night late. Thus we comytt you to the care of God. No more but that yt greveth us the losse of such person at Dublin XIIITH of September 1576.

Your poor friends and kynsfolke.

Robert Bisse
Margarer Bisse
Ciscely Fagan. [5]

1599: John the son of Henry was knighted on the 31st August in Dublin by the Earl of Essex the Lord deputy whose father was poisoned with John's sister Alice. One wonders whether the Knighting of John was in some way a long delayed recompense to the Draycott family for the death of Alice.

1632: Patrick Draycott (grandson of Henry Draycott) received pardon for accidentally causing the death of one John Lawless. The reasons given for the pardon were because he was the grandson of Henry Draycott who was held in very high esteem and also because it was the wish of several of the nobility and gentry of the Pale who were allied to him.

1639: Sir John Draycott (eldest son of Henry Draycott 1) died. He was succeeded at Mornington by his grandson John (the elder son of Henry Draycott 11). When he was about twenty eight years old he joined the Irish Army and was present at the siege of Drogheda in 1641. The following winter his home at Mornington was burned by troops of the English garrison at Drogheda.
(The forces under Colonel Wainmen advanced on Mornington, where they found the town abandoned. They raided the area and burned the houses including the house of Viscount Mornington, who was a Draycott. His library was seized, including a large parchment manuscript of an old missal consecrated to the church of Mornington).[6]

1642: It was fortunate that several of these ancient priceless manuscripts were rescured from the Draycott library, and preserved. John Draycott was outlawed for his part in the war. He died in 1663, and his son Henry claimed his estate as an innocent papist. He received a substantial part of his father's estate - Henry and his mother each received one hundred and fifty five acres in Mornington the rest of which went to Valerian Wellesley and Patrick Barnwall. His decree included Beymore and Beybeg with another six hundred and forty acres in Colpe.

In 1670, Henry married Elizabeth, daughter of Sir Thomas Leister in Middlesex.
They lived at Mornington until Henry's death in Nov. 1694. He died without issue.
The Draycott name is remembered in this area by a chalice dated 1689 given to Mornington parish.

The Draycotts of Mornington died out after five generations in Ireland.[7]

Fragmentary ruins at Donacarney, Co. Meath.

CHAPTER 4
"Rebellion-Drogheda-Years of Violence".

As a result of the conflict between the English Parliament and its allies the Scots with King Charles 1, the Irish, particularly in Ulster, took advantage of the situation and began to organise a rebellion.

In 1641 they planned a siege on Dublin Castle and to capture the principal members of Government, as well as organising a series of local risings. Their planned attack on Dublin Castle never took place due to the fact that the information was leaked to the English Parliament. But the local rising in Ulster continued according to plan under the leadership of Sir Phelim O'Neill. They attracted a lot of followers and support for their cause, which was to protect the King, and in particular to repossess their lands in Ulster and other parts of the country. When the Ulster Irish had established themselves in control of most of Ulster they marched south into Louth and Meath.

At Julianstown bridge, six miles south of Drogheda, they defeated a small detachment of Government troops marching to the relief of the town.[1] So many were killed and wounded on this occasion that the river Nanny flowing under the bridge, ran red with their blood. Around the same time the castle of Stameen was seized, with a similar blood bath, and a large quantity of corn was confiscated from the village of Colpe. In digging for building sand, many years later, the remains of human bodies mixed with fragments of armour and buckles etc. were uncovered. These finds were correctly attributed to the rebellion of 1641.[2]

Still under the leadership of Phelim O'Neill, they laid siege to Drogheda and were joined by the old English of the area; the combined forces called themselves 'the Catholic Army'.
Sir Phelim O'Neill had established his headquarters at Bewly (Beaulieu); his detachment also occupied the castle at Rathmullen together with the villages of Bettystown, Mornington, Old-bridge, Tullyallen and Ballymakenny.

On the 3rd March 1642, the Castle in Mornington belonging to John Draycott, Viscount Mornington (grandson of Sir John Draycott and great grandson of Henry Draycott) was burned by the troops of the English garrison at Drogheda. This was carried out in 'just revenge' for his fraudulent disarming of the soldiers as they were making their way from Julianstown bridge.

Draycott Castle at Mornington
There is some discrepancy as to the exact spot where the Draycott Castle stood before it was burned down in 1641/1642. The following are two examples from considered reliable sources:

According to Mary F. McCullen, (died 1970) Beamore, during the reign of Elizabeth 1, Henry Draycott remained a Catholic, but 'kept in' with the ruling powers in Dublin Castle. With some of the stones from the Abbey at Colpe he built a four storey house on the flat field, which lies between Donacarney House and the bridge at Mornington, through which the stream (the people of Beamore call 'the Bog', and the people of Mornington call the 'Colpa river') flows.[3]

According to Mr. O'Donohoe (I.T.A. General Survey 19/9/42): adjoining the Forge of Mr. Hugh Mc Cabe at Donacarney, three miles east of Drogheda, are the fragmentary ruins of 'Draycott's Castle'. This castle, originally the property of the Cusack family, was burnt by one of General Tichbourne's skirmishing parties from Drogheda on the 3rd of March, 1642.[4]
Note: According to local opinion, the ruins still visible at Donacarney, (near the place where Hughie McCabe had his forge for many years) belonged to a 'nunnery', which suffered the same fate as the Abbeys and Monasteries at the time of the Reformation. Also, according to local opinion, Henry Draycott acquired the 'nunnery' as part of his 'reward'.

Sir Henry Tichbourne belonged to an ancient Hampshire family, obtained the lands at Beaulieu from the Plunkett family (Sir Oliver Plunkett Baron of Louth) who forfeited them for their part in the 1641 Rising. On his way to Beaulieu Henry Tichbourne was equally successful in a siege in which the village of

Newtown was burned. The Civil War of 1641/42 continued with sporadic internal battles over the next seven years.

During this time Sir Henry Tichbourne travelled to England with Lord Brabazon and Sir James Ware, where they met King Charles 1 at Oxford to brief him on the situation in Ireland.

As Sir Henry Tichbourne himself described it *"that his majesty might understand the conditions of the Irish and nature and quality of their demands"*

On their return journey to Ireland the boat in which the party was travelling was captured on the Irish sea by English Parliamentarian rebels. They were brought to London, where they were placed under close arrest in the Tower. They were released in September 1645 when Sir Henry Tichbourne returned to his command in Drogheda.[5]

Cromwell/Drogheda 1649

It was not until the English Civil War came to an end with the trial and execution of Charles 1 in 1649, that events in Ireland took a decisive turn. The years of opportunity had been wasted in haggling and bargaining with Charles 1, while the really formidable enemy, the English Parliament, had built up its strength.

Cromwell was one of the main signatories on the warrant for the execution of Charles 1, in 1649. When that Parliament had disposed of Charles, and abolished the monarchy in its own favour, it turned its attention to Ireland. Their ingrained distrust of Catholicism was inflamed by exaggerated reports of brutality with which the Ulster planters had been treated in 1641. So when Oliver Cromwell landed at Dublin with a puritan army in 1649 his mission was not only conquest but also revenge.[6]

Oliver Cromwell was born at Huntingdon, England on 25th April 1599. He was the second son of Robert and Elizabeth Cromwell. He was christened 'Oliver' after his uncle, and as an extreme Puritan, his Religion was very important to him and played an enormous part in his life. At the age of twenty one, he married Elizabeth Bouchier on 22nd Aug. 1620. They had nine children. He was both a gentleman farmer and a member of Parliament, and in 1641, he was appointed Lord Lieutenant of Ireland.

Cromwell believed that God was behind him in his endeavours, and that he was partly invincible. As an extreme Puritan, he rejected any ecclesiastical authority and saw his campaign as the extermination of Catholicism, as he said himself, *"I fought with a bible in one hand and a sword in the other"*.

The storming of Drogheda in 1649, was really an extension of the 1641 Rebellion. Drogheda had proved impenetrable during the Rebellion when Sir Phelim O'Neill failed to take the town in the siege.

J.G. Simms writes :
'On Cromwell's way to Drogheda, he passed Gormanston Castle and tried to capture the infant heir of Lord Gormanston, but did not succeed'.
'Between Gormanston and Julianstown, two of his men stole a couple of hens from an old woman and Cromwell had both of them put to death in the face of his whole army, to prove his justice was impartial'.[7]

On September 1st 1649 Cromwell camped at Ballygarth. The next day he sent part of his army on to Drogheda. When Ormond heard Cromwell and his army were at Ballygarth Castle en route to Drogheda, he sent orders to Lord Aston to destroy the Castles on the Nanny river. Cromwell was too quick and had moved on with his cavalry to seize the castles at Athcarne, Dardistown and Bellewstown before the Royalist raiders could reach them.

The 'Camp Field' at Ballygarth is so called today as it is the one Cromwell used for a campsite for his army on his way to Drogheda.

On September 2nd 1649 Cromwell's Cavalry were in the immediate neighbourhood of Drogheda, on St John's Hill (Highfield) to the south west of the town to be exact. As Cromwell's army advanced, the Irish forces along the coast and in the adjoining parts of Meath (Laytown, Bettystown, Bellewstown etc.) hastened to obstruct his advance on Drogheda.

Cromwell himself spent some time on St.John's Hill, where he had a panoramic view of his prey! During this time his cannons landed at Mornington and were dragged ominously to be mounted on sites where Cromwell had now decided on for the maximum impact.

Esson Writes:

"When Cromwell examined the town he saw both its strengths and its weakness. The dominating position of Millmount and the importance of a single bridge impressed themselves on Cromwell's mind. He knew he must seize both at the same time. If Aston chose to abandon the southern garrison, a fresh assault, expensive in both casualties and time, would be necessary to reduce the northern part of the town. His main assault must carry his troops in great numbers through the breach to sweep around Millmount and to seize the bridge intact".[8]

After the final overthrow of Charles 11, son of Charles 1, at Worcester, Cromwell was made Lord Protector and ruled England until his death on the 3rd September 1658.

Much has been written about this man, who is generally regarded as a hero of the time, among historians in England.

'A man devoutly religious, constantly striving for righteousness.'(John Maidstone), a 'gentleman, and general protector' (Fleckno).

Drogheda was in fact only a minor milestone in terms of his achievements, yet like others it was a significant one. The level of emotional outcry caused by him is typified in D'Altons remarks: *The manner in which he carried out his indiscriminate slaughter on the first day and that nearly all human beings within Drogheda were murdered, some of them in cold blood four or five days after the first storming, makes a nonsense of his claims: 'and indeed being in the heat of the action, I forbad them to spare any that were in arms in the town'.* The town had been seized overnight, yet people lost their lives when the 'heat of the action' had long subsided.

Life after Cromwell

After the violent assault by Cromwell and his army, and the inevitable take over of the town, the Corporation comprised only of the Protestant gentry that had survived the onslaught, and the Cromwellian settlers who had been promised land. It comes as no surprise to the history readers of today the fact that the minutes of the Corporation from 1649 refer only briefly to the attack and slaughter of the town!

On the 10th day of October 1656 the Corporation displayed their absolute contempt for their Catholic brethren when they made an entry as follows,

Thus; 'Ordered that noe Papist from henceforth shall be made free of this Corporation'

(It was subsequently erased, as were other entries of similar text at the Open Assembly on 26th July 1672)[9]

On reading through the huge amount written about Cromwell, some of it praise and more damnation, an opinion would most certainly depend on which side of the Irish sea one came from. But from an Irish concept of how it was, it is hard to comprehend he was considered by many as a man of high principals and great righteousness and be able to justify his tyranny at Drogheda and Wexford.

The following passage from: Ireland 1649-1650 (The black curse of Cromwell)
by... Denis Esson, perhaps, would echo the sentiments of most Irish people!

Of what use are great men if they cannot rise above the narrow prejudices of their generation?

And now the Irish are ashamed
To see themselves in one year tamed:
So much one man can do
That does both act and know.

Marvel's lines may represent contemporary English opinion of Cromwell's achievements in Ireland, but in truth he had done much harm and little good. The memory of the massacres in Ireland is still alive, even after three hundred and fifty years have passed.[10]

The Battle of the Boyne 1690.

On the 1st. July 1690, King William of Orange and his 36,000 troops, faced King James 11 and his 25,000 strong army, across the Boyne at Oldbridge, just outside Drogheda.
The Williamite army battle lines of Dutch, English, German, Huguenot, French and Irish troops stretched for one and a half miles. Across the Boyne, the army of King James, lines of English, French, Irish and German stretched to the left towards the hill of Drogheda and back to the hill of Donore in the distance.

A tactical move by the Williamite forces in the early hours of the morning proved crucial to the outcome of the battle. About 10,000 Williamite solders were marched to the right to cross at the ford of Rossnaree. In response the Jacobites sent most of their best troops to counter this offensive action, leaving their defences at Oldbridge dangerously and decisively weak. Between 10.00 a.m. when William's elite Dutch Blue Guards crossed here at Oldbridge, and 2.00pm when King William had crossed one and a half miles to the left, a total of five crossings had been made.

Fierce fighting took place at each crossing with cavalry charges, artillery fire and infantry attacks. Once established, the Williamite's bridgehead weakened the Jacobite resistance and the battle moved towards Donore Hill. By late afternoon the Jacobites resistance had broken and the army had retreated towards Duleek. There was great confusion as the retreating Irish infantry got among the highly disciplined French who were arriving at Duleek at the same time from Rosnaree.
For a time there was complete disorder. However, after some time Colonel Zurlauben and the French, managed to restore order, the cavalry gained control of the pass over the Nanny river and the rest of the army got across the bridge safely. King James was advised to made haste to Dublin lest he fell into enemy hands. James together with the dragoons of Sarsfield and Maxwell departed the scene and headed for Dublin, and from Dublin to France.

Back at Duleek the French placed their five cannon on the high ground overlooking the Nanny. The French army came face to face with the Williamites as they arrived at the pass, which was a narrow bridge over the Nanny river. The French defence, together with the boggy ground, made the situation difficult, as crossing the Boyne, the Williamites were brought to a temporary halt, which miraculously assisted the safe retreat of the Irish Army. Many of the French army were later killed by the Williamites, as they continued their retreat towards Dublin. The Battle of the Boyne ended any hope of James 11 regaining the English throne. The war lasted another year and ended with the Treaty of Limerick on the 3rd October 1691. In Ireland this left the way open for the Williamite confiscation of lands and the Penal Laws.[11,12]
Enda O'Boyle describes the bridge of retreat in Duleek, today, in his account of the Battle.........
"On entering Duleek from the graveyard side, continue on to the centre of the village, which is dominated by a giant lime tree estimated as being three hundred years old. At this point turn left, continue a short distance to the bridge over the River Nanny, on a little further is the actual spot where the retreating Jacobite army crossed, enroute to Dublin, followed closely by the Williamites".

A plaque on this bridge reads:

"THIS BRIDGE WITH THE CAUSE WERE REPAIRED AND BUILDED BY WILLIAM BATH OF ATHCARNE JUSTICE AND JANET DOWDALL HIS WIFE IN THE YEAR OF OUR LORD 1587. WHO SOULES GOD TAKE TO HIS MERCIE. AMEN."[13]

The Bridge of retreat in Duleek (Battle of the Boyne 1690)

The Interchurch Group for Faith and Politics, published the following document, to mark the 300th anniversary of the Battle of the Boyne,
Battle of the Boyne, symbol past and present.[14]

Here are some passages taken from that document:
"The 300th Anniversary of any big event is certainly something to be marked. But for us in Northern Ireland the Boyne does not simply represent something in the past. It is a symbol of our values, of how we see ourselves today, three hundred years after the battle, the conflict continues!"

> *"Its near time that some small leak was sprung*
> *In the great dyke that Duchman made*
> *To damn the dangerous tide". (Seamus Heaney,*
> *Whatever you Say, Say Nothing)".*

A Christian response?

What would be a Christian way to remember the Boyne? Christian remembering needs to be based on what God has done for us and therefore what we must do ourselves. This should challenge us to respond in a new way. Remembering the past as a Christian means remembering with a desire to forgive and a will to change things for the better today. The way that the phrase "one of ours" is used in Northern Ireland often excludes "the other side". If we are really going to follow Christ we need to include the other. We need to enter into a new relationship with each other.

The Battle of the Boyne was a Protestant victory. It helped to ensure that Protestants would hold on to the position that they had gained in Ireland. Protestants owe their position in Northern Ireland today, in part, to that event.

The Battle of the Boyne was also a Catholic defeat. Defeated people are dangerous unless they are destroyed absolutely. That never happened in Ireland".

(The fortress or siege mentality of many orange men in Northern Ireland contains a fear of nationalist resurgence and a loss of their gains from 1690).

Our Legacy to the future: Victors or Victims?

"The history of the 17th century shows Catholics and Protestants fighting each other: some of them were natives to this island and some were immigrants or invaders. But all claimed to be Christian. The Protestant victory at the Boyne has left us all, both Protestant and Catholic, victims, with a legacy of bitterness, fear, division and enmity. If we do not want to leave this same legacy to our descendants, our only alternative is to create some form of new relationship of respect with each other. In the end, all of us will either become victors in Christ through a new partnership, or else we will all remain victims of our enmity with each other".

CHAPTER 5
"Penal Times and more Rebellion"

The Treaty of Limerick in 1691 marked the third great defeat for the Catholic Irish in the seventeenth-century. The Irish parliament was now entirely Protestant. Members of the Church of Ireland were restored to their positions as first-class citizens, Protestant nonconformists and Catholic were again made liable for payment of tithes to the 'established church', and a comprehensive series of new anti-Catholic laws were passed (Penal laws). By 1699 Ireland's export trade in manufactured woollen goods went into total decline.

Originally the aim of the anti-Catholic laws was to wipe out Catholic religion in Ireland, but by 1716 the laws against religious activity were almost non existent, as it proved an impossible task.

However, the penal laws which were stringently enforced, were those which excluded Catholics from parliament, government office, legal profession and from holding prominent positions in the army or navy. This was achieved absolutely by the qualifying oaths, for these professions, which no Catholic would take........

The oaths:
I do solemnly and sincerely, in the presence of God, testify and declare, that I do believe, that in the sacrament of the Lord's supper there is not any transubstantiation of the elements of bread and wine into the body and blood of Christ, at or after the consecration thereof by any person whatsoever: and that the invocation, or adoration of the virgin Mary, or any other saint, and the sacrifice of the Mass, as they are now used in the church of Rome, are superstitious and idolatrous.......

These qualifying oaths closed all chances for achievement and success in public life for the Irish Catholic, but those of them who could were free with some reservation, to accumulate wealth in other fields, trade and industry.
But for the masses of Catholic poor that formed the majority of the population of Ireland, severe poverty and wretchedness was caused, not by the penal laws, but by the tithe payments to the 'established church'. The ever rising population increased the demand for farms, as a result pushed up the already outrageous rent demands.[1]

Wolfe Tone, a liberal Protestant, speaking of these Laws, said that *'they reduced the Catholic population to a condition morally and spiritually speaking, below that of the beasts of the fields'*.
When these outrageous rents and tithes were not paid on time, the result was evictions, torturing, killings, burnings, transportations, hangings and riots on a daily basis.

Under the Penal Laws, a Catholic had no rights, civil or religious. In 1759, the Four Courts in Dublin ruled that, *'the laws did not presume a Papist to exist in the Kingdom, nor could they breathe without the connivance of the Government.'*
The Rebellion of 1798 did not just happen over night; it was the result of generations of injustices, oppression, and misrule, forced on the majority of the Irish people. To understand something about 1798 it is important to study the disastrous and inhuman conditions of the Irish 'peasant' who accounted for five-sixths of the population during the eighteenth century, while one-sixth 'the landed gentry', descendants of English and Scotch planters, lived a life of luxury and extravagance. *'Two peoples, a tyrant people and a slave people; existing on the same soil but without moral or social community; severed by a wide gulf of religious hatred, political exclusion, social enmity and legal proscription'.[2]*

The following poem appeared out of nowhere, I heard my mother recite it many times when I was a little girl. It may reflect some of the strife that existed in Ireland during that period in history. But now two hundred years on, looking back it is hard to comprehend !

'98

*'Tis the year of tears and trouble,
'tis the year of blood and hate,
of darkened hearts and roofless homes,
'tis the year of '98.*

*The people's hearts are broken,
their hopes are dead and gone,
they scarcely dare to breadth with sound,
each face so scared and wan.*

*For heavy as a thunderbolt,
swift as the lightening flash,
upon the patriots plot hath fallen,
the English vengeance lash.*

*The lands they'd hoped with arms to hold,
are but the faster bound,
and hopes that freedoms hand had raised,
are dashed again to ground.*

*The courtroom is crowded,
around the floor like statues soldiers stand.
The two whose doom this day has fixed,
are fettered hand in hand.*

*'Tis over now the foreman has spoken
the fatal words.
When hark, from out that silent crown,
a woman's voice is heard.*

*"Oh Sir my Lord, Oh Judge astor
you'll give me leave to speak,
I'm all they have, God help them now,
a mother old and weak.
One's an orphan, his mother died
and left the poor gausun,
but sure I love them both my Lord,
you'll spare them both arune"*

*" And may the Heavens be your bed,
may all the saints look down and bless you,
and you'll have the prayers of all
whose in the town."*

*Then rose a murmur strong and deep,
from out that silent crowd,
for mercy in the widow's boys
prayed earnestly aloud.*

The Judge is moved with pity,
but duty ties him down.
He tries in vain to steel his heart,
he tries in vain to frown.

"Good woman, these boys are all this day you have,
they toil that you may live.
The mercy that I can I'll show,
his life to one I'll give.

.So make your choice your foster boy,
whose mother's death did claim,
or him who is your only son,
say which you wish to name.

She bowed her aged head,
and bitter tears coursed down her cheeks.
Then she looked up and said,

"Oh Judge alanna, choose yourself,
say which you'd wish to take.
If I sent one to his death,
I'd not sleep quiet in my grave".

"Good woman, I can do no more,
one dies 'tis right and just.
Which one is saved depends on you,
so make your choice, you must"

One moment more and then she spoke,
"Oh Mike my darling boy,
its not because I love you less,
I'd die for you with joy.

But Patsy's mother is dead alana,
sure 'tis you will see her soon,
and tell her Mike I saved her boy,
God Bless you Mike arune".

A cheer arose among the crowd,
the Judge's eyes grew dim.
"Take both thy sons thou noble heart,
thou shalt not weep for them".

Then to the soldiers "Go" he said,
"oh Irish hearts so true,
its only English laws,
that find a fault, in such as you".[3]

The 1798 Rebellion

The first signs of rebellion in Meath in the 1790s became obvious at a meeting held by the Roman Catholics of Meath at Trim on 23rd October 1792.

The following gives a brief account of the United Irishmen in Meath at the time of the 1798 Rebellion.

During that sweltering summer of 1798, thousands of Irish people died fighting for freedom and the rights of man. The role of Meath in this rebellion has in the past been understated and ignored by historians. Brief as it may have been, Meath played a significant role, as events of this Great Irish Rebellion unfolded.

Tara:

Towards the end of May 1798 the United Irishmen of Meath decided to make their stand on the Hill of Tara. On Wednesday the 23rd of May, the Meath men encountered a military supply train; the escort of Scottish Fencibles together with some weapons and much ammunition were captured. On Friday the 25th of May a group of armed United Irishmen from Kildare joined the Meath Rebels. On Saturday the 26th of May over five thousand United Irishmen, mostly pikemen were on the Hill of Tara. Opposing the Rebel Army were Scottish Fencibles under the command of Captain Blanche. The local Meath Yeomanry were commanded by Lord Fingal a member of the same Plunkett family as St. Oliver and a leading Roman Catholic in the area, and Captain John Preston. Blanche launched his attack that evening, and as the five hundred Loyalists along with a cannon approached, the Rebels cheered loudly and charged the enemy cavalry and were cut down in large numbers.

Molly Weston from north Co. Dublin, together with her four brothers joined the Rebels at Tara. As the United Irishmen fled the slaughter she took command of the group stationed at the Church. They put up a magnificent and desperate defence, and nearly captured the cannon, but in their attempt, exposed themselves to a barrage of gunfire. Suffering from severe losses they were over-powered shortly afterwards. History does not record what happened to that noble heroine Molly Weston, but most likely, she lies with her brothers on Tara Hill. Although the rebels out-numbered the government forces by about ten to one, they suffered a disastrous defeat, after four hours of fighting.

Many factors contributed to this. The rebels lacked military training and discipline. They were confronted with trained military and a cannon gun, and armed only with pikes, suffering the effects of too much alcohol consumption, put deliberately their way by Lord Fingal. The rebels lost four hundred of their men, compared to about thirty of the loyalists.

The Battle of Tara was the first major engagement of the Rebellion and although the brave men of Wexford carried on the daring but futile fight, it is there on that bleak battle ground of Tara, that we draw our line on the Rebellion of The United Irishmen, 26th May, 1798.[3]

Paud O' Donohoe the blacksmith of Curragha was immortalised in verse by Patrick Archer. The following are just two of the verses taken from this famous Meath poem:

' Down on your knees, you rebel dog',
The Yeoman captain roared,
And high above his silvered crest
He waved his gleaming sword.
'Down on your knees to meet your doom;
Such is the rebels' due'
But straight as pikestaff' fore him stood
Young Paud O'Donohue.

And there upon the roadside
Where in childhood he had played
Before the cruel yeoman
He stood quite undismayed.
'I kneel but to my God above,
I ne'er shall bow to you,
You can shoot me as I'm standing,
Said Paud O'Donohoe.[4]

The Unveiling of Paud O' Donoghue Memorial

An impressive life-size bronze memorial, in honour of Paud O' Donoghue, the blacksmith of Curragha, who forged pikes for the pikemen of Meath in 1798, was unveiled by Una O'Connor, a direct descendent of Paud O' Donoghue.[5]

****

In the aftermath of 1798 the position of the gentry was consolidated. East Meath was no stranger to the 'landed gentry'. The descendants of the Scotch were Presbyterians who were numerous in north and east Meath, Kells, Moynalty, Nobber, and Kingscourt. The 'landed" gentry or 'the nobility' as they were sometimes referred to, enjoyed a good life in the fishing villages on the extreme east coast of Meath. They had privileged lifestyles, and dictated the pace, according to their requirements. On listening to some reports from local people old enough to have had parents from this period who could recall how it was for them, it seems the reign of the 'landlords' in the area was widely varied, from tyranny to generous and caring overlords.

Beaulieu House:

On a recent tour of Beaulieu House, we, the group led by James Garry who was the tour leader, walked quietly towards this silent mansion, (a giant silhouette against the sky in the twilight of the evening). As the great doors opened before us, we stepped across the threshold into a large magnificent reception area (a tall two-storey space). It was like stepping out of the present back into the past. These stately homes hold a great fascination for Irish people to day, we had entered the forbidden territory that constituted our precarious past, spanning several centuries.
The Beaulieu estate originated from the family of de Beaulieu, in Cumberland around the time of Edward 3rd, from which Sir E.T. Bewley decended. It became the Plunkett's estate from 1182, William Plunkett forfeited the lands to Sir Henry Tichborne in 1641, and from his family they passed through the female line to Aston, Tipping, Montgomery to the present owner Mrs Nesbitt Waddington (ninth-generation descendant of Sir Henry Tichborne).

The following is a brief description of Beaulieu House from the outside. It was built during the later part of the seventeenth century by Sir Henry Tichborne, and his son William. It is situated on the banks of the River Boyne, three miles down-stream from Drogheda on the Co. Louth side. This majestic house can be seen from the little bridge that joins the Colpa river to the Boyne estuary at Mornington, and it dominates the northern skyline. Beaulieu has long been considered the finest example of Irish domestic architecture to survive from the Restoration period. It is an elegant two-storey country house with a hipped dormer roof, big brick chimneystacks symmetrically massed and an emphatic eaves cornice.

Cement-rendered with pale redbrick trim, Beaulieu has two show facades, the west front and a south garden facade. The entrance is of seven bays, with the two end bays brought forward. It has corner quoins and a moulded first floor string-course. The windows are framed by flat brick surrounds, and the doorcase of fine-gauged brick consists of two Corinthian pilasters supporting a large segmental-headed pediment that bumps up to the sill of the window above. The arrangement of the dormer windows, three over the centre three bays and one above each two-bay projection, is a classic mid-seventeenth century practice and effectively balances the design.

The garden front is a simpler six-bay elevation with two doorcases, one in the centre of each principal room, both crowned by large pediments.[6]

The Brabazon Family:

The Brabazon family can be traced back to the time of Henry 1, around the time the Normans arrived in Ireland (1169)

The Brabazon family were the Earls of Meath and their estate included Kilruddery, Bray, Co Wicklow; which was built for the 10th Earl of Meath; it has been described as being 'the most successful Elizabethan revival mansion in Ireland'.

William Brabazon was created **1st Earl of Meath in 1627,** and this line of Earls continued on into the twentieth century. **The 14th and last Earl of Meath,** Anthony Wyndham-Norman Brabazon was born 3rd November 1910. He married Elizabeth Mary Bowlby the only daughter of Captain Geoffrey Bowlby. They had four children.[7]

A branch of the Brabazon family also lived in Rath House, Termonfeckin, Co Louth. The members of this Brabazon family are buried in the local Termonfeckin cemetery.[8] The Brabazon family of Mornington resided at Mornington House (Coney Hall) Mornington, Co. Meath. In nearby Mornington cemetery there is a plaque on the north side of the ruined gable of the pre-Reformation church, which bears the following inscription:

"The burial ground of James Brabazon Esq. Mornington. Chosen by him January 1794. Allied by the male line to the Earls of Meath and by the female line to the Earls of Mornington".[9]

The Earls of Mornington were the De Wellesley Family, and we can establish the connection with the Brabazon family to the Earls of Mornington through Allison De Wellesley. Mary Colley who married James Brabazon in 1686 was her grand-daughter.

The Brabazon of Kilruddery (Earls of Meath) are connected to the Brabazons of Mornington through Anthony Brabazon, who was a brother to the 1st Earl of Meath. Anthony's son James was a captain in the Army and was killed in 1676. His grandson also Anthony, born in 1688, is an ancestor of the Brabazons of Mornington.

Family tree of the De Wellesley and Brabazon families:

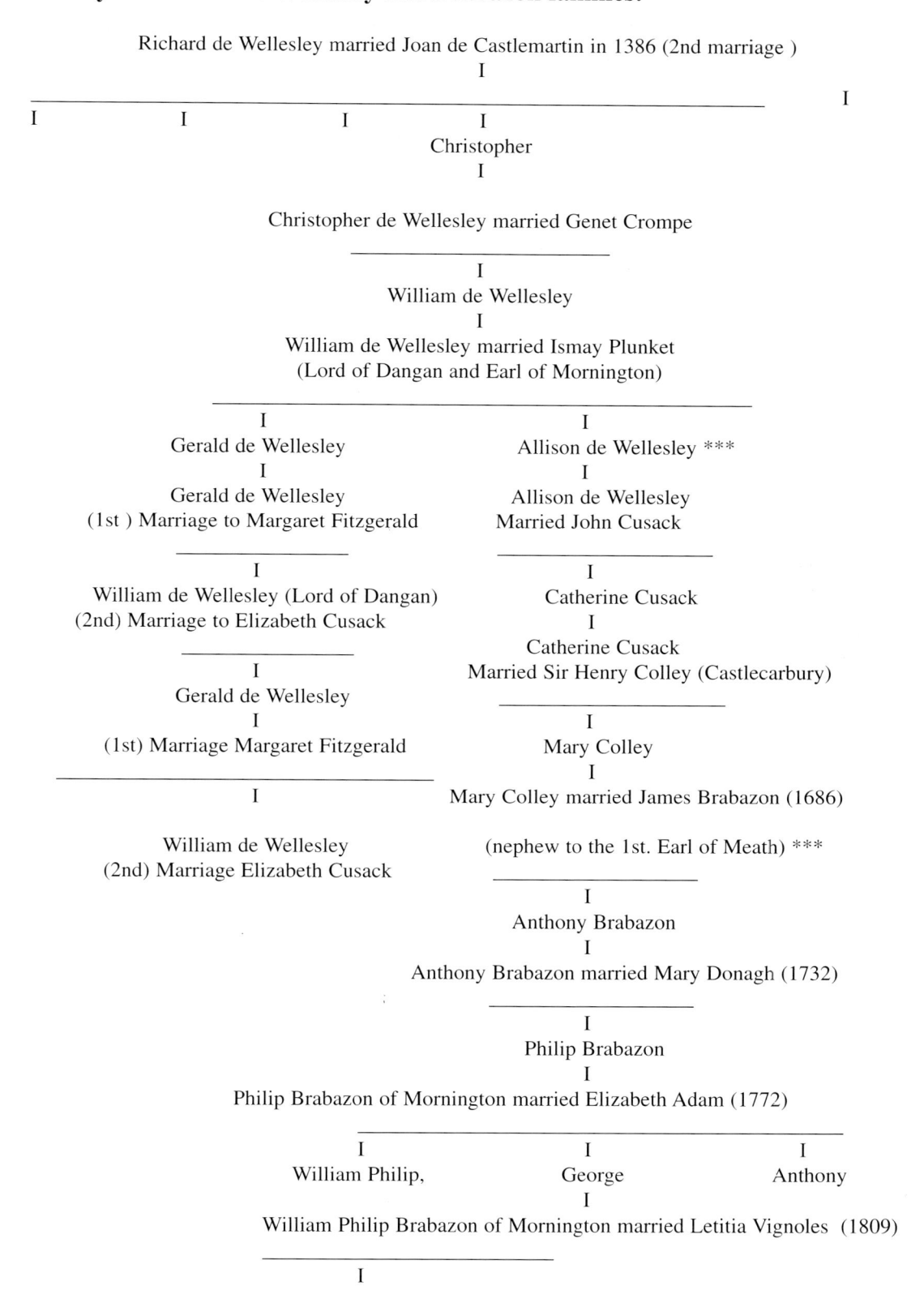

Richard de Wellesley married Joan de Castlemartin in 1386 (2nd marriage)

I — I — I — I — I — I

Christopher

Christopher de Wellesley married Genet Crompe

William de Wellesley

William de Wellesley married Ismay Plunket
(Lord of Dangan and Earl of Mornington)

Gerald de Wellesley	Allison de Wellesley ***
Gerald de Wellesley	Allison de Wellesley
(1st) Marriage to Margaret Fitzgerald	Married John Cusack
William de Wellesley (Lord of Dangan)	Catherine Cusack
(2nd) Marriage to Elizabeth Cusack	Catherine Cusack
	Married Sir Henry Colley (Castlecarbury)
Gerald de Wellesley	
(1st) Marriage Margaret Fitzgerald	Mary Colley
	Mary Colley married James Brabazon (1686)
William de Wellesley	(nephew to the 1st. Earl of Meath) ***
(2nd) Marriage Elizabeth Cusack	

Anthony Brabazon

Anthony Brabazon married Mary Donagh (1732)

Philip Brabazon

Philip Brabazon of Mornington married Elizabeth Adam (1772)

| William Philip, | George | Anthony |

William Philip Brabazon of Mornington married Letitia Vignoles (1809)

I

Family tree continued:

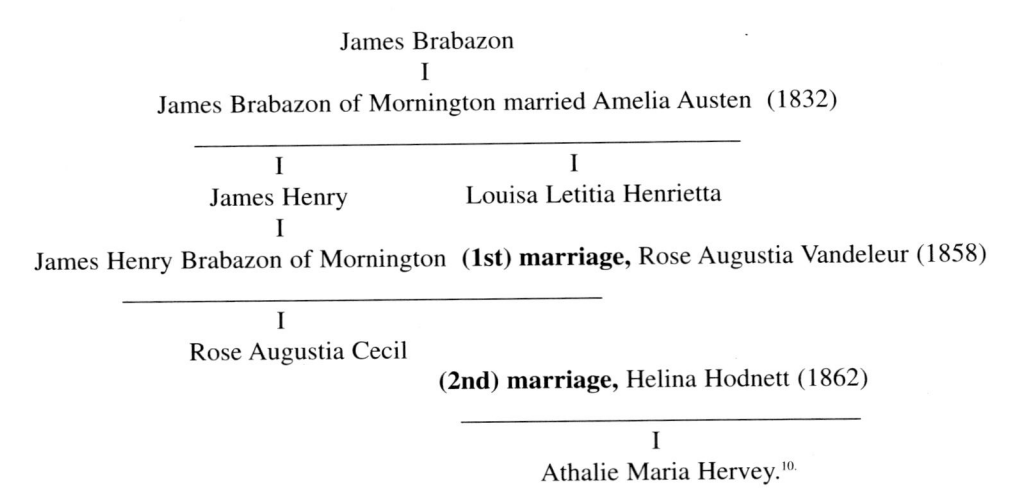

```
                           James Brabazon
                                I
        James Brabazon of Mornington married Amelia Austen  (1832)
        ─────────────────────────────────────────────────
              I                              I
           James Henry              Louisa Letitia Henrietta
              I
James Henry Brabazon of Mornington  (1st) marriage, Rose Augustia Vandeleur (1858)
        ─────────────────────────────────────────────────
              I
        Rose Augustia Cecil
                           (2nd) marriage, Helina Hodnett (1862)
                           ──────────────────────────────
                                          I
                                   Athalie Maria Hervey.¹⁰
```

James Henry Brabazon died 28th June 1913, (not in Ireland).

Captain James Brabazon (Nephew to the 1st Earl of Meath)
Captain James Brabazon was born 8th March 1661. In December 1686 he married Mary Colley, daughter of Dudley Colley Esq. of Castlecarbury. Mary died in 1693 and James died in 1728 leaving issue.
Anthony Brabazon of Carstown was born December 1688. He married Mary Donagh in 1732, they had one son.
Philip Brabazon of Mornington, Co Meath, was born in 1733. He married Elizabeth Adems, daughter of George Adems. They had three sons, Anthony, George and William Philip. Philip died in 1828.
William Philip Brabazon of Mornington was born 28th October 1783. He married Letita Vignoles the daughter of Rev. John Vignoles, March 1809. Letitia died 1859, and William Philip died December 1854, they had one son, James.
James Brabazon of Mornington J.P. Born April 1810. He married Amelia the daughter of Sir Henry E. Austin of Shalford House in Surrey. Amelia died 6th December 1881, and James died 11th July 1873. (James Brabazon, buried at St. Mary's Church of Ireland, Drogheda 1810-1873). They had a son and daughter, James Henry and Louisa Letitia Henrietta.
James Henry Brabazon of Mornington House J.P., 16th Regiment.
He was born March 1833. On the 16th March 1858 he married Rose Agusta daughter of George Vandeleur of Limerick. They had a daughter Rose Agusta Cecil, she married Willoughby Hartford Hurt-Sitwell.
James Henry's 2nd marriage was in November 1862 to Helena third daughter of William Hodnett, James Henry died 28th June 1913. They had a daughter, Athalie Marie Harvey who married Major Baudin of the Royal Bersaglieri Regt. They had a daughter Cecil Elizabeth.
Louisa Letitia Henrietta (sister of J. H. Brabazon) married Arthur C. Innes of Dromantine Co. Down. She died January 1886. They had a daughter Maria Georgina whoshe married Ralph Smyth of Newtown House. She died 2nd January 1908. [11]
James Brabazon (1833-1913) resided at Coney Hall (Mornington House) until 1880. In January of that same year, a dismissed house servant in Coney Hall, Margaret Skean murdered Emma Bouchier (who had replaced her in her duties in Coney Hall). Some time after the trial of Margaret Skean, James Brabazon left Mornington, and it is not known for certain where he spent the last thirty years of his life. He died 28th June 1913.

Mornington House /Coney Hall

Coney Hall was one of the finest old Queen Anne style residence in Co. Meath, built in very early eighteenth century. A substantial elegant spacious mansion, seated on a magnificent lawn, a short distance from the sea, with offices of all descriptions, three acres of walled round capital gardens, well stocked with fruit trees etc. A big fine yard, with stables, coach houses, barns, cow houses, farriers for making horse-shoes and looking after horses generally, wagon lodges and various other out-buildings.

Acres and acres of meadow, pasture and arable land, rolling in comfortably around this amazing house and gardens.

This estate was considered very valuable property, only two miles from the sea-port town of Drogheda, which was maintaining and enjoying a healthy state, with extensive trade in provisions and various merchandise.[12]

Mornington House (Coney Hall) Mornington, Co. Meath.

The following is a list of the proprietors of Coney Hall, and who resided there during the last three centuries.

The **Wellesley** family until 1816.[13]

The **Brabazon** family (1816-1880)

The **Gilroy** family (1885-1895 approx.) left Ireland for a new post in Sussex, England.

The property was sold to Mr. John Smith, a solicitor from Drogheda. When he died the property went to his daughter, a Mrs Byrne who was a widow and living in Liverpool. Later Mrs Byrne sold Coney Hall to a Doctor Graham who had retired from Purdesburn Hospital in Northern Ireland. When Doctor Graham died, his wife sold the property to Mrs Beresford, who was an English lady, and member of the Guinness/Mahon family, who later married Jack Graham. They had two children. Coney Hall was their home for only four years, when their family life there, came to a sudden tragic end.

In 1955, a fire, which seemed to have started in the nursery broke out in the house, and the Graham's eighteen month old baby was burned to death. Most of the house and furniture was destroyed by the fire. After this terrible tragedy, that claimed the life of their child, the Graham family moved out of the area. Mrs Pamela Graham bought Beamont House, Kilsharvan, where she lived until her death some years later. It is not known what became of Mr. Graham.

"Whitefields", Mornington:

It is not known for certain when Whitefield's house was built. The earliest date we have is of a Patrick Boyle of Whitefields, and his wife Alice, who are buried in Mornington cemetery. Alice died in December 1810, but it is not stated when Patrick died.

Mr. Cornelius Mullins of Whitefields is also buried in Mornington cemetery. He died in July 1888, and, in his will, he left St. Mary's parish heir to his possessions. His wife Ellen died one month later.15. Mrs Collins was owner of Whitefields in the early twentieth century and during her lifetime had some of the Bay View houses built in Bettystown. Mr. Allen, a retired engineer bought Whitefields and his family lived out their lives there. His wife Margrette Susanna Allen died in 1943 and her sisters, Marie and Hennrietta Anna McDowell died in 1945 and '46. All three are buried in Colpe cemetery.[16]

Mr. Joe Brown, manager of Murdocks in Drogheda, subsequently bought Whitefields, and sold the house and a few fields to Mr Paddy Monahan, who was a shipping broker. The rest of the land was sold to Durnins. After Mr Monahan's death Mrs Monahan went to live with her daughter in Cavan and the property was sold to Mrs Loraine Lyons, widow of Jimmy Lyons (junior) of Lismara. Mrs Lyons, subsequently sold Whitefields to the present owners, John and Sam Rioch.

John Drew lived and farmed the land adjoining Coney Hall. He lived with his family in the farmhouse on the farm, which incidentally was a single storey thatched house. His family are still living in this house which would be considered three hundred years old. The alterations and extensions which have taken place during the passing years added to the character of this warm and comfortable home. His son John has continued in the farming business carrying on the family tradition.[17]

Betaghstown House

Betaghstown House, (Bettystown House) is supposed to be the oldest house in the area. It was built by a man named Tomlinson in 1669 (the same year the Grammar school was built in Drogheda). Then William Shepherd bought the house from the Tomlinson family in 1755.

Note: Dennis Betagh, now living in Wellington, New Zealand, believes that Betaghstown House was built much earlier by an ancestor of his, whom, he says was a Danish Prince. The family name Betagh is of Danish origin. We are told that this mansion was confiscated by Cromwell in 1649. We have been unable to find confirmation of this.[18]

Shepherd Family

Not much is known about this family, although they were considered a prominent Anglo-Norman family in Bettystown in the eighteenth and nineteenth century. In 1718 John Shepherd held a lease of part of the premises of the Carmelites for a period of sixty one years. The family has also appeared on various records as owners of Bettystown House and Kiltrough in the mid eighteenth century. There are memorials to this family in St. Mary's church Julianstown.

The Shepherd family lived at Bettystown House for almost one hundred years, (1755-1853).

In 1853, Robert Shepherd sold it to Maxwell Wade. Robert Shepherd died in 1867, his wife Mary Jane died in 1888. In 1908, Ann Wade sold Bettystown House to Lady Matilda Scarborough. We are told she was very popular and loved by her tenants. During the period she was owner/occupier of Bettystown House and estate, she gave her rent paying tenants the option of buying the land they were renting from her. She also gave the families who lived in the cottages on the Narrowway (which was part of her estate) their cottages free gratis for their lifetime and the lifetime of their descendants. The tenants, to show their gratitude to Lady Scarborough, met her coach at Donacarney as it came from the station, they set the horses free, and pulled her carriage by hand back to Bettystown House. Sean Faulkner's grandmother was one of those tenants, Sean, now lives in his own home, built on the same site of his grandmother's cottage. Lady Scarborough left Bettystown House to a Miss Matilda Helen Mc Donnell from Portglenowen, Co Antrim. Miss McDonnell and her companion lived there until her untimely death from an infection caused by a bite she received from her pet rat. The house then became the property of John Scarborough. In 1920, John Scarborough sold Bettystown House to Francis Germain McKeever, who sold it eight years later to a Mr. Ludlow Mainwaring Jones, who died in 1940, and the property went to his son Henry Jones. In 1953, Bettystown House was sold to W. K. Allen.

The present owners are Rosemary and Charlie Allen, who run a very successful Bed and Breakfast business.

Note: According to some reports most of the owners of Bettystown House gave each of their tenants 10lbs of meat, annually, as a gesture of goodwill. This custom ended in 1920 when John Scarborough sold the property to Mr. McKeever[20].

Robert Shepherd was a subscriber to the Colpe and Kilsharven Relief Committee set up in 1847. A total 1£14-15-0 was collected. The following are names of some of the families who contributed to this relief fund:

Captain Anderson of Eastham House,
Mr. John Ryder, Farm Hill,
Mr. P. Pentlebury, Mornington,
Mr. Charles Fausset, Mornington,
Rev. J Druitt, Mornington,
Mr. N. Lubders, Colpe,
Mr. B. Labarte, Mornington.
Mr. Thomas Brodigan, Piltown,
Mr. James Heaney, Mornington,
Mr. Robert Shepherd, Bettystown House,
James Brabazon, Mornington House,
Captain Ashe, Bettystown, and many more.
Henry Moore was the Treasurer.[19]

Betaghstown or Bettystown

Bettystown is a village in the parish of Colpe in the barony of Lower Duleek. Ordnance Survey Maps of the Meath area show that this district is still known as Betaghstown and the old Manor house is also still known as Betaghstown House. Popular opinion has it that English and Welsh visitors to this small seaside resort, dropped the traditional 'agh' in favour of 'y' making it Bettystown. Again, there is some confusion as to the origin of the name Betaghstown. The following two accounts appear to have the strongest claim. Firstly, the subdivisions of a tuath (at the time of Hugh de Lacy) were called " Ballybetaghs". The "Ballybetagh" was supposed to be of sufficient size to allow grazing for four herds of seventy-five cows each "without one cow touching another".[21]

Baile na Bhiadhtaigh (or Betaghstown) means 'town of the Victualler' from early Irish and Viking times, which would make sense, since the village in question is situated near the mouth of the river Boyne (where fish and game would have been plentiful), ("Bettystown" (Town of Betty) makes a nonsense of the original and historic meaning of the word and destroys the strong link with the Irish family of that time).[22] Secondly, the family name Betagh has been associated with Ireland and Meath as far back as the fourteenth century, its origin is not certain, with some records of that period saying it was Danish and others saying it was Norman.

Betagh had certainly become a name of consequence in Co. Meath by the sixteenth century. For between 1570 and 1598, Betagh of Walterstown, Betagh of Rathalron, Betagh of Dunamore and Betagh of Moynalty all appear as gentlemen of that county. William Betagh was chief serjeant, (which means a member of the highest class of barristers, which was abolished in 1880) of the adjoining Co. Cavan and Thomas Betagh was one of the gentlemen entrusted with the task of taking a muster (assembling of men for inspection) of the inhabitants of Co. Cavan in 1587. The minutes of Court Martials held in St. Patrick's Church, Dublin, record Captain Francis Betagh of Moynalty and other Betaghs, present at those held on 20th March, and 23rd April 1652.

The case of Francis Betagh, as unjustly affected by the Acts of Settlement, is especially recorded in *Mr. O' Callaghan's Irish Brigades.* In modern times Father Thomas Betagh, S.J. (1769-1811) who was born in Kells, Co Meath was notable for his activity in the revival of Catholic education at the end of the penal period.

To conclude, Ballybetagh, south of Dublin (Betagh's town) and Betaghstown in Kildare, Louth, and Meath, were probably called from the family of Betagh, but this family name has still the same origin: their ancestors were *betaghs*.[23]

Times Past - Bettystown Square, and the Golflinks Road, Bettystown, Co. Meath.

Golf Road, Bettystown

BETTYSTOWN. CO. MEATH.

56

Returning from the rarefied atmosphere of the 'Big House' to the political state of the country we find, in 1801 the Act of Union. The Rebellion of 1798 ended in defeat for the Irish and also drew attention to the 'Irish problem' for the British Government. There was a pressing political need to prevent a recurrence of people developing notions above their station. So direct rule from London was mooted as the solution. By a process of bribery and political favour to the Irish M.P.'s, the Act of Union was passed by the Irish Parliament, and in January 1801, Ireland became part of the United Kingdom.

The act of union brought no relief or justice to the Irish people. From 1790 to 1834, Meath experienced a period of social and economic collapse, developing a climate of agitation and outrage, which in turn led to increasing violence. The deteriorating economic state was caused by the replacing of tillage land (which was a lifeline to the poorer section of the community) with grazing. The cereals market dried up in England and the Continent following the end of the wars. Landlords and tenant farmers started clearing their land of small tenants, cottiers and labourers, to make room for the profitable business of grazing cattle. This was the beginning of evictions in Meath.

In 1836, according to statements submitted the general state of the poor in various parts of Meath was very gloomy, with low prices for flax. Fruit gardens had been left uncultivated due to little demand and low prices for fruit, resulting in hundreds living well below the acceptable standard and hundreds more (farm labourers) leaving their homes and villages in search of employment in Dublin and elsewhere. However, this mode was to continue, and neither the secret societies (set up during the eviction period of the late 1820s and early 1830s) or the violence succeeded in changing anything for the underprivileged people of Meath. They finally lost their battle for survival, not to the landlords or middlemen, but to cholera in (1832), followed by the famine (1845-51).[24]

CHAPTER 6
"A Turning of the Tide?"

Daniel O'Connell was born in 1775, a son of a small landlord in Co. Kerry. He became a barrister in 1798 and was the first Catholic to enter the legal profession in Ireland after that penal law was repealed in 1792. However, Catholics still could not sit in parliament, be judges, or colonels in the army, or captains in the navy, or ministers in the government. The continuation of these 'laws' outraged the Catholic population, so the first part of the nineteenth century saw the real struggle for full Catholic emancipation. In 1823 Daniel O' Connell formed the Catholic Association, which proved a great success for two reasons. Firstly, it was aimed at the masses, which were to be organised and controlled by the clergy of the area, and secondly, there was a 'catholic rent' to be paid to the Association of 1p per month. It was so low, even the poorest of the poor could afford it. Thousands upon thousands of Catholics joined the Association and it became a very strong organisation, a political force to be reckoned with.

Daniel O'Connell became a very successful barrister, also an astute figure in the political scene in Ireland. From 1814 until his death in 1847 he worked tirelessly for the Irish cause. On the 13th April 1829 the full Catholic Emancipation Act became law. Daniel O'Connell won the confidence and trust of the great mass of Irish people, rich and poor. He was a most illustrious, prominent and popular Irish politician, of that period.[1]

****

Many emerging families date their prosperity from this period, so it is fitting to look at the history of some more local houses.

Donacarney:

The name Donacarney derived its name from the Irish 'Domhnach Cearnaigh', meaning the Church of Cearnach. St. Cearnach was a native of either Wales or Cornwall. He arrived soon after St. Patrick, and it is generally believed he was responsible for the building of the first church in this part of east Meath, hence, the name Donacarney.[2]

In 1837, Lewis in the Topographical Dictionary, describes Donacarney *"as a village of twenty five houses and one hundred and eight people"*

There is a ruined wall in Donacarney, indirectly referred to, as the gable of the *"habitable castle"* in the Down Survey, in the shadow of which a **"black smith has established his forge"**.[3]

Local blacksmith Hughie McCabe striking the anvil, in his forge at Donacarney, and Joe Winters, Fieldstown, looking on.

Robert B. Daly's Auctioneers.

Robert Bedford Daly was born, 28th February 1818, and we are told he died at Donacarney House in 1891 aged seventy three years. He is buried in St. Peter's cemetery, in Drogheda. The firm he founded Robert B. Daly's Auctioneers in Laurences Street, is one of the oldest surviving traders in Drogheda today, and possibly the fifth oldest Auctioneer firm in Ireland. He married Mary Deane, daughter of William Deane and Elizabeth Priest of Slane. They had eleven children, mostly male, who emigrated to America and Australia. One descendent was the Chief Justice of the Bahamas between 1938 and 1945.

Daly's opened a haberdashery in Laurences Street in 1846. In 1855 Daly and Deane had a wholesale and retail grocers and seed merchants at 107, West Street, Drogheda. They were already established as auctioneers at that address at that time. The business mainly dealt with estate management and land agency, looking after estates of the landed gentry and a vast amount of conacre letting.
The old estates would have been let out to tenants. Advertising was in the form of billboards, erected in the vicinity of the available property, on piers, gates, walls, trees etc.
In 1870 Robert Bedford Daly was installed as Mayor of Drogheda, for one year. Records from 1933 show land selling at ten pounds per acre![4]

Donacarney House

After the death of Robert Bedford Daly in 1891, George Henry Daly and his wife Beatrice Gertrude Delphine lived at Donacarney House for their lifetime. Beatrice died in 1932, aged seventy seven years. Olive Ismay Paine, a niece of George Daly, took up residence at Donacarney House, to nurse and care for George until his death in 1943, aged ninety years. Miss Paine was responsible for the sale of Donacarney House to Mr. Michael Connolly, a member of the Connolly Brother's family, who ran the very successful store in Shop Street, Drogheda, for many years. Wogan's furniture store now occupy this space.[5]
Joe and Rhona Connolly are the present owner/occupiers of Donacarney House. Joe was a young boy, when his parents moved to their new home in Donacarney, over fifty years ago, and it has been the Connolly's family home ever since.

Donacarney House.

Cars registered in Meath 1903 - 1916.
AI 8 -   George H. Daly, Donacarney House.
AI 299 -   George H. Daly, Donacarney House.

The following article was written about the sale of the Lordship of Donacarney.

WHO WILL LORD IT OVER DONACARNEY
One just does not know who one will be bowing and scrapping to next.
What is to become of the people of Donacarney? They wait with bated breath this week to see who will become the new Lord of their townland.
The aristocracy are selling off their titles to beat the band, and this week Lord Gormanston the Premier Viscount of Ireland - will flog the Lordship of Donacarney at an auction in London, just like that.
Jenico Nicholas Dudley Preston inherited over one hundred titles from his father, who died in the second World War, and while he lives in London, locals in Gormanston do remember the young peer being wheeled around the town in his pram.
He seems set to hang on to the title of Lord Gormanston, for the present anyway.
But it seems Donacarney is doomed to fall into the hands of the nouveau riche, Quelle Calame! the title of Lord Donacarney.
Gormanston was bestowed on the family after they fought for the crown during the Confederation of Kilkenny. They came to Gormanston as provision and wine merchants to the army, and took over the Manor House.
Gormanston Castle remained in the family for many years, but was sold to a Mr. Bingham, after the current Lord's father died in World War 11. The castle was since sold to the Franciscan Order, and opened as a college.
Lord Gormanston has been seen checking out his patch in more recent times. He certainly visited the area in the seventies, looking for people who knew his ancestors.
A local woman called Lil Murphy was called upon by Lord Gormanston and she in turn took him to visit her mother who had worked in the castle on occasion.
"He just called to the door one day and said he was Lord Gormanston. I didn't believe him at first, but as he went on I knew he was genuine. He was very pleasant really and his Polish wife was very interested in the college and the educational system here", she said.
The Lordship of Donacarney will fetch thousands of pounds, when it goes up for auction today, Wednesday. The Premier Viscount has already sold off over thirty of his titles - reportedly to pay for his children's school fees.
(Lil has since died she was tragically killed in a car accident on the 31st. Jan. 1997, one and a half hours before St. Bridget's Day, to whom Lil had great devotion, she was sixty two years of age).

Eastham House
Eastham House is situated on Eastham Road three klm south-east of Bettystown. It is an attractive house built in the late eighteenth century - five bays wide, three storeys high and two rooms deep. The windows in the upper storeys are unusual in that they have exposed sash-boxes. The entrance to the house is framed by a timber pediment door-case with fluted Tucson columns. It is very possible this house was built by the Shepherd family who were the owners of Bettystown House in 1830s.[6]
Roseville Cottage was the stables and the property of Eastham House. The Lodge where Anthony Cogan lives now also belonged to Eastham House.[7] There was also a beautiful walled in garden at Eastham House.[8] It is not certain when exactly Eastham House was built, but it is possible it was around 1780.

The Mall Mill was built by Mr John Morton in the 1850s and owned by Mr Joe Bellew in recent years. He resided at Eastham House, Bettystown, was a member of the Harbour Board and was prominent in the Milling and Exporting business. He imported many cargoes of corn direct from America.
It is believed that the Mall Mill was the local head-quarters for the Fenian Rising of 1867.[9]
In 1861 Rev. William Norton was the owner of Eastham House.
The Barrett family from Greenhills and also the Smyth family have been associated with Eastham House during the latter part of the nineteenth century and the early part of the twentieth century.
It was sold to a Mr. McCann in 1953, who rented it to the St. John of God establishment, as a summer residence.

During this period the doors had to be removed from the upstairs bedrooms in order to safeguard the patients and prevent them from locking themselves in.

The McLoughlin's bought Eastham House in 1958. Philip McLoughlin was managing director of Woodingtons factory in Drogheda.

Other families associated with Eastham House were: Mr.Young from Salthill, Co. Galway and Mr Tom Moran who owned a Bakery business in Drogheda. A Dublin-man (name unknown) also lived in Eastham House, he owned 'a string of tenement houses' as well.

The O'Brien family, the Thomas family, the Reynolds family and the Rodger family, also lived there.[10]

Stagreenan (Stagrinan)

This place name became distorted, possibly under Danish or Anglo-Norman influence, and is locally explained as Teach Grianian (Summer house) or Grennan's house. Grennan was the name of the builder of a church, the ruins of which are to be found in the Colpe area.

A Peter McEvoy is listed as owner/occupier of Stagreenan House, Mornington in 1852, although there seems to be some discrepancy with regard to dates. This man's sister Mary McEvoy married Francis Brodigan of Piltown House, and may have been the grandfather of Peter McEvoy 'The Uncrowned King of Drogheda' who lived in Stagreenan House sometime in the early 1900's.

Peter was one of Drogheda's 'characters' and is still remembered with affection. There are many stories told about this Maurice Chevalier type of character, who had a beautiful tenor singing voice. Back in a time when street music or busking was unheard of, he would stand to sing on the street for the simple pleasure of entertaining and brightening up the lives of the everyday shoppers. A huge crowd would gather to listen to him. He was also known for waiting outside the church after Mass on Sunday, handing out sweets to the children.

These stories and many more made up the fine character of Peter McEvoy. He lived at Stagreenan House for most of his life. He rode with the Louth Hunt and the Meath Harriers but spent his later years in the Central Hotel, Drogheda. He died on 18th May, 1963.[11]

The Glen House

This house was built in 1852. It was the Dower house to Stameen House, and is of similar Italianate design. It is a gabled two-storey building of rectangular plan, with a large central entrance and stairhall. Cement-rendered, with the usual projecting centre bay, bracketed eaves and corner quoin pilasters.[12]

Alen Thomas Cairnes and his wife Julia lived in Glen House (1860-1902). They had one daughter Eileen who died very young. (See Graveyard inscriptions, St. Mary's Chursh of Ireland, Mary Street, Drogheda.)

Fred Hoey also owned 'The Glen'. Dessie Grant and his family are the present owners.

Cairnes of Stameen

The Cairnes family originally came from Cairnes Castle, Midlothian, Scotland and settled in Kilnahushogue in County Tyrone where they lived at Saville Lodge. The first member of the family to come to Drogheda was born there in 1787, and was called William. He was the second son of John Elliot Cairnes, and with no prospect of inherited land, became a brewer. This job took him to Woolesey's Brewery at Castlebellingham and eventually to the foundation of the Drogheda Brewery at the Marsh Road. This was formerly operated by the Tandy family, ancestors of the famous 'Napper Tandy', but had closed down around 1800. William re-opened the brewing business and lived in the Brewery house.

At this time, John Magrane a master weaver, was living at Stameen. The flax for weaving was grown and bleached on the 'forty acres' surrounding the house, which was sometimes called the 'bleach' field. The house at Stameen became know as 'Cotton Hall'. Around 1850 John Magrane died and 'Cotton Hall' was sold to William Cairnes, who by this time was a very successful and wealthy man in the brewery business.

He engaged a noted architect from Dublin, Mr. W. F. Caldbeck, to enlarge and redesign the house. William Cairnes died in 1865 at the age of seventy eight years. His son Thomas Plunkett inherited

Stameen and carried on in the family brewery business which went from strength to strength. By all accounts Thomas Plunkett was a good Christian, and was fair and just to his fellow human beings. After his death, Stameen became the property of his eldest son William Plunkett, who was very like his father and inherited his philanthropic outlook on life.

Around 1910 William Plunkett sold much of the land at Stameen, because he was 'too busy to farm it properly'. He was married to Alice Algar. After his death in 1925 he was succeeded by his son Thomas Algar Cairnes, popularly known as 'The Colonel'. This man was a soldier at heart and spent many years in active service with the British army in India, in World War 1, and also World War 11. Farming was very difficult in the thirties, rates on buildings were high, and farm workers had to be let go. The 'Colonel' died in 1960. A family by the name of McNeece bought most of the farm and yard. They still farm the land specialising in apple growing.

The main house and lawns was bought by the Larkin/ McGovern family and turned into a luxury hotel trading under the name of ' Stameen House Hotel'.

Since then it has changed hands. It was bought by Mr.William Widmer, who created the thriving 'Boyne Valley Hotel and Sennhof Restaurant'. In March 1992, the Hotel was bought by Michael and Rosemary McNamara, and since then has been extended and modernised by them to include a Leisure Centre, one of the finest in the country. The McNamara family have been associated with Drogheda since the famous Battle of the Boyne in 1690.[13]

Mill House:

This house also belonged to the Cairnes of Stameen, it was bought by a John Hill and later sold to Raphael Hoey.

The following gravestone inscriptions of the Cairnes family can be located in St. Mary's Church graveyard, Mary Street, Drogheda.
Allen Thomas Cairnes of the Glen, born 18/3/1860, died 5/10/1902, his wife Julia Cairnes died, 3/5/1901, their daughter Eileen born 22/9/1885, died 17/2/1888.
Sarah Alice born 28/1/1862, died 2/5/1864. James Robert Arthur born 22/11/1865,
died 13/2/1867. Frederick Herbert born 13/11/1867 died 26/4/1886 (child of Thomas Plunkett Cairnes and his wife Sophia of Stameen, Co.Meath). Maryanne 'Annie' born 10/12/1863 died 13/1/1889.
'Absent from the body, present with the Lord', 2 Cor. V.V.111.[14]

Farm Hill:

On a Map dated 1771 Farm Hill is marked Prefton Park (Preston). It is our understanding that the house marked on the map was a Glebe. According to Mrs Smith (deceased) of the Bridge House, Farm Hill was a rectory for Julianstown or Colpe up to the 1830's. In 1837, Lewis stated, William Walshe was owner of Prefton (Preston) Park. Mr. Cooper from Cooperhill bought the property from William Walshe. In 1845 he reconstructed the house in preparation for his marriage to Francis Brodigan's sister. But it appears this marriage did not come to pass. Farmhill was divided into two parts, Ballymad and Prefton (Preston) Park.

Larry Moore, (who came from Co. Louth was related to Moore's of Sandyhall, Julianstown) was Sean Moore's grandfather and bought Prefton Park from Mr. Cooper.

Sean Moore's father also Larry inherited Prefton when his father died, bought Ballymad, and joined the two farms to became Farm Hill. Larry Moore's sons Sean and Paddy sold Farm Hill to the Fallon family in or about 1995.

The Threshing - in Farm Hill in 1936. The Mill belonged to Smith of Colpe. The following are the names of the men working on the mill - Jack Maguire,Beabeg, Peter Rooney, Bettystown, Jimmy Kennedy, Narrowway, Tom McQuillen - Minnistown, Joe Rafferty - Farm Hill, Sean Moore - Farm Hill and Sean Faulkner - The Narrowway.[15]

The threshing was one of the 'gems' of farm life in the forties and fifties. It would be difficult to describe in mere words the magical atmosphere that surrounded this yearly event, which normally took place in farmyards and haggards throughout rural Ireland around September.

The following few lines by Patrick Kavanagh go some way in capturing that atmosphere.

The threshing mill was set-up, I knew,
In Cassidy's haggard last night,
And we owed them a day at the threshing
Since last year. O it was delight

To be paying bills of laughter
And chaffy gossip in kind
With work thrown in to ballast
The fantasy-soaring mind. [16]

Bridge House:

In the early nineteenth century, a family by the name of Sheeler, possibly from Wales, lived in the Bridge House. John Stitt Smith and his wife Sara Jane from Forkhill Co. Armagh bought it around 1880. John Stitt Smith reconstructed the house, which was originally one storey, and built on a second storey. After John's death his son Joe inherited Bridge House. He married Molly McKeever from Collon Co. Louth in 1926.[17]

Joe J. Smith died 16th Nov. 1940 and Molly McKeever Smith died 11th Feb. 1995 at the age of ninety two Both Molly and Joe are buried in St. Mary's Church of Ireland cemetery, Julianstown. After Molly's death the property was sold.[18]

****

Farming:

While still on the subject of the 'big houses' it would be appropriate to include in this chapter, what life was like down on the farm. While fishing was considered one of the main sources of income and livelihood on the east coast of Meath, going back over hundreds of years. It would be fair to say that farming also played a major part in forming the community. From the Celtic period to the landlord and tenant days, to the farmer and farm labourer for the most part of the twentieth century, to the present day intensive farming, which has rapidly developed over the last fifteen to twenty years. Most of the well established farms in this area are tucked in comfortably around the fishing villages. Some of the people we spoke to had spent many years working on the local farms as either farm managers, farm labourers, gardeners, or herds men.

During the first half of the twentieth century, farming was mainly carried out manually and with the help of work horses. However, the type of farming varied considerably from ranch type (grazing cattle) to dairy, to mixed farming: tillage, potatoes, milking cows, sheep and store cattle, the latter being the most popular.

Farming and agriculture generally has made enormous progress in the last thirty to forty years, and, in the process has changed radically. Having been born and raised on a farm, I can still remember how it was in the forties and fifties and it might be interesting to draw up a few comparisons between then and now.

The transition period from manual farming to mechanised farming was fairly gradual, and, in general, started to take place during the fifties. But before the introduction of the tractor and the milking machine, fields were ploughed and tilled by horse drawn machines. Cows were hand milked morning and evening in a shed called a byre - today it is called a milking parlour.

There was no such thing as pasteurised milk, or milk quotas. The milk taken from the cows was put straight through a cooler/strainer into a crock, covered and left in a cool place until it was ready for use. Needless to remark everything was kept spotlessly clean. (The means to an end or method varied from farm to farm, according to their means or labour etc., but the end result was the same).

At hay-making time it was customary for the neighbours to join in and help save the hay, which nearly always ended with tea in the field.

Hens, chickens, ducks, drakes, dogs and cats roamed freely around the yard. The fowl were all housed at night time on account of the many foxes in the area. (Local folklore tells us that when a member of the Preston family of Gormanston died, anywhere in the world, the 'local' foxes gathered and howled for hours).

Animal manure was used to fertilise the fields for tillage and potato growing, similar to organic farming today; artificial manure and the wide range of chemicals that are part and parcel of farming to-day, were not readily available in Ireland back in those days. Seaweed was sometimes used as a fertiliser.

Potato harvesting was done completely by hand, picked and graded into commercial and seed potatoes. The very small potatoes (rubbish) were also gathered for animal feeding, nothing was wasted!

Shiela and Hugh Lynch picking potatoes in the 1950's.

When the corn was ripe, it was reaped by a binder, which tied it into sheaves, which were stacked up in the field. Later, it was drawn into the yard, piled high in reeks of corn, ready for the threshing, which normally took place at a later date, and could last two or three days, depending on the size of the harvest yield.

Sean Lynch cutting the corn with the 'reaper/binder' in the 1950's.

Butter was also made on a regular basis; the cream was gathered from the milk not used during the week. The cream was put into a churn and spun round until the butter was ready. This could take a couple of hours. The buttermilk was then drained from the churn. The butter was salted and removed from the churn, clapped into oblong shapes with butter clappers, and wrapped in greaseproof paper. It was called 'country butter' and was very popular at the time. The fresh buttermilk was considered a very healthy drink, something on the same lines as the popular 'natural' yoghurt being sold in supermarkets today.

Last but not least was the killing of the pig, which took place on different farms. After the killing, the carcass was placed on a large table for the purpose of salting, to preserve the meat. It was then cut up in pieces, wrapped in greaseproof paper, and hung up on the walls of the scullery, and in some cases where there was no scullery, the kitchen walls were used.
Farming in the forties and fifties was a tough life at times. However, it also had its rewards, and although the work seemed endless, the enormous pressures and stresses that exist in to-days world were almost non-existent then. Farming and nature went hand in hand, profit and loss was not so important, it was a way of life that embraced all the community, and generally speaking, people seemed to enjoy peace of mind.

In my memory the weather was consistent and very agreeable, which was a major asset, but most especially, there existed a bond and friendship between the farmer, farm worker and neighbour alike, definitely unique to that time.

Michael Lynch, with the farm horses - Hulk, Blossom and Black, in the early 1950's..

CHAPTER 7
"Famine and Disease".

Cholera:
Cholera is defined as a highly infectious intestinal disease, endemic to certain parts of Asia. The disease is marked by vomiting and diarrhoea. Cholera first appeared in Europe in 1829, and it reached England in 1831. Once this disease appeared in England, it was only a matter of time before it spread to Ireland. Cholera struck Ireland, in Dublin on 22nd March 1832. It reached Drogheda the following May. A Cholera hospital could not be set up for some days, but a soup kitchen was immediately set up in St. Patrick repository and infant school in Fair Street, Drogheda. On the 8th May the County hospital was set aside as a Cholera hospital. By the 12th May thirty seven people had died.

Drogheda and Sligo were the worst towns affected in Ireland. With regard to the town of Drogheda, the reason for this is thought to have been that the water supply for the town was polluted by the river Boyne into which sewage had seeped.
The destitution to which the working class had been reduced by Cholera was really terrible. Many families were in such a state of exhaustion. They were completely dependent on the soup kitchens, and without that support many more people would have perished.
A Dr. Jackson was in charge of the Cholera hospital set up in Fair Street. By the end of June, only two months later, three hundred and seventy-two people had died from this terrible disease. By the end of July the disease was still spreading rapidly, shops and business were closing down. Cholera raged for a period of more than four months, and out of a population of nearly seventeen thousand, it is reckoned that around one thousand five hundred people fell victim and died. Most of the victims were buried in the Chord Road Cemetery, but the small cemetery on the Marsh Road, called 'Stagrenan' was built for the purpose of burying the remainder of people who died as a result of Cholera.[1]

The Linen trade in early 19th century (Pre-Famine era):
Late 18th/early 19th centuries, show significant emphasis on a domestic industry, flax spinning, linen weaving, wool, tailor/seamstress and others. These industries were mainly ran by the female community, generally the wives and daughters of agricultural labourers and small farmers. These small industries mainly operated from the homes of the vast majority of the population of urban and rural Meath, and for two or three decades kept extreme poverty and destitution at bay. But this precarious existence could not last.
In 1815, significant changes took place in rural Meath - a move from labour intensive tillage to capital intensive livestock production. This major change in farming resulted in increased under-employment for the small farmers. By the 1830s most small tillage farms and potato gardens were a thing of the past having been taken over by the larger farms for livestock production etc. A further blow to the small farming and labouring classes in these years was the decline of the domestic linen industry. The main reason for this decline was its concentration in the northern counties of Antrim, Down, and Armagh combined with the introduction of power spinning in the early 1830s, and the effects on domestic industry were disastrous. With its gradual disappearance, a vast percentage of people faced destruction and ruin: it was only a matter of time before such an event happened.[2]

Drogheda port was one of the main exporting venues on the east coast and the town was also considered an important centre for the production of linen, which gave employment to thousands of weavers in the town and the surrounding areas. However, this situation was to change with the gradual introduction of four large textile mills, which were in full production before 1844, thousands of weavers becoming unemployed, with the exception of women, girls and children working for very low wages.[3]

****

The Famine 1845-1851

There are many books written on the great potato famine of 1845. The following passage is taken from: The Famine Story, printed by Millmount museum, on the one hundred and fiftieth anniversary of this terrible disaster.

In the summer of the year 1845 the fungus " phytophera infestans" struck Ireland for the first time causing potato blight. During the next five years repeated and more wide spread failure of the potato crop led to the deaths of one million Irish people. Two million more fled the country during the years following the first appearance of the blight.

The devastation caused by the failure of a single crop was due to the almost total dependence of a large section of the population, especially of the agricultural labourer and cottier classes, on the nutritious potato as their diet.

When the blight struck the first year it was a disaster for those who depended almost solely on it, but when it returned on a more widespread scale in the following years, it meant death to those already living at subsistence level, and emigration for those with the resources to flee disease, death and extreme poverty.

It was disaster on a massive scale. After the famine, three million of the labourers, cottiers, and small holders were literally dead or gone from the country. As a consequence, the system of land holding and tenancy was almost completely changed.

The smaller farms and cottier plots abandoned by the starving tenants or from which they had been evicted for non-payment of rent, were absorbed into larger farms or re-possessed by the landlords.

These changes also led eventually to the rapid erosion of the Irish language with the dispersal of the communities of which it was the native tongue.

The deplorable conditions of the people was further exacerbated by epidemics of dysentery and diarrhoea, which were the most frequent and fatal complications of famine fever and caused the deaths of thousands.

What caused the famine:
The failure of the potato crop on a national scale was the visible cause for this 'catastrophic disaster', which left Ireland with one million of its people dead and two million were forced to emigrate to foreign lands. Many questions have been asked and answered through the many volumes written on this terrible 'visitation'.

The general opinion appears to be that Meath was not badly affected by the Famine. This is a myth and incorrect. According to census figures recorded in 1851 the population of Meath had dropped by 43,000 over a period of ten years. The grazing lands of south Meath did not suffer as severely as the tillage lands in the northern parts of the county, where cottiers and labourers were totally dependent upon the potato crop[4]. Under the Poor Relief (Ireland) Act which became law in July 1838, each county was divided into a number of unions, each to contain a workhouse, where relief and employment should be given to the poor.

Meath was divided into five Poor Law Unions:- Trim, Navan, Kells, Oldcastle, and Dunshaughlin workhouses were built at each centre. Workhouses in Drogheda and Ardee were also intended to serve small areas of the county. Built according to a standard plan and in a gloomy and depressing style of architecture, the institutions were deliberately designed to be unattractive and to force the poor to support themselves rather then seek relief. So successful was the plan, that many preferred to die of starvation rather than darken the workhouse gate. The stigma attached to these buildings remains to this day, and even survived the change of system of administration in the 1920's.

The coastal villages of Meath, (Mornington, Colpe, Bettystown etc.) approximately three to five miles from Drogheda fell within the Drogheda Union. We can only guess that the underprivileged people of these parts suffered the same fate during the famine years as other parts of Meath. But for the most part these coastal fishing villages were saved considerable hardship, death, and destruction, because of their local mussel and fishing industry, and popular local opinion has it, that many families escaped the poorhouse and even death, with pots full of 'stewed seagulls'!

Being situated in close proximity to Drogheda was considered a huge advantage to the surrounding villages, (Colpe, Mornington, Donacarney etc.) But this changed during the famine years, as vast droves of the unfortunate Irish poor made their way from many parts of Ireland to the ports on the east coast. This resulted in considerable traffic in human misery enroute to Drogheda town, which was one of the principal embarkation points.

Housing conditions

A Doctor in Clonard attributed epidemics of typhus in his area, to bad feeding, damp bedding, and the filth of the houses, which created a very low standard of health. It could scarcely be otherwise in view of the deplorable conditions under which so many people lived.[5]

Workhouse

The regime in the Irish workhouses was so strict that prisoners in the local jails often fared better. Indeed, in some cases the workhouse inmates committed crimes in order to get transferred to jail.[6]

The mode of administration of the Poor Relief Act set up in July 1838, continued to operate until 1923, when the system was re-organised, and a number of the unions amalgamated. In 1925 the rural district councils were abolished and replaced by Boards of Health and Public Assistance in each county. Many of the workhouses became obsolete, the ones that remained, became known as County Homes and County Hospitals.[7]

Travelling back through the pages of turbulent Irish history, it is very hard to imagine ordinary everyday family life in Ireland in the 16th 17th 18th and 19th centuries, with the major portion of recorded history dealing with invasions, conquests, poverty famine and disaster. It is heartening to know it wasn't all 'doom and gloom', and the Irish did maintain a strong sense of courage, determination and endurance in the face of adversity, and most of all a love of music and storytelling, which has been passed on from generation to generation, through our national traditions (Irish music and song, dancing, set dancing, ceile, and not forgetting the shanachie).

****

At the beginning of 19th century, the most noted character in these parts was the notorious highwayman, Michael Collier or Collier the robber as he was known. Michael Collier may have been known as 'the notorious highway robber to the rich, but he was 'celebrated Collier the highwayman' to the poor. The following is a brief account of his life:

Michael Collier
Highwayman Extraordinary (1780-1849)

"Collier was then a dauntless and powerful man, exhibiting all the marks of great muscular powers; and though it was evident his best days had passed away, he yet seemed like an oak that braved the storm and stood the shock of time, defiant as ever. He was upwards of six feet high and nearly fourteen stone weight extremely broad in shoulders and made proportionately".
With these words a Drogheda solicitor described the famous highwayman, then in the last year of his life and almost seventy years of age.

There are conflicting reports as to where Michael Collier was born, some say it was at the foot of a hill on the banks of the river Nanny, and others say he was a Bellewstown man. However, one thing we can be certain of, he was a Meath man.

In his youth he fell in love with a girl whose father and three brothers were horse-thieves. They had been captured and were on their way to Trim for what was considered then a hanging offence. He engineered their escape, which made him a wanted man. He took to the hills and to the highways, and very soon established himself as a very skilful highway robber, and from the handsome booty he obtained from his activities, enabled him to live like a prince. What is to his credit is that he acted like a prince, priding himself in his unique code of conduct and helping in a practical way many less fortunate in his native countryside.

One of Colliers most famous exploits was his hold-up and robbery of the Dublin-Belfast mail coach at Bloody-Hollow on the Great North road between Drumcondra and Swords. He collected alot of coats and hats and arranged them on a hedge at the side of the steep-rising out of Bloody-Hollow. As the stage-coach was nearing, Collier leaped out in front of it and shouted "now gentlemen, resistance is useless, my men line the ditches, they only want one word from me and they will riddle you with bullets". The frightened passengers could do nothing except deliver up all their money and valuable items to the highwayman. When they did Collier stepped aside and bid them a safe journey. The next morning a flying squad of Dragoons sent out from Dublin, found six dummy figures propped up against a hedge at Bloody-Hollow. At that time, Collier was safe and sound many miles away from that spot.

Collier became hated by the well off members of society, while the poorer classes to whom he was alleged to be generous had great respect for him. Many a poor peasant or small farmer had reason to be thankful to him, as he shared some of the money he had taken from the rich landlords with them. Yet his wrong deeds deserved to be punished.

Of those who rode with him, fourteen were hanged, six were shot and two were transported, yet, he himself, seemed to live a charmed life and escaped the hangman twice.

The first time he was captured was by Lord Gormanston and his Troopers at the old Greenhills Tavern, a few hundred yards south of the entrance to the Mosney Road. He was sentenced to be hanged, but broke out of Trim Jail on the eve of his execution, and managed to escape by swimming the river Boyne to freedom.

The second time he was taken by John Armstrong (Chief of the Watch in Drogheda) and a large force of mounted Constabulary, at the Cock Pub in Gormanston, some say, it was in a cottage near the surrounding area of the Naul.

He was condemned to life imprisonment, in the penal settlements of Australia. Soon after his arrival in Australia, he was mysteriously released on condition that he joined the colonial regiment there. Some time after that he was promoted, then discharged and given a free passage back to Ireland. When he died in Drogheda in 1849, two doctors and a priest had attended at his bedside. Six men buried him by candlelight in the Cord Cemetery, they were: Brendan Reilly, Thomas Rowe, Robert Johnson, Hugh O'Neill, William Reynolds and James Fitzpatrick.[8,9]

Not alone did East Meath harbour rare outlaws, it also was the scene of a rare discovery in 1850, of the Tara or Bettystown brooch. At the time the Tara (Bettystown) brooch was found, it made no major significant impact on the poor woman looking for firewood, as to its huge historical and national importance. The tragedy of the situation was that this poor woman probably wretched from extreme poverty and starvation, scavenging for bits of food and fuel, while holding in her hand a priceless jewel, through ignorance and perhaps dementia, lost it, or gave it away, having failed to sell it for a few miserable pounds or even shillings. No amount of *pounds* would buy it today!

The Tara (Bettystown) Brooch:

The exquisite penannular brooch in the National Museum known as the 'Tara Brooch', owes its name to the fanciful imagination of a Dublin firm of jewellers rather than to any association with Tara, the ancient seat of the High Kings of Ireland.

It is generally accepted that the brooch was found in August 1850 on the beach at Bettystown, Co. Meath by a poor woman, who, with her children was gathering driftwood for fuel. According to the story, the woman offered the brooch for sale to the owner of a Drogheda junk-shop who refused to buy it because he thought it was worthless! A watchmaker in the town later acquired it and sold it at a handsome profit to Waterhouse & Co., a well known firm of jewellers in Dame St., Dublin.

The existence of the brooch was first made public in a pamphlet published in Dublin by Waterhouse, entitled "Ornamental Irish Antiques". As the 'Tara Brooch' it was exhibited at the International Exhibitions in Paris, London and Dublin, and was later sold to the Royal Irish Academy for two hundred pounds. The sale, which was completed in 1867, was made on the condition that it never be allowed leave Ireland. Sir William Wilde does not list the 'Tara Brooch' in the catalogue, (which was completed before the Royal Irish Academy made the purchase) but in listing certain silver objects, he notes that they were found 'in the excavation for the harbour wall at the mouth of the Boyne, near Drogheda, in an Oak box, and along with them the brooch called that of Tara'.

The ornament was made in the early eight century, is three and a half inches in diameter and is of white bronze, a combination of copper and tin. The face is overlaid with various ornamented patterns, which bears a remarkable resemblance to decorations on the Ardagh Chalice and the Book of Kells. To appreciate it fully one must make the journey to the National Museum, where it is properly preserved and presented. Here it enjoys the admiration of thousands each week. It has recently returned from a tour of Europe and of the United States of America.[10]

Description

It is a gilt silver ring brooch, and, in the words of the ***exhibition catalogue,***
"bears, on the front, an almost indescribable variety of ornament of animal and geometric interlacing executed in twisted, beaded and plain gold wire filigree, of granulation, amber studs, blue and red glass settings."
The back of the brooch, i.e. the private side worn next to the wearer, is as elaborately ornamented as the front, but in a different manner: *"here there are scrolls and trumpets and lentoid bosses of an earlier time. Two panels are of thin silver and one of gold foil, each with fine patterns cut through them and backed on burnished copper to look like designs in red enamel"*.[11]

The happy combination of ornaments of amber and enamel and translucent glass, have caused Petrie to declare that it is superior to any hitherto found in the variety of its ornaments and in the exquisite delicacy and perfection of its execution.[12]

The following is an extract from *Griffith's Valuation*, published in 1856. It provides us today with valuable information about the people living in the parish of Colpe then, and the value of their land holdings and dwellings. Also included in this extract is the parish of Julianstown.

BARONY OF DULEEK, LOWER
UNION OF DROGHEDA.

No. and Letters of Reference to Map.	Names. Townlands and Occupiers.	Immediate Lessors.	Description of Tenement.	Area. A. R. P.	Rateable Annual Valuation. Land. £ s. d.	Rateable Annual Valuation. Buildings. £ s. d.	Total Annual Valuation of Rateable Property. £ s. d.
1	BALLYMAD. (Ord. S. 21.) Francis Brodigan, (Also lot 1, Pilltown.)	In fee,	Land,	64 2 11	51 10 0	—	51 10 0
— a	Vacant,	Francis Brodigan,	House and office,	—	—	0 15 0	0 15 0
			Total,	64 2 11	51 10 0	0 15 0	52 5 0
1 A — B	BETAGHSTOWN. (Ord. S. 21.) Robert Sheppard, (See also lots 6 and 7.)	In fee,	Land,	57 0 18 / 38 2 9	39 0 0 / 30 0 0	— / —	} 69 0 0
— A a	Patrick Ryder,	Robert Sheppard,	House, offices, & garden,	0 0 30	0 8 0	1 2 0	1 10 0
— B a	John Byrne,	Same,	House and offices,	—	—	0 16 0	0 16 0
— b	Vacant,	Same,	House,	—	—	0 7 0	0 7 0
2 a	Thomas Killen,	Same,	House, offices, and land,	79 2 2	70 0 0	13 0 0	83 0 0
— b	Patrick M'Quillan,	Thomas Killen,	House & small garden,	—	—	0 7 0	0 7 0
— c	Anne Dalton,	Same,	House & small garden,	—	—	0 7 0	0 7 0
3 A a — B — C	Patrick M'Genniss,	Robert Sheppard,	House, offices, and land, Land, Land,	2 0 3 / 2 1 34 / 0 2 0	1 15 0 / 1 17 0 / 0 8 0	0 15 0 / — / —	} 4 15 0
4	Mary Wherty, (See also lot 10, Donacarney, Great.)	Same,	Land,	10 0 26	9 5 0	—	9 5 0
— a	John Tiernan,	Same,	House and garden,	0 0 10	0 2 0	0 6 0	0 8 0
— b	Vacant,	Same,	House,	—	—	0 6 0	0 6 0
— c	Thomas Hughes,	Same,	House,	—	—	0 6 0	0 6 0
— d	Mary Gargan,	Same,	House,	—	—	0 9 0	0 9 0
— e	Hugh Ryder,	Same,	House and garden,	0 0 30	0 8 0	0 12 0	1 0 0
— f	Vacant,	Same,	House,	—	—	0 7 0	0 7 0
— g	Jane Drew,	Same,	House,	—	—	0 7 0	0 7 0
5	Anne Reilly, (See also lot 11 A B & 17 b.)	Same,	Land,	8 2 4	7 5 0	—	7 5 0
— a	Vacant,	Anne Reilly,	House and offices,	—	—	0 10 0	0 10 0
6 a	Robert Sheppard,	In fee,	Ho., offs., & plantation,	105 2 24	114 0 0	24 0 0	138 0 0
7	Robert Sheppard,	Messrs. —— Wade,	Land,	18 2 8	18 10 0	—	18 10 0
8 a	William Murray,	Robert Sheppard,	House, offices, and land,	39 0 15	41 0 0	10 0 0	51 0 0
— b	Philip Murtagh,	William Murray,	House,	—	—	0 15 0	0 15 0
9 a	Patrick Skane,	Robert Sheppard,	House, offices, and land,	14 2 1	10 0 0	2 10 0	12 10 0
10 A a — B	Joseph M'Cann,	Same,	House, offices, and land, Land,	7 0 17 / 2 3 10	7 10 0 / 2 15 0	1 0 0 / —	} 11 5 0
— A b	Vacant,	Joseph M'Cann,	House,	—	—	4 0 0	4 0 0
— c	Joseph Connolly,	Robert Sheppard,	House and garden,	0 0 15	0 5 0	0 10 0	0 15 0
— d	William Tiernan,	Same,	House and garden,	0 0 15	0 5 0	0 15 0	1 0 0
— e	Anne Smith,	Same,	Ho., office, & sm. garden,	—	—	0 15 0	0 15 0
11 A — B	Anne Reilly,	Same,	Land,	4 0 16 / 5 3 21	4 15 0 / 6 10 0	— / —	} 11 5 0
— A a	Michael Nulty,	Same,	House, office, & garden,	0 1 0	0 10 0	0 15 0	1 5 0
— B a	Vacant,	Same,	House and office,	—	—	5 0 0	5 0 0
— b	Mary Kelly, (See also lot 13.)	Same,	House and offices,	—	—	1 0 0	1 0 0
— c	John Conorton,	Mary Kelly,	House,	—	—	0 10 0	0 10 0
— d	Mary M'Cann,	Robert Sheppard,	House and office,	—	—	0 10 0	0 10 0
— e	Vacant,	Mary M'Cann,	House,	—	—	1 0 0	1 0 0
— f	Thomas M'Cann,	Robert Sheppard,	House and offices,	—	—	1 5 0	1 5 0

VALUATION OF TENEMENTS.

PARISH OF COLPE.

No. and Letters of Reference to Map.		Names. Townlands and Occupiers.	Immediate Lessors.	Description of Tenement.	Area. A. R. P.	Rateable Annual Valuation. Land. £ s. d.	Buildings. £ s. d.	Total Annual Valuation of Rateable Property. £ s. d.
		BETAGHSTOWN—*continued.*						
—	g	Vacant,	Thomas M'Cann,	House,	—	—	0 12 0	0 12 0
12		Thomas M'Cann,	Robert Sheppard,	Land,	8 3 26	9 0 0	—	9 0 0
13		Mary Kelly,	Same,	Land,	6 3 19	7 15 0	—	7 15 0
14	a	Patrick M'Cann,	Mary Kelly,	House, offices, and land,	1 3 6	2 0 0	1 15 0	3 15 0
15		Gerald Simcock,	Robert Sheppard,	Land,	24 1 37	27 0 0	—	27 0 0
—	a	Christopher Tyrrell,	Gerald Simcock,	House,	—	—	0 10 0	0 10 0
—	b	James Daly,	Same,	House,	—	—	1 5 0	1 5 0
—	c	Vacant,	Same,	House,	—	—	1 5 0	1 5 0
—	d	Patrick Kelly,	Robert Sheppard,	House and garden,	0 0 12	0 3 0	2 7 0	2 10 0
—	e	Vacant,	Same,	House,	—	—	1 5 0	1 5 0
—	f	Vacant,	Same,	House,	—	—	2 0 0	2 0 0
—	g	Vacant,	Same,	House,	—	—	2 10 0	2 10 0
—	h	Vacant,	Same,	House,	—	—	1 5 0	1 5 0
16	a	Gerald Simcocks, (See also lot 10 g Townland of *Mornington*.)	Rev. John Brabazon,	Hotel (*part of*) offs. & gar.	0 2 0	0 10 0	10 0 0	10 10 0
—	b	Vacant,	Same,	House and offices,	—	—	8 0 0	8 0 0
—	c	Vacant,	Same,	House and offices,	—	—	8 0 0	8 0 0
—	d	Vacant,	Same,	House and office,	—	—	8 0 0	8 0 0
—	e	William Campbell,	Same,	House and offices,	—	—	8 0 0	8 0 0
				Waste of houses, yards, &c.,	1 0 6	—	—	—
		ESTHAM-SQUARE.						
17	a	Edward Fogarty,	Bridget Wherty,	House, office, & gardens,	0 1 30	0 15 0	4 0 0	4 15 0
—	b	Anne Reilly,	Ralph Smyth,	House, offices, & garden,	0 0 20	0 5 0	6 0 0	6 5 0
—	c	Joseph Ashe,	Same,	House, offices, & garden,	0 0 20	0 5 0	7 0 0	7 5 0
—	d	William Wynne,	Same,	House and garden,	0 0 10	0 2 0	2 13 0	2 15 0
—	e	Thomas Clinton,	Same,	House, offices, & garden,	0 0 16	0 4 0	3 6 0	3 10 0
—	f	Francis Anderson,	William Murray,	House (*servants*),	—	—	4 0 0	4 0 0
—	g	William Murray,	P. —— M. O. Hanlon,	Offices,	—	—	1 0 0	1 0 0
—	h	William Kelly,	Reps. John Shegog,	House, offices, & garden,	0 1 0	1 10 0	5 0 0	6 10 0
				Waste of houses, roads, &c.,	0 3 30	—	—	—
18		William Murray,	P. —— M. O. Hanlon,	Land,	3 1 19	3 5 0	—	3 5 0
19	a	Francis Anderson,	Ralph Smyth,	House, offices, and land,	22 3 23	27 0 0	20 0 0	47 0 0
20	a	David Lucas, (See also lot 15, *Donacarney, Great.*)	George H. Pentland,	House, offices, and land,	24 1 21	28 10 0	21 0 0	49 10 0
21	{A B}	Hugh Woods, (See also lot 9, *Donacarney, Great.*)	Reps. William H. Batt,	Land,	{11 0 35 4 2 10}	{11 10 0 5 10 0}	—	}17 0 0
22		Nicholas Woods,	Same,	Land,	8 0 18	9 5 0	—	9 5 0
23		Patrick Carroll,	Same,	Land,	10 2 24	12 0 0	—	12 0 0
—	a	Vacant,	Patrick Carroll,	House,	—	—	0 8 0	0 8 0
—	b	Andrew Morgan,	Same,	House,	—	—	0 8 0	0 8 0
—	c	James Donegan,	Same,	House,	—	—	0 8 0	0 8 0
—	d	James Donegan,	Nicholas Woods,	Forge,	—	—	0 7 0	0 7 0
—	e	Peter Farnan,	Same,	House,	—	—	0 8 0	0 8 0
—	f	John Murphy,	Same,	House,	—	—	0 9 0	0 9 0
—	g	Mary Hammel,	Same,	House,	—	—	0 6 0	0 6 0
—	h	Martin Gallagher,	Hugh Woods,	House,	—	—	0 7 0	0 7 0
—	i	Patrick Toner,	Same,	House,	—	—	0 9 0	0 9 0
24	a	Richard Heney,	Reps. William H. Batt,	House, office, and land,	1 3 24	2 0 0	0 15 0	2 15 0
25		Dublin and Drogheda Railway Company,	In fee,	Railway (228 *lin. perches*),	7 2 6	—	—	12 15 0
				Total,	537 3 0	514 17 0	209 0 0	736 12 0
		BEY BEG. (*Ord. S.* 20 & 27.)						
1	a	Henry Smith,	In fee,	House, offices, and land,	323 3 25	325 0 0	33 0 0	358 0 0
—	b	John M'Ardle,	Henry Smith,	House, office, & garden,	0 0 10	0 3 0	0 11 0	0 14 0
—	c	Patrick Berrill,	Same,	House, office, & garden,	0 0 10	0 3 0	0 11 0	0 14 0
—	d	John Caulen,	Same,	House and garden,	0 0 10	0 3 0	0 10 0	0 13 0
—	e	Patrick Caulen,	Same,	House,	—	—	0 6 0	0 6 0
2	a	Andrew Morgan,	Same,	House, office, and land,	10 2 0	10 15 0	0 10 0	11 5 0

VALUATION OF TENEMENTS.

PARISH OF COLPE.

No. and Letters of Reference to Map.		Townlands and Occupiers.	Immediate Lessors.	Description of Tenement.	Area. A. R. P.	Rateable Annual Valuation. Land. £ s. d.	Buildings. £ s. d.	Total Annual Valuation of Rateable Property. £ s. d.
		BEY BEG—continued.						
3	a	Nicholas M'Cullen,	Henry Smith,	House, offices, and land,	14 3 33	16 0 0	1 10 0	17 10 0
4 A	}	Patrick M'Cullen,	Same,	Land,	1 2 21	2 0 0	—	} 12 15 0
— B	a			Offices and land.	11 1 39	10 0 0	0 15 0	
—	b	James Caulen,	Same,	House, offices, & garden,	0 3 26	1 4 0	0 12 0	1 16 0
5	a	Patrick M'Cullen,	Same,	House, office, and land,	3 0 16	3 0 0	1 5 0	4 5 0
6	a	James Faulkner,	Same,	House, offices, and land,	30 0 23	22 2 0	1 18 0	24 0 0
7	a	Peter Taaffe,	Same,	House, offices, and land,	6 0 33	6 5 0	1 5 0	7 10 0
8	a	Michael Quinn,	Same,	House, office, and land.	2 2 31	2 10 0	1 5 0	3 15 0
				Total,	405 2 37	390 5 0	43 18 0	443 3 0
		BEY MORE. (Ord. S. 20 & 27.)						
1	a	John Cooper,	Oliver Cramer,	House, offices, and land,	102 1 11	260 0 0	13 10 0	273 10 0
—	b	John Magrath,	John Cooper,	House and garden,	0 1 0	0 8 0	0 12 0	1 0 0
—	c	Thomas Dillon,	Same,	House and office,	—	—	0 14 0	0 14 0
—	d	James D'Arcy,	Same,	House,	—	—	0 9 0	0 9 0
—	e	Patrick M'Cann,	Same,	House,	—	—	0 9 0	0 9 0
—	f	John Maxwell,	Same,	House,	—	—	0 9 0	0 9 0
2	a	John Cooper,	Oliver Cramer,	Office and land,	41 1 14	46 0 0	0 8 0	46 8 0
—	b	Patrick Dobson,	John Cooper,	House,	—	—	0 8 0	0 8 0
3	a	John Cook,	Same,	House, offs., & orchard,	2 2 8	6 0 0	2 0 0	8 0 0
4	a	Frederick Cooper,	Same,	House and orchard,	1 1 25	3 5 0	1 5 0	4 10 0
—	b	Thomas D'Arcy,	Frederick Cooper,	House,	—	—	0 7 0	0 7 0
—	c	Edward Stafford,	Same,	House,	—	—	0 7 0	0 7 0
5		Frederick Cooper,	John Cooper,	Orchard,	1 2 36	4 0 0	—	4 0 0
6	a	James M'Cullen,	Oliver Cramer,	House, offices, and land,	66 1 26	75 0 0	4 0 0	79 0 0
—	b	Patrick Fay,	James M'Cullen,	House,	—	—	0 9 0	0 9 0
7	a	Matthew Dorman,	John Barlow,	House, office, and land,	17 2 4	17 10 0	1 0 0	18 10 0
—	b	Patrick Dorman,	Matthew Dorman,	House,	—	—	0 9 0	0 9 0
—	c	John Boylan,	Same,	House,	—	—	0 9 0	0 9 0
—	d	Michael Boylan,	Bernard Dorman,	House,	—	—	0 8 0	0 8 0
8	a	John Flanigan,	John Barlow,	House, offices, and land,	22 1 19	20 10 0	0 15 0	21 5 0
—	b	Mary Hammel,	John Flanigan,	House,	—	—	0 6 0	0 6 0
—	c	Mary Reilly,	Same,	House,	—	—	0 7 0	0 7 0
—	d	Nicholas Hickey,	Same,	House,	—	—	0 7 0	0 7 0
—	e	Patrick M'Loughlin,	Same,	House,	—	—	0 7 0	0 7 0
—	f	Thomas Brennan,	Same,	House,	—	—	0 6 0	0 6 0
9	a	Mary M'Donagh,	John Barlow,	House, offices, and land,	71 0 14	71 0 0	4 0 0	75 0 0
10	a	William Ball,	Same,	House, offices, and land,	318 3 14	367 0 0	18 0 0	385 0 0
—	b	Owen Wherty,	William Ball,	House and garden,	0 1 0	0 10 0	0 9 0	0 19 0
—	c	Thomas Ring,	Same,	House,	—	—	0 8 0	0 8 0
—	d	Mary Kane,	Same,	House,	—	—	0 6 0	0 6 0
11		Patrick Mathews,	John Barlow,	Land,	70 3 2	87 0 0	—	87 0 0
—	a	Patrick Dolan,	Patrick Mathews,	House and garden,	0 0 10	0 2 0	0 10 0	0 12 0
—	b	Laurence Kelly,	Same,	House,	—	—	0 8 0	0 8 0
—	c	Bridget Kelly,	Same,	House,	—	—	0 7 0	0 7 0
				Total,	806 3 23	958 5 0	54 9 0	1012 14 0
		COLP, EAST. (Ord. S. 20 & 21.)						
1	a	Nicholas Kelly,	William E. Smythe,	House, offices, and land,	83 2 21	74 10 0	2 10 0	77 0 0
2 A — B	} a	James Garvey,	Same,	House, offices, and land, Land,	18 0 35 89 2 33	18 15 0 75 0 0	2 0 0	} 95 15 0
3	a	John Taaffe,	Same,	House, offices, and land,	16 0 8	13 3 0	0 12 0	13 15 0
4	a	Owen Carroll,	Same,	House, offices, and land,	181 0 34	179 15 0	6 5 0	186 0 0
5	a	Hugh M'Cabe,	Same,	Offices and land,	5 3 10	6 13 0	0 12 0	7 5 0
6		Dublin and Drogheda Railway Company,	In fee,	Railway (197 lin. perches),	2 3 14	—	—	11 0 0
				Total,	397 2 1	367 16 0	11 19 0	390 15 0
		COLP, WEST. (Ord. S. 20 & 21.)						
1	a	Peter Mathews,	Maria S. Hutchinson,	House, offices, and land,	1 1 24	1 5 0	5 0 0	6 5 0
2 A — B	} a	James Mathews,	Same,	Land, Herd's ho., off., & land,	83 1 36 103 2 14	100 0 0 120 0 0	— 1 5 0	} 221 5 0

VALUATION OF TENEMENTS.

PARISH OF COLPE.

No. and Letters of Reference to Map.	Names. Townlands and Occupiers.	Immediate Lessors.	Description of Tenement.	Area. A. R. P.	Rateable Annual Valuation. Land. £ s. d.	Buildings. £ s. d.	Total Annual Valuation of Rateable Property. £ s. d.
	COLP, WEST— continued.						
— A a	Mathew Cooney,	James Mathews,	House,	—	—	0 7 0	0 7 0
— b	James Johnston,	Same,	House,	—	—	0 7 0	0 7 0
— c	Vacant,	Same,	House,	—	—	0 6 0	0 6 0
— d	Vacant,	Same,	House,	—	—	0 5 0	0 5 0
— e	Michael Tracy,	Same,	House,	—	—	0 7 0	0 7 0
— f	Matthew Tracy,	Same,	House,	—	—	0 8 0	0 8 0
— g	Thomas Hoey,	Same,	House,	—	—	0 8 0	0 8 0
— h	Patrick Brangan,	Same,	House,	—	—	0 8 0	0 8 0
— i	. . . .	Same,	Church and grave-yard,	0 2 16	1 0 0	10 0 0	11 0 0
— B b	Michael Black,	Same,	House,	—	—	0 12 0	0 12 0
3 A / B	William Kearns,	Maria S. Hutchinson,	Land,	32 3 38 / 5 2 8	37 0 0 / 6 0 0	—	} 43 0 0
	(See also lots 1 & 7, Stameen.)						
4	Michael Walsh,	William E. Smith,	Land,	31 0 23	41 0 0	—	41 0 0
— a	Peter M'Cullagh,	Michael Walsh,	House and offices,	—	—	1 5 0	1 5 0
5 a	Ralph Smith,	William E. Smith,	Herd's ho., offs., & land,	41 1 6	52 15 0	0 15 0	53 10 0
6	Dublin and Drogheda Railway Company,	In fee,	Railway (214 lin. perches)	4 0 14	—	—	12 0 0
			Total,	309 0 19	359 0 0	21 13 0	392 13 0
			EXEMPTIONS: Church and grave-yard,	0 2 16	1 0 0	10 0 0	11 0 0
			Total, exclusive of Exemptions,	308 2 3	358 0 0	11 13 0	381 13 0
	DONACARNEY, GREAT. (Ord. S. 21.)						
1	William Boylan,	Henry Smith,	Land,	1 2 20	2 0 0	—	2 0 0
	(Lot 5, Donacarney, Little.)						
— a	Patrick Kirwan,	William Boylan,	House,	—	—	0 8 0	0 8 0
— b	Bridget Garrigan,	Same,	House,	—	—	0 7 0	0 7 0
— c	William Donegan,	Same,	House,	—	—	0 9 0	0 9 0
— d	Alice Gargan,	Same,	House,	—	—	0 6 0	0 6 0
— e	Catherine Carolan,	Same,	House,	—	—	0 7 0	0 7 0
— f	James Leech,	Same,	House,	—	—	0 8 0	0 8 0
— g	James Donnelly,	Patrick Boylan,	House and office,	—	—	0 8 0	0 8 0
— h	Thomas Arnold,	Same,	House,	—	—	0 9 0	0 9 0
— i	William Brabazon,	In fee,	Garden,	0 1 20	0 10 0	—	0 10 0
— j	Henry Fox,	William Brabazon,	House and garden,	0 1 0	0 7 0	0 13 0	1 0 0
— k	Rose Donegan,	Same,	House,	—	—	0 7 0	0 7 0
— l	Vacant,	Same,	House and garden,	0 0 20	0 5 0	0 10 0	0 15 0
— m	Patrick M'Cabe,	Same,	House, forge, & sm. gar.,	—	—	0 10 0	0 10 0
— n	Judith Clinton,	Same,	House,	—	—	0 8 0	0 8 0
— o	James M'Ardle,	Same,	House and garden,	0 0 10	0 3 0	0 7 0	0 10 0
— p	George Verdon,	Same,	House & small garden,	—	—	0 7 0	0 7 0
— q	William M'Cabe,	Same,	House, office, & garden,	0 0 10	0 3 0	0 17 0	1 0 0
— r	George Richardson,	Henry Smith,	House, office, & garden,	0 0 36	0 8 0	0 12 0	1 0 0
	(Also lot 11.)		Waste,	0 3 24	—	—	—
2 a	Henry Garvey,	William Brabazon,	House, offices, and land,	3 3 21	4 15 0	5 0 0	9 15 0
3	William Brabazon,	James Brabazon,	Land,	1 2 8	1 15 0	—	1 15 0
— a	Vacant,	William Brabazon,	House and offices,	—	—	4 10 0	4 10 0
4	William Brabazon,	James Brabazon,	Land,	73 3 20	67 0 0	—	67 0 0
5 A / B	Nicholas Woods,	William Brabazon	Land,	8 3 8 / 16 3 11	10 0 0 / 17 5 0	—	} 27 5 0
6 a	Nicholas Woods,	Same,	House, offices, and land,	50 1 1	50 0 0	1 15 0	51 15 0
7	John Tiernan, jun.,	Same,	Land,	30 2 9	29 0 0	—	29 0 0
	(Also lot 13 A B C.)						
8 A a / B	Patrick Carroll,	Same,	House, offices, and land, / Land,	25 0 20 / 19 3 38	25 0 0 / 22 0 0	2 10 0	} 49 10 0
9 a	Hugh Woods,	Same,	House, offices, and land,	41 0 11	37 0 0	3 0 0	40 0 0
	(Also lot 35, Mornington.)						
10 a	Mary Wherty,	Same,	House, offices, and land,	3 1 18	3 0 0	1 5 0	4 5 0
11 a	John Tiernan,	Henry Smith,	House, offices, and land,	31 1 17	34 8 0	1 2 0	35 10 0

VALUATION OF TENEMENTS.

PARISH OF COLPE.

No. and Letters of Reference to Map.	Names. Townlands and Occupiers.	Names. Immediate Lessors.	Description of Tenement.	Area. A. R. P.	Rateable Annual Valuation. Land. £ s. d.	Rateable Annual Valuation. Buildings. £ s. d.	Total Annual Valuation of Rateable Property. £ s. d.
	DONACARNEY, GREAT—*continued.*						
— b	John Clinton,	John Tiernan,	House,	—	—	0 8 0	0 8 0
— c	Vacant,	Same,	House,	—	—	0 8 0	0 8 0
— d	Michael Merryman,	Same,	House,	—	—	0 6 0	0 6 0
— e	Nicholas Wherty,	Same,	House,	—	—	0 12 0	0 12 0
— f	Vacant,	Same,	House,	—	—	1 0 0	1 0 0
— g	Bernard Halfpenny,	Same,	House,	—	—	0 6 0	0 6 0
— h	Patrick Murphy,	Same,	House,	—	—	0 6 0	0 6 0
— i	Simon Tiernan,	Henry Smith,	House,	—	—	0 10 0	0 10 0
12	Simon Tiernan,	John Tiernan,	Garden,	1 0 12	2 10 0	—	2 10 0
13 A			Land,	2 3 30	3 0 0	—	
— B a	John Tiernan, jun.,	Henry Smith,	House, offices, and land,	4 3 18	5 5 0	2 0 0	} 15 15 0
— C			Land,	5 0 18	5 10 0	—	
14	George Richardson,	Same,	Land,	0 2 3	0 10 0	—	0 10 0
15	David Lucas,	George H. Pentland,	Land,	10 3 17	12 0 0	—	12 0 0
			Total,	335 2 20	333 14 0	32 11 0	366 5 0
	DONACARNEY, LITTLE. *(Ord. S. 21.)*						
1	James Carroll, *(Also lot 2, Mornington.)*	Burton Tandy,	House, offices, and land,	22 0 0	25 0 0	16 0 0	41 0 0
—	John Flood,	James Carroll,	House, office, & garden,	0 0 10	0 1 0	0 12 0	0 13 0
2	Rose Heany,	Burton Tandy,	Land,	2 0 29	2 10 0	—	2 10 0
— a	Edmund Thornton,	Rose Heany,	House,	—	—	0 5 0	0 5 0
— b	James Ward,	Same,	House and garden,	0 0 10	0 2 0	0 8 0	0 10 0
— c	Anne M'Cabe,	Same,	House and garden,	0 0 15	0 3 0	0 9 0	0 12 0
3	John Woods, *(Also lot 5, Mornington.)*	Burton Tandy,	Land,	149 2 30	170 0 0	—	170 0 0
— a	Patrick M'Ardle,	John Woods,	House and garden,	0 0 14	0 4 0	0 10 0	0 14 0
— b	John Murphy,	Same,	House and garden,	0 0 10	0 3 0	0 7 0	0 10 0
— c	Vacant,	Same,	House and garden,	0 0 10	0 3 0	0 7 0	0 10 0
— d	Patrick Carroll,	Same,	House and garden,	0 0 12	0 3 0	0 7 0	0 10 0
— e	Patrick Whitehorn,	Same,	House and garden,	0 0 10	0 3 0	0 7 0	0 10 0
— f	Michael M'Grane,	Same,	House and garden,	0 0 12	0 3 0	0 9 0	0 12 0
— g	Hugh M'Cabe,	Same,	Forge,	—	—	0 9 0	0 9 0
— h	Patrick Wherty,	James Carroll,	House,	—	—	0 12 0	0 12 0
— i	Denis Wherty,	Same,	House and garden,	0 0 12	0 3 0	0 9 0	0 12 0
— j	James Wherty,	Denis Wherty,	House,	—	—	0 6 0	0 6 0
4 A a	Patrick Boylan,	Henry Smith,	House, office, and land,	5 2 22	6 12 0	0 15 0	} 8 5 0
— B			Land,	0 3 13	0 18 0	—	
5 a	William Boylan,	Same,	House, offices, and land,	18 2 3	20 10 0	3 15 0	24 5 0
			Total,	199 2 12	226 18 0	26 7 0	253 5 0
	KILTROUGH. *(Ord. S. 20 & 27.)*						
1 a	John M'Loughlin,	Maria S. Hutchinson,	Offices and land,	26 0 26	33 10 0	0 10 0	34 0 0
— b	Edward Meehan,	John M'Loughlin,	House,	—	—	0 10 0	0 10 0
— c	Margaret Halligan,	Same,	House and garden,	0 0 10	0 3 0	0 10 0	0 13 0
— d	Margaret Morgan,	Same,	House,	—	—	0 10 0	0 10 0
2 a	John M'Loughlin,	Maria S. Hutchinson,	House, offices, and land,	109 2 17	91 0 0	3 0 0	94 0 0
			Total,	135 3 13	124 13 0	5 0 0	129 13 0
	MORNINGTON. *(Ord. S. 21.)*						
1	James Mathews,	Maria S. Hutchinson,	Land,	40 0 17	48 0 0	—	48 0 0
2 A				76 1 29	80 0 0	—	
— B	James Carroll,	Burton Tandy,	Land,	27 1 24	35 0 0	—	} 116 5 0
— C				1 0 4	1 5 0	—	
— B a	Peter Young,	James Carroll,	House,	—	—	0 7 0	0 7 0
3 A a	Michael Carroll,	Burton Tandy,	House, offices, and land,	27 1 24	33 0 0	2 15 0	} 52 5 0
— B			Land,	14 1 35	16 10 0	—	
4	Michael Carroll,	Same,	Land,	20 2 32	9 10 0	—	9 10 0
— a	James Campbell,	Same,	House, office, & garden,	0 1 30	0 10 0	0 12 0	1 2 0
5 a	John Woods,	Same,	House, offices, and land,	10 1 18	12 0 0	9 10 0	21 10 0
— b	John Mathews,	John Woods,	House,	—	—	0 12 0	0 12 0
— c	Michael Butler,	Same,	House,	—	—	0 12 0	0 12 0
— d	Denis Durna,	Same,	House,	—	—	0 12 0	0 12 0
— e	Patrick M'Cullagh,	Same,	House,	—	—	0 12 0	0 12 0

VALUATION OF TENEMENTS.

PARISH OF COLPE.

No. and Letters of Reference to Map.	Townlands and Occupiers.	Immediate Lessors.	Description of Tenement.	Area. A. R. P.	Rateable Annual Valuation. Land. £ s. d.	Buildings. £ s. d.	Total Annual Valuation of Rateable Property. £ s. d.
	MORNINGTON— *continued.*						
6	Rose Heney,	Burton Tandy,	Land,	6 2 22	4 10 0	—	4 10 0
7 *a*	John Stuart,	Rose Heney,	House & small garden, Waste,	— 2 1 25	— —	1 5 0 —	1 5 0
8 *a*	Rev. Joseph Druitt,	James Brabazon,	House, offices, and land,	16 3 23	21 0 0	10 0 0	31 0 0
9 *a*	Charles Fawcett,	Same,	House, offices, and land,	92 3 28	105 0 0	5 5 0	110 5 0
- *b*	Patrick Tiernan,	Charles Fawcett,	House and garden,	0 0 30	0 7 0	0 10 0	0 17 0
- *c*	James Mathews,	Same,	House and garden,	0 0 30	0 7 0	0 10 0	0 17 0
- *d*	Anne Murphy,	Same,	House,	—	—	0 6 0	0 6 0
10 *a*	Catherine Finnegan,	James Brabazon,	House and land,	3 1 7	2 15 0	5 0 0	7 15 0
11 *a*	James Maguire,	Same,	House, office, and land,	7 1 15	7 5 0	1 10 0	8 15 0
- *b*	Vacant,	James Maguire,	House,	—	—	4 10 0	4 10 0
- *c*	James Begg,	Same,	House,	—	—	0 15 0	0 15 0
- *d*	Maria Bray,	Same,	House,	—	—	2 10 0	2 10 0
12 A *a*	John Connors,	James Brabazon,	House, offices, and land,	6 2 1	5 0 0	1 10 0	} 9 10 0
- B			Land,	5 3 9	3 0 0	—	
13 A *a*	Peter Reynolds,	Same,	Office and land,	16 0 31	8 0 0	0 10 0	} 25 10 0
- B *a*			House, offices, and land,	0 2 30	0 8 0	1 15 0	
- C			Land,	17 2 27	14 17 0	—	
- A *b*	James Reynolds,	Peter Reynolds,	House,	—	—	0 15 0	0 15 0
- B *b*	Vacant,	Same,	House,	—	—	1 0 0	1 0 0
- *c*	Vacant,	Same,	House,	—	—	1 0 0	1 0 0
14	James Reynolds,	James Brabazon,	Land,	6 1 32	2 10 0	—	2 10 0
- *a*	Vacant,	James Reynolds,	House,	—	—	0 7 0	0 7 0
15 *a*	Thomas Duffy,	James Brabazon,	House, offices, and land,	5 0 17	3 5 0	1 15 0	5 0 0
- *b*	Vacant,	Thomas Duffy,	House,	—	—	1 5 0	1 5 0
16 *a*	Richard Victory,	James Brabazon,	House, offices, and land,	6 2 10	4 0 0	1 0 0	5 0 0
17	John Reynolds, (*See also lot 31.*)	Same,	Land,	3 3 13	{ 0 17 0 0 17 0	— 0 8 0	0 17 0 1 5 0
a	Patrick Reynolds,	John Reynolds,	House and land,				
18 *a*	Richard Lynch,	James Brabazon,	House, offices, and land,	3 3 5	1 10 0	1 5 0	2 15 0
19 A	Margaret Victory,	Same,	Land,	3 1 11	2 0 0	—	} 3 15 0
- B *a*			House, offices, and land,	0 3 38	0 13 0	1 2 0	
- *b*	Vacant,	Margaret Victory,	House,	—	—	0 15 0	0 15 0
20 *a*	John Garvey,	James Brabazon,	House, office, and land,	1 0 29	0 15 0	1 5 0	2 0 0
- *b*	Margaret Burns,	John Garvey,	House,	—	—	0 6 0	0 6 0
21	Henry Garvey, (*See also lot 26 c.*)	James Brabazon,	Land,	1 0 3	0 13 0	—	0 13 0
22 *a*	Mary Crawley,	Same,	House, office, and land	1 0 3	0 13 0	0 12 0	1 5 0
- *b*	Vacant,	Mary Crawley,	House,	—	—	0 12 0	0 12 0
23 A B *a*	Patrick Smith,	James Brabazon,	House, offices, & land,	16 1 18	{ 3 5 0 3 5 0	1 5 0 1 5 0	4 10 0 4 10 0
b	Martin Carr,		House, office, & land,				
- *c*	Vacant,	Patrick Smith,	House,	—	—	1 0 0	1 0 0
- *d*	Vacant,	Martin Carr,	House,	—	—	0 15 0	0 15 0
- *e*	Richard Farrell, (*See lot 24.*)	James Brabazon,	House, offices, & garden,	0 0 10	0 2 0	1 0 0	1 2 0
- *f*	Vacant,	Richard Farrell,	House,	—	—	0 15 0	0 15 0
- *g*	Patrick Carr,	James Brabazon,	House and garden,	0 0 10	0 2 0	1 0 0	1 2 0
- *h*	Vacant,	Patrick Carr,	House,	—	—	1 0 0	1 0 0
- *i*	Patrick O'Brien,	James Brabazon,	House,	—	—	0 12 0	0 12 0
24	Richard Farrell,	Same,	Land,	2 1 17	0 17 0	—	0 17 0
25 *a*	Patrick Courtney,	Same,	House, offices, and land,	3 0 10	1 10 0	1 15 0	3 5 0
26 *a*	John Goff,	Same,	House, offices, and land,	4 1 15	1 15 0	1 0 0	2 15 0
- *b*	Vacant,	John Goff,	House,	—	—	1 0 0	1 0 0
- *c*	Henry Garvey,	Same,	House,	—	—	0 7 0	0 7 0
27 A	Patrick Lynch,	James Brabazon,	Land,	2 2 24	1 0 0	—	} 2 15 0
- B *a*			House, office, and land,	1 2 15	1 0 0	0 15 0	
- *b*	Vacant,	Patrick Lynch,	House,	—	—	0 15 0	0 15 0
28 *a*	Nicholas Ward,	James Brabazon,	House and land,	4 2 28	{ 0 14 0 0 14 0 0 7 0	0 6 0 0 5 0 0 6 0	1 0 0 0 19 0 0 13 0
b	Patrick Ward,		House and land,				
c	Maurice Ward,		House and land,				
29 *a*	Andrew Cavanagh,	Same,	House and land,	10 0 36	3 0 0	0 5 0	3 5 0
- *b*	Edward Smith,	Andrew Cavanagh,	House,	—	—	0 5 0	0 5 0
30 *a*	Michael Clarke,	James Brabazon,	House and land,	3 2 26	1 5 0	0 10 0	1 15 0
31 *a*	John Reynolds,	Same,	House, office, and land,	5 0 8	1 15 0	0 10 0	2 5 0
32 *a*	Francis Sheeler,	Same,	House, offices, and land,	56 2 19	64 0 0	0 15 0	64 15 0
- *b*	Patrick M'Ginn,	Francis Sheeler,	House,	—	—	0 15 0	0 15 0
- *c*	James Hoey,	Same,	House,	—	—	1 0 0	1 0 0
- *d*	John Dolan,	James Brabazon,	House and garden,	0 0 10	0 3 0	0 7 0	0 10 0

VALUATION OF TENEMENTS.

PARISH OF COLPE.

No. and Letters of Reference to Map	Names. Townlands and Occupiers.	Immediate Lessors.	Description of Tenement.	Area. A. R. P.	Rateable Annual Valuation. Land. £ s. d.	Buildings. £ s. d.	Total Annual Valuation of Rateable Property. £ s. d.
	MORNINGTON—continued.						
— c	John Pierce,	James Brabazon,	House and garden,	0 0 25	0 6 0	1 6 0	1 12 0
— f	John Duffy,	Same,	House & small garden,	—	—	1 0 0	1 0 0
33 a	John Drew,	Same,	House, offices, and land,	54 2 22	57 0 0	1 10 0	58 10 0
34	John Drew,	Same,	Land,	33 2 21	29 0 0	—	29 0 0
35	Hugh Woods,	Same,	Land,	15 1 32	11 10 0	—	11 10 0
36 A			Land,	6 1 10	0 5 0	—	
— B	James Brabazon,	Christina P. Leslie and John Gardner,	Strand,	8 3 6	—	—	270 0 0
— C			Strand,	2 0 14	—	—	
— D a			House, offices, and land,	442 2 7	219 15 0	50 0 0	
— b	Ballast Board,	James Brabazon,	Light keeper's house and offices,	—	—	1 10 0	1 10 0
—	James Brabazon,	As lessor,	Half rent rateable, £4.				
— c	Ballast Board,	James Brabazon,	Light keeper's house and offices,	—	—	1 5 0	1 5 0
—	James Brabazon,	As lessor,	Half rent rateable, £4.				
— d	Vacant,	James Brabazon,	House,	—	—	2 10 0	2 10 0
— e	Nicholas Brennan,	Same,	Herd's house,	—	—	1 0 0	1 0 0
— f	George M'Alester,	Same,	House and offices,	—	—	1 0 0	1 0 0
— g	Anne King,	Same,	House and garden,	0 0 10	0 2 0	0 15 0	0 17 0
— h	Vacant,	Same,	House,	—	—	1 0 0	1 0 0
— i	Vacant,	Same,	House,	—	—	1 0 0	1 0 0
— j	Patrick Clarke,	Same,	House and garden,	0 0 20	0 4 0	1 0 0	1 4 0
— k	Vacant,	James Smith,	House,	—	—	1 5 0	1 5 0
— l	Vacant,	Same,	House,	—	—	0 15 0	0 15 0
— m	Thomas Corrigan,	James Brabazon,	House,	—	—	1 0 0	1 0 0
— n	Vacant,	Thomas Corrigan,	House,	—	—	1 0 0	1 0 0
— o	Vacant,	Same,	House,	—	—	0 10 0	0 10 0
— p	Vacant,	Same,	House and office,	—	—	1 5 0	1 5 0
37	Michael Arnold, (See also lot 40.)	James Brabazon,	Land,	3 0 12	1 10 0	—	1 10 0
— a	James M'Cullagh,	Michael Arnold,	House,	—	—	0 6 0	0 6 0
38	John Mullins, (See also lot 43 c.)	James Brabazon,	Land,	12 1 8	9 0 0	—	9 0 0
39	Francis Anderson,	Same,	Land,	10 1 21	10 5 0	—	10 5 0
40 a	Michael Arnold,	Same,	House, offices, and land,	5 3 23	2 10 0	3 10 0	6 0 0
— b	Vacant,	Michael Arnold,	House and office,	—	—	3 10 0	3 10 0
— c	Vacant,	Same,	House,	—	—	3 0 0	3 0 0
— d	Vacant,	Same,	House,	—	—	2 0 0	2 0 0
— e	Vacant,	Same,	House,	—	—	2 5 0	2 5 0
— f	Vacant,	Same,	House,	—	—	4 0 0	4 0 0
— g	Gerald Simcocks, (See also lot 16, Betaghstown.)	Rev. John Brabazon,	Hotel (part of),	—	—	36 0 0	36 0 0
41 a	William Price,	James Brabazon,	House, office, and land,	1 3 17	1 0 0	1 0 0	2 0 0
— b	Patrick M'Cann,	William Price,	House,	—	—	0 15 0	0 15 0
— c	Vacant,	Same,	House,	—	—	0 15 0	0 15 0
42 a	Ellen Clinton,	James Brabazon,	House and land,	1 1 36	0 16 0	0 6 0	1 2 0
— b	Vacant,	Ellen Clinton,	House,	—	—	0 6 0	0 6 0
— c	Vacant,	Same,	House,	—	—	0 6 0	0 6 0
43 a	Patrick Mullins,	James Brabazon,	House, offices, and land,	5 3 13	3 0 0	0 15 0	3 15 0
— b	Vacant,	Patrick Mullins,	House,	—	—	0 15 0	0 15 0
— c	John Mullins,	Same,	House and offices,	—	—	0 15 0	0 15 0
— d	Vacant,	Same,	House,	—	—	1 0 0	1 0 0
	VILLAGE OF MORNINGTON.						
44 1	James Kelly,	James Brabazon,	House, offices, & garden,	0 1 0	0 12 0	1 13 0	2 5 0
— 2	Catherine Farrell,	Patrick M'Donagh,	House,	—	—	0 5 0	0 5 0
— 3	Patrick M'Donagh,	James Brabazon,	House and garden,	0 0 39	0 12 0	1 8 0	2 0 0
— 4	Thomas Whitehorn,	Same,	House, office, & gardens,	0 1 26	0 17 0	2 13 0	3 10 0
— 5	Simon Finnegan,	Same,	House and garden,	0 2 10	1 5 0	1 10 0	2 15 0
— 6 {a b}	Peter Farrell,	Same,	Garden, / House and garden,	0 2 4 / 0 0 7	1 3 0 / 0 2 0	— / 1 0 0	2 5 0
— 7	Rose Heaney,	Maria S. Hutchinson,	House, offices, & garden,	0 0 31	0 7 0	10 3 0	10 10 0
— 8		Same,	R.C. Chapel & grave-yd.	0 1 7	0 10 0	20 0 0	20 10 0
— 9	Vacant,	James Brabazon,	House and land,	1 0 36	2 5 0	1 10 0	3 15 0
— 10	Mary Caulfield,	Same,	House and garden,	0 0 23	0 6 0	1 14 0	2 0 0
— 11	Robert Young,	Same,	House and garden,	0 0 24	0 6 0	1 14 0	2 0 0

VALUATION OF TENEMENTS.

PARISH OF COLPE.

No. and Letters of Reference to Map.	Names. Townlands and Occupiers.	Immediate Lessors.	Description of Tenement.	Area. A. R. P.	Rateable Annual Valuation. Land. £ s. d.	Rateable Annual Valuation. Buildings. £ s. d.	Total Annual Valuation of Rateable Property. £ s. d.
	MORNINGTON—*continued.* **VILLAGE OF MORNINGTON.**						
— 12	Catherine Mathews,	James Brabazon,	House,	—	—	0 10 0	0 10 0
— 13	John Dignan,	Same,	House and garden,	0 0 27	0 7 0	0 13 0	1 0 0
— 14	Vacant,	James Maguire,	House,	—	—	0 13 0	0 13 0
— 15	Susan Montgomery,	Same,	House and garden,	0 0 23	0 6 0	0 14 0	1 0 0
— 16	John Brady,	Same,	House and garden,	0 0 12	0 3 0	0 14 0	0 17 0
— 17	Vacant,	James Brabazon,	House, office, & gardens,	0 0 30	0 7 0	0 13 0	1 0 0
— 18 {a b}	Patrick Coyle,	Same,	House, office, & garden, Small garden,	0 0 20 —	0 5 0 —	2 5 0 —	} 2 10 0
— 19	Mary Brady,	Same,	House, office, & garden,	0 0 36	0 8 0	1 7 0	1 15 0
— 20	Joseph Doherty,	Same,	House and garden,	0 0 31	0 7 0	2 3 0	2 10 0
— 21	Thomas Sheeran,	Same,	House and garden,	0 0 32	0 7 0	1 5 0	1 12 0
— 22	Vacant,	Joseph Doherty,	House,	—	—	0 10 0	0 10 0
— 23	Bridget M'Cullen,	Margaret Long,	House,	—	—	1 10 0	1 10 0
— 24 {a b}	Margaret Long,	James Brabazon,	House, office, & garden, Garden,	0 0 33 0 0 10	0 8 0 0 2 0	1 0 0 —	} 1 10 0
— 25 {a b}	Bartholomew La Barte,	Patrick Coyle,	House, offices, & garden, Garden,	0 1 8 0 0 12	0 12 0 0 3 0	9 15 0 —	} 10 10 0
— 26 {a b}	Michael Mackin,	James Maguire,	House, office, & garden, Garden,	0 1 3 0 0 10	0 10 0 0 3 0	2 17 0 —	} 3 10 0
— 27 {a b}	Alice Brennan,	James Brabazon,	House, offices, & garden, Garden,	0 1 10 0 0 8	0 13 0 0 2 0	1 5 0 —	} 2 0 0
— 28	Nicholas Lauders,	Same,	House and garden,	0 0 27	0 7 0	1 13 0	2 0 0
— 29	James Connolly,	Same,	House and garden,	0 0 24	0 6 0	0 10 0	0 16 0
— 30	Jane Dea,	Rose Heaney,	House,	—	—	0 10 0	0 10 0
— 31	Matthew Halfpenny,	Same,	House,	—	—	0 10 0	0 10 0
— 32	Vacant,	Same,	House and garden, Waste of houses, &c.,	0 1 22 4 0 4	0 15 0 —	3 10 0 —	4 5 0 —
			Total,	1155 0 24	871 10 0	293 15 0	1165 5 0
			Exemptions: Light-keeper's house and offices (36 b), Light-keeper's house and offices (36 c), R.C. Chapel & grave-yd.	— — 0 1 7	— — 0 10 0	1 10 0 1 5 0 20 0 0	1 10 0 1 5 0 20 10 0
			Total of Exemptions,	0 1 7	0 10 0	22 15 0	23 5 0
			Total, exclusive of Exemptions,	1154 3 17	871 0 0	271 0 0	1142 0 0
	NEWTOWN. *(Ord. S. 20.)*						
1 A — B — C	Francis Brodigan,	In fee,	Land,	11 3 29 13 0 35 49 2 37	20 10 0 23 15 0 88 0 0	— — —	} 132 5 0
— B a	Andrew Smith,	Francis Brodigan,	House,	—	—	0 9 0	0 9 0
— b	Vacant,	Same,	House,	—	—	0 9 0	0 9 0
— c	Patrick Smith,	Same,	House,	—	—	0 8 0	0 8 0
— d	Vacant,	Same,	House,	—	—	0 8 0	0 8 0
2 A a — B	John M'Enteggart,	Same,	House, office, and land, Land,	7 2 38 5 0 32	11 10 0 8 15 0	0 10 0 —	} 20 15 0
3	Patrick Beahan,	Same,	Land,	18 3 8	32 10 0	—	32 10 0
— a	John Lucar,	Patrick Beahan,	House, offices, & garden,	0 1 0	0 15 0	12 5 0	13 0 0
4	Peter Flynn,	Reps. —— Skelly,	Land,	6 1 6	10 10 0	—	10 10 0
— a	Patrick King,	Peter Flynn,	House,	—	—	0 12 0	0 12 0
5 A a — B	Thomas M'Enteggart,	Francis Brodigan,	House, offices, and land, Land,	1 2 4 1 1 36	1 10 0 2 10 0	1 5 0 —	} 5 5 0
— a	Samuel Trisdall,	Thomas M'Enteggart,	House,	—	—	0 6 0	0 6 0
— b	James Plunket,	Same,	House,	—	—	0 6 0	0 6 0
6 a	Christopher Carolan,	Francis Brodigan,	House and gardens,	0 1 15	0 12 0	0 8 0	1 0 0
— b	James Donnelly,	Same,	House,	—	—	0 8 0	0 8 0
— c	Denis Coyle,	Same,	House and garden,	0 0 6	0 2 0	0 12 0	0 14 0
— d	Patrick Murray,	Same,	House and garden,	0 0 8	0 3 0	0 9 0	0 12 0
— e	Ellen Reid,	Same,	House,	—	—	0 6 0	0 6 0

VALUATION OF TENEMENTS.

PARISH OF COLPE.

No. and Letters of Reference to Map.		Names. Townlands and Occupiers.	Immediate Lessors.	Description of Tenement.	Area. A. R. P.	Rateable Annual Valuation. Land. £ s. d.	Buildings. £ s. d.	Total Annual Valuation of Rateable Property. £ s. d.
		NEWTOWN— *continued.*						
—	f	Patrick Morris,	Francis Brodigan,	House,	—	—	0 6 0	0 6 0
—	g	Catherine Miles,	Same,	House and garden,	0 0 12	0 5 0	0 5 0	0 10 0
—	h	James Harland,	Same,	House and garden,	0 0 10	0 4 0	0 16 0	1 0 0
—	i	Peter Farrell,	Same,	House and garden,	0 0 12	0 5 0	1 0 0	1 5 0
—	j	Bridget Murray,	Same,	House and garden,	0 1 0	0 10 0	1 0 0	1 10 0
—	k	John Branagan,	Bridget Murray,	House,	—	—	1 0 0	1 0 0
—	l	George Henry,	Francis Brodigan,	House and garden,	0 1 0	0 10 0	1 0 0	1 10 0
—	m	Thomas Hughes,	Same,	House,	—	—	0 8 0	0 8 0
—	n	Michael Conroy,	George Henry,	House,	—	—	0 12 0	0 12 0
—	o	Peter Duffy,	Same,	House,	—	—	0 12 0	0 12 0
—	p	Eliza Connigan,	Same,	House,	—	—	0 12 0	0 12 0
—	q	John Garvey,	Francis Brodigan,	House and garden,	0 0 22	0 7 0	0 10 0	0 17 0
—	r	Bridget Levins,	Same,	House,	—	—	0 7 0	0 7 0
—	s	Patrick Fogarty,	Christopher Carolan,	House,	—	—	0 7 0	0 7 0
7		Mary Caraher,	Francis Brodigan,	Waste, &c., Garden,	0 3 2 / 0 2 7	1 10 0	—	1 10 0
—	a	Vacant,	Mary Caraher,	House,	—	—	1 10 0	1 10 0
8	a	Patrick M'Govern,	Emily O. Farrell,	House and garden,	1 2 25	3 10 0	1 15 0	5 5 0
—	b	Margaret Neale,	Patrick M'Govern,	House,	—	—	0 15 0	0 15 0
—	c	John M'Ardle,	Same,	House,	—	—	0 12 0	0 12 0
9	a	Mary Bones,	Francis Brodigan,	House and garden,	1 0 34	3 8 0	0 12 0	4 0 0
10	a	Patrick Tallon,	Same,	House, office, & garden,	0 2 37	1 15 0	1 0 0	2 15 0
—	b	Peter Fitzpatrick,	Patrick Tallon,	House & small garden,	—	—	0 15 0	0 15 0
11	a	John M'Glen,	Francis Brodigan,	House and land,	0 3 3	1 8 0	0 7 0	1 15 0
—	b	Patrick Kennedy,	John M'Glen,	House,	—	—	0 7 0	0 7 0
—	c	Bryan Reilly,	Same,	House,	—	—	0 5 0	0 5 0
12		Dublin and Drogheda Railway Company,	In fee,	Railway (154 lin. perches), Dublin and Drogheda Railway (33 lin. perches, Navan branch),	5 3 35 / 0 2 0	—	—	8 10 0 / 1 5 0
				Total,	129 2 13	214 14 0	35 14 0	260 3 0
		PAINESTOWN. *(Ord. S. 20 & 21.)*						
1		John M'Cullen,	Rev. John Smith,	Land,	26 2 35	33 0 0	—	33 0 0
2	A a	Michael Stafford,	Same,	House, offices, and land,	24 0 29	25 0 0	3 5 0	} 31 15 0
—	B			Garden,	1 0 1	2 10 0	—	
—	C			Garden,	0 2 1	1 0 0	—	
3	a	Michael Kelly (*Michael*),	Same,	House, offices, and land,	10 1 12	9 0 0	1 0 0	10 0 0
4		Rev. John Smith,	In fee,	Land,	17 1 18	15 10 0	—	15 10 0
—	a	Patrick M'Eneiry,	Rev. John Smith,	House and garden,	0 0 12	0 3 0	0 15 0	0 18 0
—	b	Vacant,	Same,	House,	—	—	0 15 0	0 15 0
—	c	James Smith,	Same,	House,	—	—	0 8 0	0 8 0
—	d	Anne Logheran,	Same,	House,	—	—	0 8 0	0 8 0
5	a	Patrick Kelly,	Miss Farrell,	House, office, & garden,	0 3 15	2 2 0	0 13 0	2 15 0
—	b	John Taaffe,	Patrick Kelly,	House,	—	—	0 8 0	0 8 0
6	A a	Michael Kelly (*Pat*),	Francis Brodigan,	House, offices, and land,	5 3 23	6 10 0	1 5 0	} 22 5 0
—	B			Land,	17 2 10	14 10 0	—	
—	a	James Durnin,	Michael Kelly (*Pat*),	House, forge, & garden,	0 0 28	0 7 0	0 13 0	1 0 0
—	b	Patrick Johnston,	Same,	House,	—	—	0 10 0	0 10 0
—	c	Lawrence Greene,	Same,	House and garden,	0 0 30	0 8 0	0 7 0	0 15 0
—	d	John Hammell,	Same,	House and garden,	0 0 10	0 3 0	0 7 0	0 10 0
—	e	James Cooney,	Same,	House and garden,	0 0 10	0 3 0	0 7 0	0 10 0
—	f	John Mathews,	Same,	House and garden,	0 0 10	0 3 0	0 7 0	0 10 0
7	a	Mary Kelly,	Francis Brodigan,	House, offices, and land,	18 3 28	20 5 0	1 5 0	21 10 0
8	A a	Thomas M'Coy,	Same,	House and land,	0 1 21	0 7 0	0 15 0	} 5 5 0
—	B			Land,	1 0 12	0 18 0	—	
—	C			Land,	2 3 18	3 5 0	—	
9	a	Michael Campbell,	Same,	House, office, & garden,	1 1 13	2 15 0	1 0 0	3 15 0
10	A	John M'Loughlin,	Same,	Land,	1 3 7 / 4 3 34	2 0 0 / 5 15 0	—	} 7 15 0
—	B							
	A a	Jn. M'Loughlin's lodgers	John M'Loughlin,	House,	—	—	0 15 0	0 15 0
11	a	Anne Kelly,	Francis Brodigan,	House, offices, and land,	23 3 27	30 0 0	2 0 0	32 0 0
				Total,	160 1 4	175 14 0	17 3 0	192 17 0

VALUATION OF TENEMENTS.

PARISH OF COLPE.

No. and Letters of Reference to Map.		Names. Townlands and Occupiers.	Immediate Lessors.	Description of Tenement.	Area. A. R. P	Rateable Annual Valuation. Land. £ s. d.	Buildings. £ s. d.	Total Annual Valuation of Rateable Property. £ s. d.
		PILLTOWN. *(Ord. S. 21.)*						
1	a	Francis Brodigan,	In fee,	Ho.,offs.,gate lodge,&ld.	173 3 25	160 0 0	46 0 0	206 0 0
—	b	Mary Madden,	Francis Brodigan,	House,	—	—	0 8 0	0 8 0
—	c	Patrick Pasty,	Same,	House,	—	—	0 7 0	0 7 0
—	d	William Halpin,	Same,	House,	—	—	0 7 0	0 7 0
2	a	Patrick Connolly,	Same,	House and land,	4 0 0	3 7 0	0 8 0	3 15 0
—	b	Alice Connolly,	Same,	House,	—	—	0 8 0	0 8 0
3		Alice Connolly,	Same,	Land,	3 0 35	2 15 0	—	2 15 0
4	a	Peter M'Grath,	Same,	House and land,		2 0 0	0 8 0	2 8 0
—	b	Thomas Clarke,	Same,	House and land,	4 2 2	1 0 0	0 12 0	1 12 0
—	c	John Kane,	Same,	House and land,		1 0 0	0 12 0	1 12 0
5	a	William Kelly,	Same,	House,offices, and land,	78 2 25	62 0 0	3 0 0	65 0 0
6	a	Patrick Stephens,	Same,	House,offices, and land,	5 3 36	4 3 0	0 12 0	4 15 0
7	a	Judith Stephens,	Same,	House,offices, and land,	10 0 27	7 3 0	0 12 0	7 15 0
8		Dublin & Drogheda Railway Company,	In fee,	Railway (77 lin. perches), Land,	1 0 20 6 3 32	— 5 15 0	— —	4 5 0 5 15 0
				Total,	288 2 2	249 3 0	53 14 0	307 2 0
		STAGREENAN. *(Ord. S. 20.)*						
1	a	Robert M'Conkey,	Rev. Wm. E. Barlow,	House, offices, and land,	52 2 12	67 10 0	30 0 0	97 10 0
—	b	. . . .	Same,	Grave-yard,	0 1 20	0 7 0	—	0 7 0
2	a	Peter M'Evoy,	Same,	House, offices,and land,	52 0 20	70 0 0	25 0 0	95 0 0
3	a	James Carroll,	Same,	Office and land,	5 0 12	5 0 0	1 0 0	6 0 0
4	a	Margaret Dowd,	Same,	Herd's ho., offs., & land,	20 0 6	28 10 0	1 10 0	30 0 0
				Total,	130 0 30	171 7 0	57 10 0	228 17 0
				EXEMPTIONS:				
				Grave-yard,	0 1 20	0 7 0	—	0 7 0
				Total, exclusive of Exemptions,	129 3 10	171 0 0	57 10 0	228 10 0
		STAMEEN. *(Ord. S. 20 & 21.)*						
1	a	William Kearns, *(See also lot 7.)*	Reps. Thomas Wade,	Ho.offs.,gate lodge,&ld.	83 1 15	130 0 0	40 0 0	170 0 0
—	b	William Kearns,	Same,	Herd's house,	—	—	0 6 0	0 6 0
—	c	Vacant,	William Kearns,	House,	—	—	0 18 0	0 18 0
2	A B	Thomas Sherlock,	Reps. Thomas Wade,	Land,	10 2 31 30 1 36	15 0 0 38 0 0	— —	} 53 0 0
3	a	Thomas Sherlock,	Same,	House,offices, and land,	61 1 10	80 0 0	17 5 0	97 5 0
—	b	Bryan Cassidy,	Thomas Sherlock,	House,	—	—	0 12 0	0 12 0
—	c	Joseph Magrane,	Same,	House,	—	—	0 12 0	0 12 0
—	d	Patrick Doner,	Same,	House and garden,	0 0 10	0 2 0	0 16 0	0 18 0
—	e	Christopher Clarke,	Same,	House,	—	—	0 11 0	0 11 0
—	f	Catherine Carolan,	Same,	House,	—	—	0 11 0	0 11 0
—	g	Commissioners of Boyne Navigation,	Same,	Quarry,	2 0 0	—	—	10 10 0
		Thomas Sherlock,	*As lessor,*	*Half rent rateable, £15.*				
4	a	Francis Chadwick,	Reps. Thomas Wade,	Herd's ho., offs., & land,	32 0 15	40 0 0	3 15 0	43 15 0
5	a	Peter Verdon,	Same,	House,offices, and land,	42 2 37	68 0 0	9 15 0	77 15 0
6	a	John Chadwick,	Thomas Sherlock,	House,offices, and land,	13 0 38	19 0 0	20 10 0	39 10 0
7	A B C	William Kearns,	Same,	Land,	3 3 12 70 3 13 0 0 31	5 8 0 88 0 0 0 2 0	— — —	} 93 10 0
8	a b	Mary Crosbie, Thomas Myles,	Same,	House, office, & land, House, office, & land,	7 1 13	3 15 0 3 15 0	0 10 0 0 15 0	4 5 0 4 10 0
9		Dublin and Drogheda Railway Company,	In fee,	Railway (81 lin. perches),	3 1 24	—	—	3 0 0
				Total,	361 2 5	491 2 0	96 16 0	601 8 0

81

VALUATION OF TENEMENTS.

PARISH OF COLPE.

No. and Letters of Reference to Map.	Names. Townlands and Occupiers.	Immediate Lessors.	Description of Tenement.	Area. A. R. P.	Rateable Annual Valuation. Land. £ s. d.	Buildings. £ s. d.	Total Annual Valuation of Rateable Property. £ s. d.
	STAMEEN—continued.		Exemptions: Quarry,	2 0 0	—	—	10 10 0
			Total, exclusive of Exemptions,	359 2 5	494 2 0	96 16 0	590 18 0

PARISH OF JULIANSTOWN.

No. and Letters of Reference to Map.	Townlands and Occupiers.	Immediate Lessors.	Description of Tenement.	Area. A. R. P.	Land. £ s. d.	Buildings. £ s. d.	Total. £ s. d.
	BALLYMAD. (Ord. S. 21 & 28.)						
1 a	James Meade,	Joseph Osborne,	Office and land,	57 3 1	39 0 0	0 10 0	39 10 0
2 a	William Kelly,	Same,	Land,	54 0 36	41 5 0	—	41 5 0
— a	Vacant,	William Kelly,	House,	—	—	0 13 0	0 13 0
— b	Vacant,	Same,	House,	—	—	0 7 0	0 7 0
			Total,	111 3 37	80 5 0	1 10 0	81 15 0
	GLEBE. (Ord. S. 28.)						
1 a	Rev. Henry Moore,	In fee,	House, offices, and land,	16 1 35	20 0 0	15 0 0	35 0 0
			Total,	16 1 35	20 0 0	15 0 0	35 0 0
	JULIANSTOWN, EAST. (Ord. S. 28 & 21.)						
1 a	Michael Balfe,	Thomas Pepper,	House, offices, and land,	80 2 32	55 10 0	1 10 0	57 0 0
2 a	Michael Balfe,	Same,	House, offices, and land,	113 3 25	100 0 0	4 10 0	104 10 0
— b	Edward Barrett,	Michael Balfe,	House,	—	—	0 10 0	0 10 0
3	Thomas Seagrave,	Thomas Pepper,	Land,	9 2 31	11 5 0	—	11 5 0
			Total,	204 1 8	166 15 0	6 10 0	173 5 0
	JULIANSTOWN, SOUTH. (Ord. S. 28.)						
1	Thomas Pepper,	In fee,	Land,	51 1 35	45 0 0	—	45 0 0
2 a	Thomas Seagrave,	Thomas Pepper,	House, offices, and land,	7 3 11	12 10 0	2 10 0	15 0 0
			Total,	59 1 6	57 10 0	2 10 0	60 0 0
	JULIANSTOWN, WEST. (Ord. S. 28 & 21.)						
1 A	John Moran,	Anna M. Disney,	Land,	25 3 32	24 0 0	—	} 41 10 0
— B a			Ho., offs., mill, kiln, & gar.	0 3 3	0 10 0	17 0 0	
2 a	William Moore,	Same,	Farm-ho., office, & land,	129 1 3	101 0 0	3 0 0	104 0 0
— b	Matthew Taaffe,	William Moore,	House,	—	—	0 10 0	0 10 0
3 a	William Moore,	Anna M. Disney,	House, offices, and land,	95 3 10	116 0 0	11 10 0	127 10 0
— b	Vacant,	William Moore,	House,	—	—	0 10 0	0 10 0
— c	Patrick Farrell,	Same,	House,	—	—	0 10 0	0 10 0
— d	James Potter,	Same,	House and garden,	0 2 0	1 0 0	0 13 0	1 13 0
— e	John Hughes,	Same,	House,	—	—	0 10 0	0 10 0
— f	Patrick Taaffe,	Same,	House and garden,	0 0 15	0 6 0	0 10 0	0 16 0
— g	Thomas Nulty,	Same,	House,	—	—	0 6 0	0 6 0
— h	Thomas Doonan,	Same,	House and garden,	0 0 16	0 6 0	0 10 0	0 16 0
— i	John M'Donnell,	Same,	Garden,	0 0 18	0 7 0	—	0 7 0
4 a	John Coogan,	Anna M. Disney,	House, offices, & garden,	1 0 13	1 10 0	6 0 0	7 10 0
5	John Coogan,	William Moore,	Land,	4 0 13	6 10 0	—	6 10 0
6 a	William Dillon,	Same,	House, offices, and land,	2 3 6	3 0 0	2 15 0	5 15 0
7 a	Richard M'Keon,	Thomas Pepper,	House and garden,	2 1 38	5 15 0	0 15 0	6 10 0
— b	Vacant,	Same,	House and yard,	—	—	5 0 0	5 0 0
— c	Vacant,	Same,	House, office, and yard,	—	—	2 0 0	2 0 0
— d	Richard M'Keon,	Same,	House,	—	—	1 0 0	1 0 0

VALUATION OF TENEMENTS.

PARISH OF COLPE.

No. and Letters of Reference to Map.	Townlands and Occupiers.	Immediate Lessors.	Description of Tenement.	Area. A. R. P.	Rateable Annual Valuation. Land. £ s. d.	Buildings. £ s. d.	Total Annual Valuation of Rateable Property. £ s. d.
	JULIANSTOWN, WEST—*continued*						
— c	James M'Elroy,	Thomas Pepper,	House,	—	—	0 15 0	0 15 0
— f	John M'Donnell,	Same,	House,	—	—	1 2 0	1 2 0
— g	Eliza Tiernan,	Same,	House,	—	—	1 5 0	1 5 0
— h	John Savage,	Same,	House,	—	—	1 0 0	1 0 0
— i	Peter Donner,	Same,	House,	—	—	1 0 0	1 0 0
— j	John Ruddy,	Same,	House and office,	—	—	1 15 0	1 15 0
— k	Michael Farrelly,	Same,	House,	—	—	1 5 0	1 5 0
— l	Charles Mallen,	Same,	House,	—	—	1 5 0	1 5 0
— m	James Murray,	Same,	House,	—	—	1 15 0	1 15 0
8 a	. . . . .	Same,	Church and yard,	1 0 0	1 0 0	5 0 0	6 0 0
— b	John M'Mullen,	Rev. Henry Moore,	House and garden,	0 1 5	0 10 0	1 0 0	1 10 0
·· c	Church Educ. Society,	In fee,	School-house,	—	—	1 0 0	1 0 0
— d	James Cordington,	Rev. Henry Moore,	House & small garden,	0 0 8	0 3 0	0 12 0	0 15 0
— e	James Dolan,	Same,	House & small garden,	0 0 8	0 3 0	0 12 0	0 15 0
— f	Peter Fox,	Thomas Pepper,	House,	—	—	1 0 0	1 0 0
— g	Henry King,	Same,	House,	—	—	1 0 0	1 0 0
— h	Richard Allen,	Same,	House,	—	—	0 15 0	0 15 0
— i	Christopher Griffin,	Same,	House and garden,	0 0 24	0 9 0	1 6 0	1 15 0
			Waste,	0 2 4	—	—	
9	William Moore,	Rev. Henry Moore,	Glebe-land,	1 1 24	1 15 0	—	1 15 0
			Total,	266 2 0	264 4 0	76 6 0	340 10 0
			EXEMPTIONS: Church and grave-yard,	1 0 0	1 0 0	5 0 0	6 0 0
			School-house,	—	—	1 0 0	1 0 0
			Total of Exemptions,	1 0 0	1 0 0	6 0 0	7 0 0
			Total, exclusive of Exemptions,	265 2 0	263 4 0	70 6 0	333 10 0
	MINISTOWN. (*Ord. S.* 21 & 28.)						
1 a B	Peter Kelly,	Trustees of James J. Taylor,	House, offices, and land,	28 1 23	19 12 0	0 13 0	20 5 0
2 a	Anne M'Donagh,	Same,	House, office, and land,	4 1 26	2 18 0	0 7 0	3 5 0
— b	Michael Walsh,	Same,	House and garden,	0 0 24	0 5 0	0 8 0	0 13 0
3 A a	Brien M'Kenna,	Same,	House, offices, and land,	13 0 10	9 6 0	0 8 0	} 16 0 0
— B			Land,	8 1 21	6 6 0	—	
4 a	John Reilly,	Same,	House, offices, and land,	19 0 2	13 18 0	0 17 0	14 15 0
5 a	Catherine Delahunt,	Same,	House, office, and land,	13 2 37	9 15 0	0 10 0	10 5 0
— b	Michael Bannon,	Same,	House,	—	—	0 6 0	0 6 0
— c	Peter Woods,	Catherine Delahunt,	House,	—	—	0 7 0	0 7 0
— d	Thomas Kelly,	Same,	House,	—	—	0 7 0	0 7 0
— e	Hugh M'Cabe,	Same,	Forge,	—	—	0 6 0	0 6 0
— f	Matthew Garvey,	Same,	House,	—	—	0 6 0	0 6 0
6 A a	John Kinchella,	Trustees of James J. Taylor,	House, offices, and land,	5 1 32	3 15 0	0 10 0	} 6 0 0
— B			Land,	2 1 17	1 15 0	—	
7 A a	Thomas Branagan,	Same,	House, offices, and land,	79 2 29	61 10 0	1 15 0	} 131 15 0
— B			Land,	92 1 14	68 10 0	—	
— A b	Thomas Allen,	Same,	Ploughman's house,	—	—	0 10 0	0 10 0
8 A a	Mary M'Ardle,	John Hammel,	House and land,	4 0 37	3 10 0	0 10 0	} 5 5 0
— B			Land,	1 3 7	1 5 0	—	
9	John Hammel,	In fee,	Land,	4 3 32	3 0 0	—	3 0 0
10	Dublin and Drogheda Railway Company,	In fee,	Railway (158 *lin. perches*),	2 0 11	—	—	9 0 0
— A b	Peter Hughes,	Mary M'Ardle,	House,	—	—	0 10 0	0 10 0
			Total,	280 0 2	205 5 0	8 10 0	222 15 0
	NINCH. (*Ord. S.* 23 & 24.)						
— A a — B — C	} Edmund Doran,	In fee,	{ House, offices, and land, Garden, Garden,	170 0 20 1 3 2 7 3 36	170 0 0 5 0 0 16 0 0	20 0 0 — —	} 211 0 0
— A b	Vacant,	Edmund Doran,	House,	—	—	0 8 0	0 8 0
2 a	Patrick Farrell,	Edmund Wynne,	House, office, and land,	13 2 4	12 2 0	0 8 0	12 10 0
3 A a — B a	} James Walsh,	John Hammel,	{ House, offices, and land, Office and land,	217 1 20 111 1 11	215 0 0 95 0 0	13 0 0 0 10 0	} 323 10 0

VALUATION OF TENEMENTS.

PARISH OF COLPE.

No. and Letters of Reference to Map.	Townlands and Occupiers.	Immediate Lessors.	Description of Tenement.	Area. A. R. P.	Rateable Annual Valuation. Land. £ s. d	Buildings. £ s. d	Total Annual Valuation of Rateable Property. £ s. d
	NINCH—*continued.*						
— A b	John Kelledy,	James Walsh,	House and garden,	0 1 10	0 9 0	0 7 0	0 16 0
— c	John Richie,	Edmund Doran,	House and garden,	0 1 0	0 6 0	0 10 0	0 16 0
— d	Vacant,	Same,	House and garden,	0 1 0	0 6 0	0 10 0	0 16 0
— e	Thomas White,	James Walsh,	House and garden,	0 0 10	0 2 0	0 10 0	0 12 0
— f	Thomas Devin,	Same,	House and garden,	0 0 10	0 2 0	0 10 0	0 12 0
— g	Thomas Flynn,	Same,	Herd's house,	—	—	0 8 0	0 8 0
— h	Vacant,	Same,	House,	—	—	0 8 0	0 8 0
4 A / — B } a	Thomas Hand,	John Hammel,	{ Land, / House, offices, and land,	9 1 33 / 3 3 30	6 5 0 / 4 10 0	— / 0 15 0	} 11 10 0 / 13 15 0
5 a	James Boyle,	Same,	House, office, and land,	17 2 38	13 0 0	0 15 0	13 15 0
— b	Vacant,	James Boyle,	House,	—	—	2 0 0	2 0 0
— c	Vacant,	Same,	House,	—	—	2 0 0	2 0 0
— d	Vacant,	Same,	House,	—	—	3 10 0	3 10 0
6	John Murphy,	John Hammel,	Land,	31 2 37	28 15 0	—	28 15 0
	MURPHY'S COTTAGES.						
— a	Vacant,	John Murphy,	House and office,	—	—	10 0 0	10 0 0
— b	Vacant,	Same,	House and office,	—	—	8 0 0	8 0 0
— c	Vacant,	Same,	House,	—	—	7 0 0	7 0 0
— d	Vacant,	Same,	House and office,	—	—	7 0 0	7 0 0
— e	Vacant,	Same,	House and office,	—	—	8 0 0	8 0 0
— f	Vacant,	Same,	House,	—	—	6 0 0	6 0 0
— g	Vacant,	Same,	Offices,	—	—	3 0 0	3 0 0
— h	Vacant,	Same,	Offices,	—	—	2 0 0	2 0 0
— i	Vacant,	Same,	House and office,	—	—	24 0 0	24 0 0
— j	Vacant,	Same,	House and office,	—	—	22 0 0	22 0 0
— k	Vacant,	James M'Donagh,	House and offices,	—	—	18 0 0	18 0 0
7 A / — B } a	James Finnin,	John Hammel,	{ House, offices, and land, / Land,	23 1 21 / 4 3 10	13 15 0 / 5 15 0	1 0 0 / —	} 20 10 0
8	Joseph M'Cann,	Same,	Land,	20 0 32	12 10 0	—	12 10 0
9 a	Hugh Smith,	Ralph Cusack,	House, offices, and land,	5 1 15	4 5 0	0 15 0	5 0 0
— b	Vacant,	Hugh Smith,	House,	—	—	2 10 0	2 10 0
10	Ralph Cusack,	In fee,	Land,	15 1 38	15 0 0	—	15 0 0
11 { a / b	John Heney / James Heney,	Ralph Cusack,	{ House, office, & land, / House, office, & land,	5 1 32	{ 3 0 0 / 3 0 0	0 15 0 / 0 15 0	3 15 0 / 3 15 0
— c	Vacant,	James Heney,	House,	—	—	1 10 0	1 10 0
— d	Vacant,	Same,	House,	—	—	1 10 0	1 10 0
12 a	John Mulvanny,	Judith Cooke,	House, office, and land,	3 2 27	4 5 0	8 0 0	12 5 0
— b	Catherine Farrelly,	John Mulvanny,	House,	—	—	0 15 0	0 15 0
— c	William Kearney,	Same,	House,	—	—	0 15 0	0 15 0
— d	John Murphy,	Same,	House,	—	—	0 12 0	0 12 0
— e	Vacant,	Same,	House,	—	—	0 12 0	0 12 0
13 a	David Abbott,	Judith Cooke,	House, offices & garden,	1 1 23	1 15 0	4 5 0	6 0 0
— b	Peter Thompson,	David Abbott,	House & small garden,	—	—	1 10 0	1 10 0
— c	Charles Child,	Same,	House & small garden,	—	—	1 10 0	1 10 0
— d	Matilda Thompson,	Same,	House,	—	—	1 10 0	1 10 0
— e	Mary Ailward,	Same,	House,	—	—	6 0 0	6 0 0
14 a	Dublin & Drogheda Railway Company,	In fee,	{ Railway station & office, / Railway (279 *lineal perches*),	5 1 22	—	1 0 0 / —	1 0 0 / 15 0 0
15	John Hammel,	In fee,	Land (*detached*),	15 1 16	6 15 0	—	6 15 0
			Total,	686 1 17	636 17 0	196 13 0	848 10 0
	ROGERSTOWN. (*Ord. S. 27, 28, 21.*)						
1 a	Patrick Markey,	Edmund Doran,	House, offices, and land,	518 3 13	435 0 0	15 0 0	450 0 0
— b	Patrick Johnson,	Patrick Markey,	House,	—	—	0 8 0	0 8 0
— c	Nicholas Kelly,	Same,	House and office,	—	—	0 8 0	0 8 0
— d	Vacant,	Same,	House,	—	—	0 8 0	0 8 0
— e	Michael Connor,	Same,	House,	—	—	0 8 0	0 8 0
— f	Vacant,	Same,	House,	—	—	0 8 0	0 8 0
— g	Peter Duffe,	Same,	House,	—	—	0 8 0	0 8 0
— h	Mary Neill,	Same,	House,	—	—	0 12 0	0 12 0
— i	John Woods,	Same,	House,	—	—	0 8 0	0 8 0
— j	William Neill,	Same,	House,	—	—	0 7 0	0 7 0
— k	Catherine Carroll,	Same,	House,	—	—	0 5 0	0 5 0
			Total,	518 3 13	435 0 0	19 0 0	454 0 0

VALUATION OF TENEMENTS.

PARISH OF COLPE.

No. and Letters of Reference to Map.	Names. Townlands and Occupiers.	Immediate Lessors.	Description of Tenement.	Area. A. R. P.	Rateable Annual Valuation. Land. £ s. d.	Buildings. £ s. d.	Total Annual Valuation of Rateable Property. £ s. d.
	SEVITSLAND. *(Ord. S. 21.)*						
1 A	William Boylan,	Michael Chester.	Land.	44 3 39	32 5 0	—	} 51 5 0
– B a			Offices and land.	27 0 0	18 10 0	0 10 0	
2	Dublin & Drogheda Railway Company,	In fee.	Railway (63 lin. p rches).	0 3 34	—	—	3 10 0
			Land,	1 1 16	1 0 0	—	1 0 0
			Total.	74 1 9	51 15 0	0 10 0	55 15 0
	SMITHSTOWN. *(Ord. S. 28, 27, 20, & 21.)*						
1 a	James Meade,	Joseph Osborne.	House, offices, and land.	86 0 5	67 10 0	4 5 0	71 15 0
2 a	Laurence Moonan.	Same.	House, offices, and land.	71 1 23	58 0 0	3 10 0	61 10 0
3	Laurence Moonan,	Same.	Land,	37 0 31	36 10 0	—	36 10 0
– a	Michael Duff,	Laurence Moonan.	House and garden,	0 0 10	0 3 0	0 7 0	0 10 0
4 a	Francis N. Osborne,	Joseph Osborne,	House, offices, and land.	312 0 30	349 0 0	21 0 0	370 0 0
– b	John Brien,	Francis N. Osborne.	House and office,	—	—	0 14 0	0 14 0
– c	Catherine Campbell,	Same.	House,	—	—	0 10 0	0 10 0
– d	Michael Singleton,	Same.	House,	—	—	0 7 0	0 7 0
– e	Anne Collins,	Same.	House,	—	—	0 7 0	0 7 0
– f	Vacant,	Same.	House,	—	—	0 7 0	0 7 0
– g	William Gallagher,	Same.	House and garden,	0 0 33	0 10 0	0 10 0	1 0 0
5 A	Henry Ludgate,	Joseph Osborne.	Land,	2 3 2	2 15 0	—	} 6 15 0
– B a			House, offices, & garden,	0 1 33	1 0 0	3 0 0	
6 a	Luke Stephenson,	Same.	House, offices, & garden,	3 0 0	7 10 0	2 10 0	10 0 0
– b	Constabulary Force,	Same,	Police-barrack,	—	—	3 0 0	3 0 0
	Joseph Osborne,	*As lessor,*	*Half annual rent rateable, £3.*				
– c	Anne Madden,	Joseph Osborne.	House and yard,	—	—	2 5 0	2 5 0
– d	. . . .	Same.	Petty sessions-house,	—	—	2 5 0	2 5 0
	Joseph Osborne,	*As lessor,*	*Half annual rent rateable, £3.*				
7 a	James English,	Joseph Osborne,	House, offices, and land,	5 0 31	8 10 0	0 15 0	9 5 0
			Total.	518 1 38	531 8 0	45 12 0	577 0 0
			EXEMPTIONS:				
			Police-barrack,	—	—	3 0 0	3 0 0
			Petty sessions-house,	—	—	2 5 0	2 5 0
			Total of Exemptions,	—	—	5 5 0	5 5 0
			Total, exclusive of Exemptions.	518 1 38	531 8 0	40 7 0	571 15 0

Richard Griffith, Commissioner of Valuation.
Dated : September, 1854, General Valuation Office, Dublin.
Published in 1856.[13]

CHAPTER 8
"A Flavour of Mornington".

1850-1891

The forty years between the Famine and the fall of Parnell are dominated by two great questions, the land and national independence. The struggle of the tenant farmers for security in their holdings and the national struggle for independence, each expressed itself in two ways, one constitutional and parliamentary, the other revolutionary and conspiratorial. Neither of the two methods of action proved effective when used separately.

But in 1879 a common front between constitutional and revolutionary nationalists was achieved through the transcendent political genius of Charles Stewart Parnell, and the passion for social justice of Michael Davitt. The struggle for land and national independence became merged in a mass movement without precedent in Irish history. Two resounding successes were achieved for the cause of the tenant farmers in the 'land-war' of 1879-82, and 1886, when the British Liberal party under the leadership of Gladstone, acknowledged the justice and the necessity of giving Ireland self-government. Although these questions were still a long way from being resolved, the consequences of the 'new departure' of 1879 were to have a deep and lasting influence on the whole future of Ireland and of Anglo-Irish relations.

The fall of Parnell commenced in 1890 when he was sued for adultery by a former member of his party W.H. O'Shea whose wife had become Parnell's mistress.

The British reaction to the O'Shea case was one of violent hostility to Parnell's continued leadership of the Irish party. The Liberal party was threatened with a split, and because of 'this', Gladstone demanded Parnell's temporary retirement from leadership of the Irish party. Parnell's refusal brought about a bitter split in his party, and his own downfall. He died a year later (6th October 1891).

Gladstone's second home rule bill (1893) was passed the house of Commons, but was overwhelmingly defeated by the house of Lords. He was then eighty four years.

Parnell's achievement as a statesman, damaged though it was by his fall, was far from being undone, nor has it ever been undone. He brought Ireland's claims home to the British people as no Irish leader had ever succeeded in doing, and he is rightly remembered for the spirit of splendid defiance with which he voiced the Irish demand for independent nationhood. His superb leadership during ten critical years created conditions that prepared the way for the final stages in the struggle for independence.[1]

The shock of the Famine and its resultant emigration took many decades to recover from. Nevertheless, the people who remained focused their energies on reform of the land tenancy system, and on securing more control over their own affairs. Thus, Law Reform and Repeal of the Act of Union became the rallying cries.

Church building demonstrated the ability of the natives to achieve significant developments, as did the Railway construction, industrialisation and the founding of the G.A.A. Gradually self-belief started to take root again. This became very apparent in the coastal fishing villages of Mornington, Bettystown and Laytown etc., with the opening of schools, the building of churches, the development of beautiful sandy natural beaches into popular seaside resorts, the building of Hotels, and Bettystown's golf course. Mornington's fishing industry, which included mussel fishing in the Boyne estuary, provided the people of Mornington with a way of life that has lasted for centuries. All this and more brought employment and prosperity to these areas.

Mornington, near Drogheda.

Mornington Village and Boyne Estuary over forty years ago.

Mornington Village and Boyne Estuary to-day.

Salmon

The Boyne fishing industry has a long history, dating back hundreds of years. Fishermen harvested salmon as far back as the twelfth century. The salmon fishing season opens on the 12th February and closes on the 12th. August, (this has now changed to a much later date, sadly, due to the decline in the industry). The families of the fishermen, are also very involved and have provided the necessary back up, vital to the success of the industry, from generation to generation. This close-knit fishing community of Mornington looked forward eagerly each year to the opening of the season. Salmon fishing involves the use of drift nets, with two men to each boat. The salmon caught was usually bought by an agent, a local man named Dessie Smith, who exported it to London, where they commanded highest prices for quality. The children also enter into the enthusiasm and excitement, fishing for pinkings and tadpoles, and enjoyed the happy atmosphere, almost as much as Christmas. Everything that was planned or bought depended on the salmon harvest, for the people of Mornington it was their insurance. It was well known that they could obtain credit anywhere on the strength of the salmon.

Once the season started, the topic of conversation at the weekends in the local pub was always centred around the catch for the week - who caught what, and the size etc. Just as the opening of the season was eagerly awaited, so too did the children look forward to the closing, when they all congregated on the banks of the river, to help bring in the boats and nets, and put them away, ready for the next year. In the 1920's, there were ninety six fishing boats at Mornington. At that time fishermen came from Drogheda, because, by fishing at Mornington, they had the first chance to catch the salmon as they made their way up river. The salmon came from the feeding grounds of Greenland, back to where they were spawned, their original birthplace.

Up to twenty years ago the Boyne Salmon Fishery was one of the best in Europe. Hundreds of men fished for salmon at any one time during the forties, fifties and sixties. When mono filament netting was introduced, its widespread use at sea prevented most salmon from getting back to their river of origin. Consequently catches in the river dropped dramatically, however, new regulations have been drawn up to prevent this continuing. Due to the gradual decline in catches and restrictive regulations there are now only fifty licensed salmon fishermen.[1a].

Dessie Smith holding a forty two lb. salmon in 1954.

All eyes south, watching for a jumper- July 1989. (Front)

Mussels

The recorded history of the Mornington mussel fishery could be more informative than it is. It is very possible the mussel industry was in existence, in the Mornington area for hundreds of years. But the records available at present only go back to the 1880's. It is generally accepted that it was the Romans who first introduced mussels to the British Isles, in fact North Wales. Mussels won't grow just anywhere. They need a certain amount of fresh salty water, and also a good food supply. This makes the Boyne estuary an ideal habitat for the mussel. The Boyne river flows into the sea at Mornington, and is one of the longest rivers in Ireland, and therefore, considerable quantities of fresh water flow into the Estuary. The harvesting season for mussels is from Sept. to the following April. The month of May is the prime spawning period, though there may be intermittent spawning up to August-September, depending on water temperatures.

Mussel Fishing Technique

The method used to harvest the mussels involves a lot of physical work. The local men have their own currach style boat. The boat is anchored in the estuary, and a mussel rake is used from the boat. The fisherman throws the mussel rake into the water, still holding the end of the handle, and proceeds to dredge along the river bed. He then deposits the haul of mussels into his boat. There may be four to five hundred casts during the fishing spell. This particular method is not used in any other Irish mussel fishery, and in fact there is only one other river in the British Isles where this method is used, the Conway river in North Wales. Mechanical dredges that were being used in other Irish fisheries were tried out on the Mornington fishery in 1969. The dredges became damaged and unworkable, the reason being the ground structure was too hard and gravely, with a lot of very large stones.

Larry Reynolds and Paddy Clynch, sorting the mussels from the stones - Mornington 1966.

Mussel Fishing- has been a way of life in Mornington for decades. During the 1880's and up until 1923 the fishermen used to scull their boats from Mornington to the harbour in Drogheda. They would have already graded their mussels by hand on the mussel bank, have them bagged and sewn when full, ready to load onto a ship, destined for England. The grading in those days was all done by hand. The womenfolk of this small fishing village played a major part in the success of this unique industry. They would kneel down inside the load of mussels on the beach or bank and sort out the commercial size mussels, put them into a bucket, and from there into a sack.

There was no shelter whatsoever from the elements. Irrespective of lashing rain, gales of wind, snow, and frost, the mussels had to be graded and sold, to keep the food on the table for this hard working fishing community. Even if it wasn't raining, it was almost impossible to remain dry. The graders would be bent over the heaps of mussels for five to six hours per day and could hardly straighten themselves up when finished.

Up to the introduction of the grader in the seventies, not only the fishermen's wives would be grading the mussels, but also any of their children who would be old enough. In the end, even though it was an old tradition, fishermen and their wives and families, were glad to see the back of the old hand grading system.

It wasn't an easy life by any standards, but this fishing community could take the hard life in their stride. It was the serious disasters, which threatened this old mussel fishing industry, and their livelihood, which caused this community worry and frustration. But they fought against the 'injustices' for their 'rights' as fishermen.

Development of the area for Industrial, Residential, or Port use, has to be done with extreme care to avoid damage to the sensitive mussel fish industry, and the fishermen are very cautious and suspicious of such planning.

"We can never forget how the fishery enabled our predecessors to survive. We were blessed to have been born and bred on the banks of one of the finest mussel fisheries in Europe, if not the world. In the bad old days, when poverty was rampant in Ireland, a shilling or two could be earned to keep the wolf from the door".

Leo Boyle - holding an empty mussel rake.

They survived those difficult years, and are very proud of their past. Some of the older members in the community who are still with us, feel very strong and passionate about the mussel beds, marshes, and their old and noble way of life. They very much want it preserved for posterity as well as prosperity, and they love to talk about 'times past' and the 'good' hard old days!
The fishermen feel that the fishery is on the verge of a major breakthrough to the European market.
It is not generally known that mussels contain as much protein as does a T/bone steak, approximately one hundred and forty grams of protein per kg of mussels.[2].

'Twas down where the fisherfolk gathered
I wandered far from the throng,
I heard a fisher girl singing,
and this refrain was her song.

Swift wings you will borrow,
make straight for the shore,
we'll marry to-morrow,
and you'll go sailing no more.
Red sails in the sunset,
way out on the sea.
Oh, carry my loved one,
home safely to me.

He sailed at the dawning,
all day I've been blue.
Red sails in the sunset,
I trust in you.
By........Jimmy Kennedy and Hugh Williams[2a]

Following on in the same vein, another 'celebrity' from these parts and this period, deserves a mention: The beautiful restaurant 'The Estuary' previously known as the 'The Anchorage' which also traded as a well known and loved restaurant, due to the fact that this old house, was in the early 1900's, the home of two famous sons of Mornington, Captain Joe and Denis Lyons.

Captain Denis Lyons was one of a family of six children, his father was a seaman, who it appears, did everything in his power to prevent any of his sons following in his footsteps. In Denis's early life, the high seas beckoned him to a life of risk, danger, and most of all adventure. He worked with his father, and learned from him, all the sailing skills, serving his time, as it were. His father was a hard task master and would have been a very difficult role play to follow. A young Denis took it all in his stride, the rough with the smooth; learned all that he could, and eventually became a much respected captain of his ship and a much loved man of the sea whose knowledge stood the test of time.

He tells his own story in 'My Life at Sea' by Captain Denis Lyons.
The following are a couple of excerpts, taken from the book, just to give you a little taste of what life was like for our 'celebrated hero' at sea:

Two Happy years:
"I passed about two happy years on board this splendid ship, crossing and re-crossing the Atlantic, ballast to the westward and maize homewards. The Captain took me out of the forecastle and put me in the petty officers' room with the carpenter and boatswain. In 1879, the first year the sailing ships in the Western Ocean trade began to feel the inroad of steamers on their preserves. We lay at Guonoes Creek, Brooklyn, N.Y., for six months, (a whole winter), awaiting a rise in freights. As a matter of fact, all the American ports were crowded up with ships, I must call it a ship strike for want of a better word. When Spring came we chartered for the east coast of Scotland, for less money than was offered and refused when we first arrived. This was the beginning of the end of the fine fleet of grain ships that crossed and re-crossed the Western Ocean from New York, Philadelphia and Baltimore.
The compound engine, and later the triple expansion, put the marine steam engine into ships, and made the tramp steamer more economical than her rival propelled by sails".

"When I was on the ship 'Stamboul' we went from New York to the east coast of Scotland, with a cargo of about two thousand three hundred tons of maize (Indian corn). This cargo was for a distillery at the town of Alloa, what the distillers wanted with the corn was of course their own business. We lay in the Firth of Forth opposite Boness, not able to get to our own port of discharge, our cargo went into lighters and was then taken to its destination. Our Captain felt himself in a fix as to how we were to get our supply of fresh water for our return voyage. He must have told this to the manager of the whiskey mill, as they obliged by lending several large spirit barrels. These were filled with water and taken down in the barges when they were on the return journey, hoisted on board and emptied into our tanks.

It may appear strange to the well fed and housed seafarers of to-day, that we had no complaints, although there was a strong smell and taste of the 'real Macoy' from tea, coffee, pea soup, etc. Ay, even from the drinking water! as a matter of fact, all on board appeared to like the soup very much, and felt a bit put out when our tanks were again filled with fresh water in the U.S.A.".[3]

I can't help feeling lonesome
For the old ships that are gone,
For the sight of Tropic sunsets,
And the hour before the dawn;
And the white sails pulling
Stoutly to a warm and steady draught,
The smell of roasting coffee,
And the watches mustering aft.

I'd like to sail off shore again
Upon some 'Blue Nose' barque,
And hear a rousing shanty
In the windy, starry dark;
Or first a clewed-down topsail
In a black South-Easter's roar,
But there ain't no good a-wishing,
For those days will come no more.

by....Frederick W. Wallace[4]

The following passage written as a tribute, on the death of Captain Denis Lyons, in the Drogheda Independent 18th June 1938 says it all.[5]

Capt. Denis Lyons
'The Anchorage', Mornington.

"The death of Captain Denis Lyons occurred at his residence on Tuesday night last. One of three brothers, who from an early age adopted the sea as their profession, all of them becoming masters with wide experience of navigation in all the seven seas. In the early days of sail he served before the mast, along the coasts of the Americas, and his keen mind was such that he learned something new from everywhere he went. His memory was remarkable, he could name every man from Drogheda who had gone to sea in the past forty of fifty years, and in most cases, knew what had become of them.

When steam spoiled the romance of the sea, he captained many famous ships and his later years were spent on the Drogheda-Liverpool service, in charge of such well-known vessels as the 'Colleen Bawn', 'Tredagh', 'Iverna', the new 'Colleen Bawn' and the 'Mellifont'.

He had retired from the sea several years, but never lost his abiding interest in everything connected with the life.

He watched with interest the development of the Port of Drogheda, and from time to time, in letters to the Press, gave very valuable advice on technical navigation matters, upon which his knowledge was vast and his conclusions reliable.

A steadfast and loveable little gentleman, a man whose nobility of character was written on his face, whose search across the vast horizons of the immense seas, had brought him that tranquillity of soul, which brings greater happiness, than power, wealth or fame. Those who were privileged to be his friends shared when talking to him, some of his mental peace. They will miss him.

He has gone on his last voyage, his port of call the haven of Peace. God be with him".

My love is a tall ship, at a sweet brigantine,
One of the old girls, seldom now seen,
And she heaves to the wind boys, see how she glides,
With stars in her hair, and mist in her eyes.
by....... Jimmy Crowley [6]

Frances Moran is a member of the well known Moran family of Mornington and next door neighbours to Captains Joe and Denis Lyons. When we had the pleasure of meeting this gentle old lady, she was residing in St. Ursula's private nursing home in Bettystown. We were surprised to find Frances's memory so good considering her very advanced years. She was delighted to share with us memories from her long life, and seemed to have no problem recalling interesting happenings in her past.

Frances who was born in 1907 came from a large family of nine children most of whom lived long lives. She was reared in a fine house, near the old church and graveyard in Mornington. This house was owned by a Protestant Minister before her grandfather or great grandfather bought it in 1841 approximately. During the 1840's her family started a public house business, which is still in operation today, known as 'Moran's Pub'.

Their father was an invalid when the children were young. They had a housekeeper called Mary Matthews, who helped their mother care for them. Frances remembers as a child growing up in Mornington, most people were poor, but it was a close knit community, where everybody helped one another.

Mornington was primarily a fishing village, life there evolved around the tides. When the tide was right, men went fishing twice a day, and most times brought back big catches of fish. According to Frances, some of the salmon caught were very large, over 20 lbs in weight.

There was also a lot of mussel fishing in the area, this presented very hard work for the local women, as they had the job of separating the good mussels from the bad ones, which meant, their hands were in freezing water for many hours.

The view from their home of sailing ships going up and down the river was spectacular, with large sails blowing in the wind. It was wonderful to watch especially at night, when the ships were all lit up. Another memory was watching the lights from the lighthouses, guiding the ships home safely.

When they were children, their housekeeper would take them and their dog for a picnic down by the river. The dog used to swim in the water, and the children used to watch him, it was from the dog that they all learned how to swim. When they were older and stronger swimmers, they used to go diving at what was known as the 'minister's hole'.

Frances had her primary education in Donacarney school and her secondary education in the Sacred Heart school in Drogheda. After her education was completed, she secured a very good job as an agricultural adviser, which she enjoyed very much.[7]

Tragic death of Mr. Nicholas Moran, Julianstown, 1909.

Widespread regret was expressed when it became known about the unfortunate circumstances, which brought about the untimely death of Mr. Nicholas Moran. The deceased, who was well-known in Drogheda and throughout the counties of Meath, Louth and Dublin, had been in Drogheda transacting business. When driving into a yard to stable his horse, in Shop Street, an impetuous pony caused the trap in which Mr. Moran was sitting to collide with the entrance gate, with the result that the shaft was smashed. It was temporarily repaired to enable Mr. Moran proceed home.

He left Drogheda about 3pm but at Mr Osborne's house at Smithstown, the shaft broke again, the pony bolted at a reckless pace in the direction of Mr. Moran's home. While this mad pony, completely out of control, attempted to turn at Moran residences in Julianstown collided with the gate pier and turned a somersault. As Mr. Moran was flung to the ground, his head hit a sharp stone projecting from the wall, his skull was badly fractured and he was unconscious. Dr. Hunt, who was in the area, came on the scene immediately, found Mr. Moran in a very serious condition, and he was removed to the local hospital, where everything humanly possible was attempted to alleviate the suffering of the injured man. Mr. Moran never regained consciousness, and died a couple of days later. His two sons Frank and John were with him.

Mr. Moran was sixty one years at the time of his death; he owned a milling concern in Julianstown, as well as being a successful farmer. He was open-hearted and generous, and enjoyed widespread popularity from all walks of life. Medical evidence having been given, a verdict of death from misadventure was returned.[8] Frank Moran was living in Mornington at the time of his father"s death, and the above mentioned Frances was then two years old.

The 'Minister's Hole',is an unusual name by any standards. However, it appears there is an explanation which may have little to do with reality, and much to do with local folklore and intrigue. The local vicar Rev. Joseph Druitt, from Mornington, loved to swim, and made a point of swimming each day at this spot. Alas, the minister died in somewhat mysterious circumstances, and at the time of his death, rumour had it, that he drowned in this pool, which resulted in the above name. It was a favourite place for swimming in the old days and existed for over a hundred years before the introduction of the 'swimming pool', and can be found at the end of a derelict causeway in the Boyne estuary.

Here, the late Jimmy Martin, former member and swimmer of the 'river rescue club' of the mid 1950's, gave swimming instructions, and no doubt, the boys and girls of those days must still remember their first lessons in 'water rescue'.[9]

Death of the Rev. Druitt, Vicar of Colpe

We regret to record the demise of the Rev. Joseph Druitt, which took place at the Glebe, Mornington, on the 25th October 1869, at the age of fifty six years. Born in Co. Cavan, where his father was a rector, educated in the royal school there, and in Trinity College. He entered the church, and in the year 1841, was appointed vicar of the united parishes of Colpe and Kilsharvin, in which ministry he continued until his death. His funeral was largely and respectably attended by members of his own and other creeds. The funeral arrangements conducted under the superintendance of Mr. Thomas Butterly, were carried out in a manner highly creditable to that gentleman.[10]

The Boyne Yacht Club, Mornington

On the 5th May 1955, a meeting took place of like-minded enthusiasts, at Alex Moore's residence on the Dublin Rd. for the purpose of forming a Yacht club.
Present at this meeting were as follows:-
Paddy Holden, Alex Moore, Frank and Jim McIvor, and Des Gogarty.
A club was duly formed and immediately put in motion. It was not long until other sailing enthusiasts joined the newly formed club. Archie Lappin and Chris Reid helped in the building of the club house on Crook Rd., Mornington, and membership grew rapidly to embrace different walks of life.

The regattas and competitions organised by the club brought great fun and enjoyment to the participant and all who were involved. Added to this gala scene were races, arranged between clubs, in Skerries, Howth, Dunlaoghaire and Carlingford. Come hail, rain or snow, the race went on and those taking part had to be of a tough hardy nature in order to enable them to weather the 'storm' if necessary.

Every Thursday evening and Sunday afternoon members met at the Yacht Club, and a good social life emerged, with dances and a bar facility, but most were geared towards sailing. In the early sixties, Frank and Jim McIvor built their own boat, a catamaran, a very fast twin hulled boat, a novelty at the time, as most of the other boats were National 18 inch. Mr. Shane Bogne was involved in excavating the area in front of the club, to make space for moorings. This was all carried out with the co-operation of the local fishermen and pilot, John 'the Neighbour' Reynolds.

The Yacht Club went from strength to strength in the sixties and into the seventies. But Disaster struck the club in 1973, when four young members lost their lives at sea. In January of that year Peter Lappin (son of founder member Archie Lappin) and Bernard O'Reilly, Clogherhead, both drowned off Balbriggan, in a freak accident. Both young men were very experienced sailors. In July of the same year (1973) Charlie Moore (son of founder member Alex Moore) and Derek Kearney Sunnyside Villas, Drogheda, were both drowned off Gormanston, during a race from Mornington to Rock a Bill, a sudden storm arose. These two tragedies took their toll on the club, plus many members now had cruisers, which because of lack of moorings on the Boyne, had to go to Howth or Dunlaoghaire. Also the new training-walls at the mouth of the river made the current stronger and very difficult to manage.

In the late seventies, a proposal to move to Clogherhead was passed, but it was never implemented. In 1979/80 the committee decided to wind up the Club, they sold the premises to a Mr. Reynolds of Mornington. At a presentation in Egan's Black Bull, Dublin Rd., the proceeds of the sale were handed over to the R,N.L.I. represented by Mr. Paddy Hodgins, Harbour Master, Clogherhead, and Mr. Andy Collier, Chairman.

The twenty five eventful years (1955-1979/80) of the Yacht Club in Mornington were full of fun and adventure for the sailing enthusiast. Not to mention the skills and stamina required for this tough competitive sport, definitely not for the faint hearted, with local races organised between members, just off the bar on the Baltray side of the river. The fun and enjoyment was also swept along by the tide of activity, with many reports of boats breaking loose and ending up in Wales and the Isle of Man. It must have been a sad day in Mornington, for many people on the social scene as well as the sailing, when the club closed and ceased to exist.[11]

Left to right - young boy Noel Smith, Dr. Connolly, Michael McCullough, Noreen McCullough, Alex Moore, and Sam Williams, in the early sixties.

Life Boat Station (Boat House)

A derelict building beside Maiden Tower was a lifeboat station up until it closed in 1926. It was known as the Mornington of Drogheda No. 2 station. In the fifty odd years of its existence it was responsible for saving thirty eight lives from ships and boats which were wrecked or grounded near the river mouth. A shipwreck lies on the fore-shore as a reminder of the powers of the elements, it is the wreck of the four hundred and fifty ton 'Irish Trader' which was blown ashore in February 1974, with its cargo of fertiliser. Attempts to re-float this ship failed, and eventually the 'Trader' was abandoned to end its days there..........an attraction for the inquisitive and an eyesore for the conservationist.[12]

In 1980, an attempt to re-float the 'Irish Trader' failed.

Maiden Tower and Lady's Finger

Maiden Tower has always been a well known and much loved landmark in the Mornington area, situated on the southern shore of the mouth of the river Boyne. Unfortunately the tower has become very dilapidated and in serious need of renovations and repair. There are fifty five spiral steps in the centre leading to the top, which is well worth the climb, to experience the breathtaking view of the rolling Irish sea, the Boyne estuary and the beautiful plains of Meath and Louth.

The Maiden Tower, which stands on oak piles, now covered in sand, was evidently built to guide ships entering the Boyne estuary. Nothing for definite is known of the tower's history, but traditions tells us, it was erected during the reign of Elizabeth 1 of England, and the tower was named after this unmarried monarch. The Tower was originally brightly coloured (white) making it very conspicuous and thus rendering a service to seafarers navigating ships bound for Drogheda Port. It is said that in the past when a mariner brought both the Tower and the nearby stone structure called Lady's Finger into line, the course of the ship marked the precise angle necessary to strike the bar. This method has long since ceased, because with the building of the river walls in 1765, the entrance to the river Boyne changed.[13]

Description

A tall slender beacon or lighthouse tower, about 12ft (3.6m) square in plan and 62ft (18.9m) in height, it tapers to a battlement parapet. Limestone rubble dashed over the original limewash. Inside, it is simply a spiral stair, light coming through deep embrasures in the wall, with a pair of windows near the top on the east and west sides. Originally a trap door provided access to the platform and parapet. Isaac Butler visited it in 1744 and took an accurate account of the building, which has remained substantially the same today. The battlement parapet is nineteenth century, the fabric of the tower built with the typical Irish masonry technique of tapering the stair to a fine rising point instead of a newel, may well have been constructed several centuries earlier.[14]

Legend and Folklore

The Maiden Tower has been associated with stories of romance, love and intrigue, and these stories have been told over and over again, however, once more won't hurt anyone. Legend tells us that the tower was built by a beautiful maiden to watch the return of her sweetheart who was engaged in battle in a far distant country. His parting words to his loved one were "there'll be white sails, blowing from my ship, if I'm alive, if I'm killed in battle, my ship will hoist red sails". (source unknown). Awaiting the return of her beloved was long and dreary. Day by day as the promised time drew near, she watched anxiously hoping for her beloved's ship to appear over the horizon, at last through the morning mist the 'fair weary one' caught a glimpse of a speck upon the horizon. With beating heart and straining eyes, she watched it, as it gradually drew nearer, unbounded joy filled her heart as she recognised the ship of her loved one.

But her joy was short-lived, as the knight drew closer, sighting the Boyne and his destination, he saw there a watch tower of menacing significance. An enemy, he felt sure had done this, so immediately hoisting his red sails, he prepared his ship for battle. By this time, his 'fair lady love' could see the sails, and at the sight of the dreaded 'red sails', she cried in mournful wail "my beloved is dead" and alas! falling over the battlement of the tower in despair, she met her death. So ended the tragic tale.[15]

There is another story told, also associated with the famous Tower, which is based on fact and perhaps a greater source of wonder and sadness:

In the spring of 1819 the people living on the north side of Bettystown saw smoke coming from the topmost battlement of the Maiden Tower. On investigating, they found there, a care-worn ageing woman. She had gathered bundles of grass grown by the sea, on which to make her bed. She had lit a fire from driftwood, collected from the beach, and her furniture consisted of the bare necessities, which also included a spinning wheel.

Here she sat and sang while she spun her flax. On being questioned as to her motive for being in her unusual set up, she said she was weary of the world, and had been directed by a vision to that spot, where she would find peace and solitude. And so, she was determined to spend the remainder of her life there. She spoke clearly about revelations made to her, and because of this, she became, not only an object of curiosity but also of sympathy and reverence. In a very short space of time she had won the hearts of many of the local people, who constructed a shed roof and chimney over her humble abode, a proper bed, table and chairs were also provided for her simple comfort. She appeared quite at home in her aerial habitation she seldom came down, except to go to Mass on Sunday.

During the summer of 1819, her situation was not only agreeable but flattering. Visitors flocked in their crowds to see and talk to the strange lady, and as few intruded on her privacy without leaving a little money or food her necessities were well taken care of. On those occasions she would not allow any males to enter through the door to the platform which was now her home. With a certain wildness in her eyes, and an occasional significant glance at a heavy stool placed near her, was sufficient to repel the most courageous.

Her appearance and manners were respectable, and she was scrupulously neat in her dress. She presented herself as a native of Drogheda, but had left the place in her early youth. She had many long and sad stories to tell about her life and her travels.

The Spring and Summer of 1819 passed all too quickly followed by the harsh severe winter weather. The novelty of this strange lady living in the tower had 'worn off ' the people in the surrounding villages and towns. But, the landlord of the area a Mr. Philip Brabazon, out of compassion for this woman, made sure she was well cared for. After Mr. Brabazon died, she found herself very much alone and unable to cope with life, her spirits weakened, and her health deteriorated. She was forced to leave her home in the tower, and found refuge in an institution in Drogheda, where she ended her days.[16]

In 1897 there was a hut made of tin or galvanise, which acted as a hospital. The ships coming into Drogheda port stopped there in order to drop off any sailors who had contacted a fever on the journey. In this place of quarantine he was cared for by a nurse, appointed by the Board of Guardians, the fore-runner of the County Council. The sailor would be picked up by his ship on it's way back out to sea. The caretaker was Mary Reynolds. Board of Guardians ran the workhouse in Drogheda, and the master of the workhouse or secretary, kept a manual of the day to day running of the workhouse.[17]

The Lady's Finger

This structure is a solid round tower about 40ft high and 7ft in diameter, its based on a square pediment and tapering cone-like to its summit. It does not look like a finger. Like Maiden Tower, nothing is known of its history, but it is possible that it maybe a phallic symbol of some period in history; regardless of possibilities, tradition tell us it played a significant role with the Maiden tower in guiding the ships home safely to Mornington.[18]

Maiden Tower and Lady's Finger, Mornington

CHAPTER 9
"Open for the Season"

HOTELS,
Neptune Hotel

In 1815 Charles Bianconi started his fast, efficient and cheap transport system, and was said at the time to be 'the man who put Ireland on wheels' yet, this service never extended to Drogheda. Travellers from Dublin to Drogheda, Dundalk and Belfast used the privately owned stage coaches.

In those days the Imperial Hotel stood where the Post Office now is in West Street Drogheda. This hotel was owned by Thomas Simcocks, who also owned the Neptune Hotel Bettystown. At that time it was known as the Neptune Lodge. Mr. Simcocks the proprietor, organised a horse-drawn coach service to operate twice daily between his hotels for his patrons.[1]

The village of Bettystown grew up around the Neptune Lodge.
By 1853 this Lodge was recorded as a hotel.[2]

List of Proprietors: Neptune (Lodge) Hotel
Thomas Simcocks............early 19th century
Gerald Simcocks.............1848- 1873
K. Burke (Proprieties) 1874- 1886
Connolly & Denis ....1887- Misses Gogarty....early twentieth century .

The Crinion family, were the owners of the Neptune Hotel for over seventy years, from 1925 ending in 1997. Kieran then sold it to the present owner, Denis Reddan.

The following are a sample of some of the advertising of this fine Hotel, over a hundred years ago. The advertisements, give a very clear description of 'what's on offer' in the hotel, and also include details of attractive leisurely activities which could be enjoyed outside the immediate area of Bettystown seaside resort and the Neptune Hotel.

The Neptune Hotel, Bettystown in the 1950's

THE NEPTUNE HOTEL
BETTYSTOWN

K. BURKE, PROPRIETIES

This Hotel is situated at the seaside, within three and a half miles of Drogheda. It is fitted and furnished in the best manner, and affords accommodation for forty to fifty persons. There are large public and private dining and sitting rooms. The general sanitary arrangements throughout the buildings include the modern improvements, and are of the most perfect character.

Extensive grounds, including a tennis court, connect the Hotel with a strand several miles in length affording unrivalled facilities for surf bathing.

Hot and cold salt water baths on the premises, ready for use at all hours of the day.

Special rates for sojourners of a week or upward.

Wines of the choicest brands, liquors of the purest quality, and prime cigars constantly kept in stock.

SPECIAL SUMMER SERVICE.

A large waggonette leaves the Hotel twice a day - 9 a.m. and 2 p.m.- for Drogheda, returning from Miss Warren's West Street, at 11 a.m. and 6 p.m.
Moderate charges in every department

SEPARATE HOUSES FOR FAMILIES

In the vicinity of, and belonging to the Hotel, are commodiously furnished houses for families. They have enclosed grounds, containing nine rooms each, and face the sea.

The morning hours at Bettystown and Laytown are almost sacred to the children. They throng the beach for the bath, and afterwards busy at play. Indeed it is only simple justice to say that here is a perfect paradise for little ones. There are no pitfalls, no dangers of any kind to cause anxiety to parents or nursemaids. In the evening strolling parties, equestrians, and pony-carts make a very lively scene. The sand hills rise to heights which render their shelter exceedingly agreeable for invalids, and for those who desire comfortable lounging places, in which to read, watch the in flowing tide, or to impatiently await the dinner hour, a most satisfactory consequence of the invigorating air. If it be possible to grow weary of the sand and the sea, and long for other recreation, there are charming walks and drives inland, including Ballygarth Castle, a mile and a half and Gormanston, three miles.[3]

Note: According to Willow Keneghan (a local Bettystown man) the Neptune Hotel was a very popular hotel in those days. The wealthy people from Dublin, and indeed other parts of the country, came for their holidays every year.

One of the reasons for the big attraction to the hotel was that they lay on salt water and seaweed baths. In order to provide this service at minimum cost a pipe was used to pump the salt water from the sea into the hotel, and this proved very successful.[6]

SEA BATHING

PURE SEA WATER, HOT, COLD, AND SHOWER BATHS,
OPEN FROM SIX O'CLOCK IN THE MORNING UNTIL TEN AT NIGHT

The Neptune Hotel, Bettystown.
NOW OPEN FOR THE SUMMER SEASON, REPLETE WITH EVERY ACCOMMODATION

THE GROCERY, TEA, WINE, AND SPIRIT ESTABLISHMENT attached to the Hotel will be found supplied with goods of the best quality, on the most Moderate Terms.

FINEST TEAS, PORT, SHERRY, AND CLARET WINES,
MARTELL'S AND HENNESSY'S BRANDIES,
JAMESON & SON'S WHISKEY ON SHERRY HOGSHEAD,
BASS & CO's PALE ALE,
GUINNESS'S XX PORTER, ALL ON DRAUGHT AND BOTTLES

FRESH BREAD EVERY MORNING.

GOODS ORDERED DELIVERED.

Well appointed conveyances ply, as usual, between the Imperial Hotel, Drogheda, and Neptune, Bettystown at 9am., and 7 pm., Hotel Drogheda, at 11 am., 4 and 7 pm.
The Billiard Room opens on 20th June. Two large Terrace Houses and three Neat Cottages to be Let, furnished or unfurnished, by Month or Season.

THOMAS SIMCOCKS, Proprietor.[4]

****

THE NEPTUNE HOTEL, BETTYSTOWN, CO. MEATH.

(Standing on the Finest Strand in the Three Kingdoms)

IS NOW IN PERFECT WORKING ORDER. THE PRESENT OWNERS,

MESSERS CONNOLLY AND DENIS.

**Having made Extensive Alterations and Improvements, are determined to have this Favourite Hotel conducted in every detail second to none in the Kingdom.
For Terms, &c. apply to the Manageress.**

The Salt-Water Baths attached to above are also PERFECT.
Brakes will ply between Neptune and Drogheda on and after Monday, 27th.

In connection with the above Hotel (though distinctly separate) is a Grocery, Wine, Spirit, and Italian Warehouse, where goods of all kinds of Very Best Quality can be had at Very Lowest City Prices.[5]

****

The Strand Hotel

The Neptune Hotel was not always the only hotel in Bettystown. The Beach Inn, almost opposite the Neptune Hotel on the other side of the square was once 'The Strand Hotel' owned by Mr. McDonnell, approximately seventy years before Mr. McLoughlin bought the premises. A Mr. Flanagan was also associated with the above hotel, and in 1901 he had his name in Irish over the bar door. Also, around this time there was a private road in front of the Strand Hotel, with gates at one end, which were closed for one week each year, to preserve ownership. This practice ended in the 1920's. Mr. Peter Garvey from Carrickmacross was also associated with the 'Beach Inn' during the sixties and early seventies. It was then sold to the Rooney family. Mr. White owns the entire building now part of which has been up for sale.[7]

Strand Hotel, Bettystown, Co. Meath, early twentieth century.

The Village/Northlands Hotel

The original name for the Village Hotel was 'The Cowslip Lodge'.
Built in the early part of the 1800's by Carrolls. We are told, a Mr. G. H. Pentland lived at the Cowslip Lodge in 1837.
The following, are a list of names of people who resided there when it was a private residence, and ultimately a hotel, the period in question, middle to late 1800's to early 1900's:.......Mr. Moran, Mrs. Osborne and Mr. Adams.
A family by the name McCaul bought the 'The Cowslip Lodge' from Mr. Adams and renamed it 'Northlands'. The Northlands became known as the 'Hydro', meaning spa waters.
According to local opinion the Northland's Hotel was a very popular venue for the young and the not-so-young during the war years, as many people came long distance to enjoy the dances and 'good drink' (goes without saying!) there. Also to listen and dance to the music of the 'Charlton' the 'Jacksons' and the 'Hillbillies', which were the popular bands at the time.
A cousin of the McCaul family, Patrica, married Mr. Jimmy Collins, a member of the Shop Street Collins family and an engineer with Meath County Council. She became Dr. Patrica McCaul Collins, who is remembered with great affection locally.

Note: A bomb was dropped in the vicinity of this hotel (around the same time). A German who wanted to get rid of his cargo! or so we are told.[8]

The Hoey family from Dublin bought the Northlands from the McCauls. A daughter from this family married Patrick Stanley from Drogheda. After a few years, the Hoeys sold the Northlands to a Mr. Farrell from Athboy, who ran it for approximately three years.

A Mrs. Andrews and her daughter were also associated with this hotel in the fifties.

Dr. McAllister bought the hotel in 1960, and stayed for eight years. On the 20th April 1965 the Northlands became the Village Hotel, and was the 'in' place in those days.[9]

Michael Keogh (bar manager of the new Neptune Hotel, until recently) learned the trade in the Northlands/Village Hotel in the sixties and seventies. He was employed first as the head chef and later became the manager, under the ownership of Dr. McAllister and later when it was sold to a Mr John Jones (deceased). Michael left in 1979, when the Hotel changed hands again, this time to a Mr. Fred Brady.

The Village was sold again in 1983, and the following are some of the names associated with it since then.

Salviana Traders Limited (Vincent Hoey & Assoc.).

Mr. Gerry Keogh.

The final curtain fell on the Village Hotel, after it was destroyed by fire in 1992/93.

The site was bought a couple of years ago by the O'Connor building contractors.[10,11]

The Village Hotel - before it was destroyed by fire.

Alverno House (Hotel), Laytown

Alverno was built sometime in the middle 1800's, and was originally meant to be a convent for the Sisters of Mercy. On completion the Bishop of Meath, would not give permission for it to be used as a convent, he considered it an unsuitable location, Laytown being a seaside resort.[12]

In 1852, part of the lands at Laytown, consisting of five acres, one rood and thirty two perches was sold by - The Commissioners of Incumbered Estates in Ireland, to Ralph Smith Cusack Esq. for the sum of three hundred and thirty pounds.

According to an Indenture made in 1864, on the same piece of land at Laytown, an agreement was drawn up between three parties.......William Oliver Parker and Graves Swan Warren Esqres first part, Ralph Smith Cusack Esq. second part, and Robert Taylor Esq. third part.

After the death of Mr. Robert Taylor in 1872, he bequeathed all his property and premises in Laytown, to James Mortimer and George Allman.

In 1897, according to an Indenture made at that time between Darcy W. Thompson and William F. Forrest (the newly appointed trustees of Robert Taylor's estate) and Mr.Patrick McCullen of Beamore. The property and premises consisting of five acres, one rood and thirty two perches, were sold at a public auction to Mr. Patrick McCullen for four hundred and forty pounds, to hold forever, subject to the tenancy of Richard James Kennedy under the lease since 1864 that was made between Robert Taylor and Richard James Kennedy for a term of one hundred and fifty years, at a rent of twenty one pounds, to be paid twice yearly.[13]

James R. Kennedy, rated tenant/occupier in 1852. Founding director of the Drogheda Independent, also Town Councillor, 1884.
Richard J. Kennedy, Mayor of Drogheda, 1886-1888.[13a]

The following passage was written by a writer, who it appears had the pleasure of spending some time in the Alverno Hotel.

"Taking it all in all," he says, "I cannot convey to you my admiration and esteem for it. At the outset it is notable that not one visitor here, and they are many and of the most respectable class, has left it for the last five weeks; that the invalids have become convalescent, and the strong still stronger; that they all, Catholic and Protestant, live and mix together on terms of the most social unity, viewing all of them to make each other happy and cheerful. It is indeed a most engaging family, and the servants are so obliging that you cannot from the time you put your foot in here experience anything but a true home feeling. Need I say that the rooms and beds are exceptionally good; that the meats are fine, and the cookery excellent. The worthy and public spirited proprietor, Mr. Kennedy, and his good sisters are unceasing in their endeavours to cater for the wants of their visitors. You have not seen the hotel itself? Well, 'tis a noble, lofty pile, standing on a most healthy eminence above the cleanly kept cottages and gardens belonging to the coastguard station. It looks out on the near and deep blue sea, and up the Nanny river, and the sweet woods of Ballygarth. To the south, around the lovely crescent which begirds the sea, the eye will fondly linger from where the peaks of the Skerries shine while in the wave, down to Balbriggan, famous the world over for its unrivalled hosiery. On to Gormanston which, though its great castle be now desolate, is surrounded by hundreds of acres of the richest fruit gardens.
Then look to the northern coast, starting with Clogher Head, you see the Magnificent range of the blue northern mountains, the whole forming a panorama of exquisite and rare interest.
If you would like to enjoy a luxurious hour, go down, as I do every day and sit upon 'the banks', watch the billows breaking, while on the velvet strand where groups of children are safely disporting themselves, and listen to the soft tumult of the incoming tide and the long waves sobbing upon the shore.
Here at your very door, there is every convenience for bathing, boating or driving. The railway station is just hard by - you reach Drogheda in ten minutes, Dublin in an hour, Navan, Kells, Oldcastle and the nearer northern towns- are within easy and cheap reach of you".

JAMES KENNEDY,

(R.J. KENNEDY,)

FAMILY GROCER, WINE, SPIRITS, AND PROVISION MERCHANT

NORTH QUAY, DROGHEDA,
AND
L A Y T O W N.[14]

That how it was at the "Alverno Hotel" in Laytown, Co. Meath, over a hundred years ago, and that was advertising at its purest, without a doubt!

Laytown, Co. Meath - The Alverno Hotel towering in the background

THE "ALVERNO" HOTEL
LAYTOWN.

The above Hotel has now been OPENED for the Season under the personal supervision of Mr. R.J. Kennedy

The Hotel is the only one at Laytown, and is sumptuously appointed. Visitors and Tourists specially catered for. Splendid Grounds, Select Bar and Billard Room.

Car Service to Golf Links,
At Moderate Prices
For an ideal Summer Resort, recommend your friends to:

THE ALVERNO HOTEL, LAYTOWN, CO. MEATH

R.J. Kennedy, Proprietor.

****

David and Margaret Sheridan were also owners of the above hotel in the early twentieth century. It continued to thrive under their management, and they are still remembered by some members in the community. David Sheridan died in 1963 at the age of ninety nine years.
In 1952, the Monahan family bought the Alverno Hotel, and continued to run it as a hotel until 1988.[15] In 1992, the hotel was bought by Hugh and Margaret O'Donaghue from Dermot Monahan, they have great plans for the future of the old hotel, but at present are running it as a successful licence premises. Hugh and Margaret are no strangers to Laytown, Hugh's father was Laytown station master for many years.[16]

Paddy Monahan, a member of the above family who was also well known locally for his skills on the local St. Mary's football team in the forties now lives in Baltray. He is, no doubt, enjoying a quiet life, far from the maddening crowds of Hotel/Pub life.

While still on the subject of good food and pleasant surroundings it would be very difficult to leave Laytown, without mentioning the late Francie Stafford who died 2nd March 1976. Especially when it was high quality food and fresh vegetables, first class pub beer/ale and stout, that was the order of the day. A service to the Laytown people with his own unique personal touch, in a traditional atmosphere was second to none. The following passages go a little way to describe the character of the man who is still remembered with affection by those who had the good fortune to know him.

"Many old soldiers of the Second Division battalions and of the FCA will remember with affection the famous Francie Stafford and his thatched pub at Laytown.
Francie is not too well in the Mother Mary Martin hospital in Drogheda, and gone are the days, when you sit on a bench with a pint, being careful that the sheep carcass hung over your head did not drip blood into your glass! These were the simple pleasures of the ordinary people."[17]

In the good ould days, when the boys gathered in their 'favourite pub' to quench their thirst, and indulge themselves in an atmosphere of pure pleasure, time usually went by very quickly! At closing time, the boys would make no effort to leave, Francie would close the door, top up the glasses, and so the evening continued into the 'wee' hours totally undisturbed. Until one night there was a loud knock on the door, the local sergeant (at the time) stepped into the smoked filled room. But alas, the room was empty, except for Francie in his butcher's coat and his cleaver stuck in his belt, he was giving nothing away, that goes without saying. The sergeant asked where the culprits were, pointing to the full glasses on the table, to which Francie replied, "ah sergeant, you may have found the honey, but the bees have flown".[18]

"Old Soldiers of the eighteenth and twenty second Battalions, and indeed odds and ends of all the regiments and Corps ever stationed at Gormanston Camp on either regular or Reserve training will be pained to hear that Francie Stafford of Laytown is dead. A bachelor, he was one of the amenities of the Laytown area. At the height of his remarkable powers, ran a pub, a vegetable shop, all most pleasantly intermingled. Francie's pride and joy, which he showed to only a favoured few, was the biggest collection of spiders in Ireland. There was a one time bottling shed in his yard where the cobwebs were a foot thick, and within the black fur lived, what must be presumed, a cannibal colony of thousands of spiders.[19]

Note: In the 1920's Mr. John Kenehan, Willow Kenehan's father, owned the above thatched pub before it was bought by the Stafford family in 1928.

The corner, Laytown, Co. Meath - over one hundred years ago.

James Stafford & Sons Limited
Phone-Bettystown 10

==========================
HIGH-CLASS GROCERS
AND VICTUALLERS
*
WINE, SPIRIT AND

PROVISION MERCHANTS

OIL, FRUIT AND
VEGETABLE STORE

==========================

Laytown and Julianstown
1 mile from Mosney (along the beach)[20]

****

Staffords labels - Guinness and Ale

Francie Stafford and staff, bottling the beer - 1948

James Darkie Stafford, outside Stafford's Bar and Grocery, Laytown - 1948.

After Francie Stafford died in 1976, the Pub and Grocery business in Laytown was sold. The new owners were Michael and Kathleen Gilna (both now sadly deceased) from Dublin. In 1980, a new lounge was added and alterations made to the bar. Their son Jimmy, married to local girl Emer O'Reilly, took over the business in 1986. The pub continued to be a very popular venue on the east coast true to its humble beginnings. On the 1st October 1995, disaster struck again in Laytown, when the pub was burnt to the ground by fire.

Jimmy and Emer rebuilt the pub now called 'The Cottage Inn', and opened their Bar, Lounge and Off Licence to the public in June '98, a restaurant to open in '99, and further exciting plans are in the pipeline.

The Nanny Water Cottage, and the Nanny River winding its way to the sea at Laytown, Co. Meath.

CHAPTER 10
"Good Sports"

Proximity to the sea and a prevailing holiday atmosphere has encouraged many outdoor pursuits. The Horse racing, Tennis, and Golf has flourished along the coastline. Let us start with Orkney Villa, it was built by Mr. Tom Gilroy a retired banker of Scottish origin, who founded the County Louth Golf Club in 1892. Mr. Gilroy lived for a time in Coney Hall (Mornington House), before he built Orkney Villa in an isolated position overlooking the Boyne, an unusual place to build a house, but Tom Gilroy, was, by all accounts an unusual man.

The house, Orkney Villa played its part in history and was featured as a 'haunted house' in fictitious stories around the beginning of this century. One story in particular comes to mind 'The old house by the Boyne' by Mrs J. Sadlier.[1] This house was also used as the head quarters of the local security force in the second world war because of its obvious impressive view of the sea. The McGrane family are the present owners.[2]

Mr. Tom Gilroy, a native of Dundee, was born on the 2nd October 1852. He was playing golf from the age of six or seven years, and it soon became obvious that he was very talented, and one day would be a great golfer. Jack Butchart (whose son would later become professional at Newcastle) took him in hand, coaching him together with George Morris (a brother of Tom Morris).

Tom Gilroy was educated at St. Andrews, where he often played golf with the young Tom Morris.

From the moment of his arrival, in 1885, it was clear that Tom Gilroy set out to foster the game of golf in Ireland. By 1893, his handicap at the Royal Dublin was plus four, and he was widely acknowledged as the greatest golfer in Ireland.[3]

Golf was first introduced and played in Laytown and Bettystown area in the 1880's by Tom Gilroy and his family and continued so into late 1895, when the family emigrated to England.

But it appears the 'golfer' was no stranger to Laytown in the 1880's. According to Robert Browning in his book 'A History of Golf' on page 157: "There is also a tradition of golf being played early in the 19th century (1850) at Laytown in Co. Meath". It is believed that those memories are some way related to Tom Gilroy and his family in the 1880's. Present research shows no proof of its existence in this area, prior to the 1880's.

Tom Gilroy of Mornington was a major pioneer of Golf in the 1890's, and was one of the key figures in the spread of early golf in Ireland. In 1885 he settled at Mornington four miles from Drogheda. He helped to lay out the original Phoenix Park course in 1885, he laid out his own course near Laytown in 1886, and assisted W.H. Mann in laying out the North West Club's course in 1891. Tom Gilroy laid out the original nine holes at Baltray in 1892.

In an article on Tom Gilroy in the Golf magazine 17th Feb. 1893, the writer states: "There may be seen at (Mornington) fluttering in the breeze.....the flags of an excellent fourteen-hole course, which Mr. Gilroy has laid out upon his property, the tee for the first hole being about a two hundred yard distance from the entrance gates of Mornington House/Coney Hall, where Tom Gilroy now resides".

In the 13th Sept. 1913 addition of "The Irish Field", the following article was written: "The golf course at Bettystown is to be extended to eighteen holes. When this is accomplished it will undoubtedly be one of the best seaside golf courses in the country".

Late in 1895, Tom Gilroy accepted the post of secretary of Seaford Golf Club in East Sussex and much to the regret of the Irish Golfing world he left Mornington, and moved there with his family.[4]

In March 1909 a meeting was held in the office of George Henry Daly Auctioneer, Laurence Street, Drogheda. This meeting was called to establish the Golf Club in Bettystown and name it. It was chaired by Mr. Daly himself, the motion of the meeting was passed and the club was named accordingly, Laytown and Bettystown Golf Club.

The following Officers and Committee members were elected:

Captain	Mr. P. J. Tallon.
Hon. Treasurer	Mr. J. Lyons.
Hon. Secretary	Mr. J. F. Smyth.
Trustees	Mr. P. Lynch, Mr. J. Lyons, Mr. C. Gogarty and Mr. P. J. Delany.
General Committee	Mr. J. Markey, and Mr. J. R. Smith.

In the months that followed, the Trustees obtained a lease on the sand dunes stretching from the village of Bettystown to the North Lighthouse in Mornington on the banks of the river Boyne. This lease was for a period of thirty five years and was renewed in 1937. The Golf club went from strength to strength, and in April 1923 the Irish Field reported that a club pavilion was in the process of being erected. One year later, July 1924, the same paper reported that an additional nine holes had been opened.

In the considerable short period of fifteen years, the Laytown and Bettystown Golf Club had developed into a major force in Irish Golf, it is a great tribute to the remarkable men who guided it through a very difficult time in Irish history.

Green keeping

It is a fact of history that the vast majority of courses laid out in the British Isles, in the latter part of the nineteenth and the early part of the twentieth century, were links courses. The natural seaside grasses were short and with the absence of machinery to cut grass to suit the game, it was played on the grass as it was.

The most destructive natural problem on the golf course was the rabbit. There were thousands of them, and they appeared to be increasing every year. Every hill, bank and sand dune was honeycombed with rabbit burrows. The destruction they caused was enormous. Every known remedy of destroying them was tried. People were encouraged to catch them with traps and snares, also with lamps and dogs at night. There was a great demand for rabbits as a food during the war and a big export trade built up with England during that period. Still the rabbits increased and multiplied in population.

In the late forties the rabbits died in their thousands from some unknown disease, it was a complete mystery! it wasn't until months later it was identified as Myxomatosis. Some of the rabbits escaped the infection and the rabbit population started to build up again. The 'disease' struck again in the late fifties, but was not as deadly as before. The rabbits are still around, but seem to be confined to the area of the furze bushes around the twelfth hole.

Note: Sand Dunes

(In recent times the sand dunes between Bettystown and Mornington have been much in the news and a topic of discussion in the coastal area. As an aside to the arguments about the preservation of the dunes, the following extract from Thompson's Statistical Survey of the County of Meath (1802) makes interesting reading:

"There is only one rabbit warren in the county of sufficient extent to entitle it a particular notice in this survey. It extents along the seashore from the mouth of the Nanny River to the mouth of the River Boyne and belongs to Mr. Brabazon of Mornington. The rabbits burrow in a heap of sand blown off the seashore by the easterly winds and feed on a salt marsh running parallel to it, being prevented from going on the uplands and corn grounds by broad drains, which are constantly full of water. The rabbits are taken by pass-nets placed between them and the burrow on their hasty return from feeding at night being alarmed by the barking of dogs, kept for that sole purpose.

They are all disposed of in the Dublin market, the skin being generally more valuable than the flesh, and they (rabbits) are sold by the warreners at, from one shilling and sixpence to two shillings a pair. I have been informed this warren is worth three hundred pounds per annum to Mr. Brabazon, and the ground so employed is not valued at one shilling per acre".

Golf Clubhouse, Bettystown

Front Row: J. Mc Guirk, Vera Somers, Ida Delaney, _____, _____, C.H. Walsh, Josie Delaney, Sheila Walsh, Maureen Taylor and Blauna Delany.
Middle Row: Mrs. P. J. McPhelimy, John McGuirk, _____, Pat Gray, P.J. McPhelimy, John Drew, Den Somers, O.T. Somers, Con McLoughlin, Peter Gray, Sean Rooney, J.P. McDonough, Tom Delany, Tom Lynch, Maureen Gray and Charlie Crinion.
Back Row: Sean Taylor; R.J. O'Malley and P.B. Delany.

L - R: **1st Row:** Owen Somers, Jimmy Flynn, John Gallagher, Anne Corrigan, Sheena O'Brien-Kenny, AnneMarie Bellew and Valerie Flynn.
L - R: **2nd Row:** Susan Taylor, Catherine Craig, _____, Stanley McIvor, John Taylor, _____, Miriam Somers, _____, Kevin Byrne.
L - R: **3rd Row:** Pamela Hoey, Paula Gannon, Toss Delany and Kevin Somers, _____.

However, it is very obvious the Laytown and Bettystown golf course survived the hand cutting mower, the horse drawn mower and the rabbits, and lived to see the day when the club had a fully mechanised green keeping staff.

Clubhouse

Even though the clubhouse was erected in 1923, with refreshments available, there was no facilities or amenities whatsoever with regards to lighting, toilets or water etc., until about 1936 when electricity was installed in the area, and more modern living condition could be established. With the electricity came the mains water, and in 1939 a sewerage system was installed in the club served by a septic tank. The ladies locker room was destroyed by fire in the mid fifties and the first of the modern developments took place. A new locker room was built for the ladies. It served the purpose for over thirty years, and was still in use up to recently. It is now the caddycar store and also for general use.

The ladies membership was very low during the period from 1930 to 1960, but none the less very active. They held their weekly competitions even though they had only ten to twelve entries. They played during spring summer and autumn but winter play was out. They all carried their own bags, as caddy cars were not common then. However, one well known lady was observed in the mid fifties wheeling a pram on the course with a baby in it along with her bag of clubs! She is still playing good golf to the present day.

Major renovations took place on the clubhouse over the years. By the late eighties, the old clubhouse building had reached the end of the road. The facilities were not in keeping with the increased membership and the building was in need of extensive repairs. The committee considered all the options and decided that a complete new clubhouse was the answer. Many different designs were discussed, and the final outcome is the present clubhouse, which is now one of the finest in the country.

The Tennis Club:

The tennis club as it exists today is about thirty years old. Tennis had been played in the area for many years but no separate tennis club existed. It was known as the Tennis section of the Golf club. This facility was available to all members of the Golf club and visitors. In 1966 the conversion of the grass courts to hard courts took place, and the following year the first tennis pavilion was built. The formation of a separate club did not take place, until some years later.

When the separate Tennis club was established on a sound footing the club made great progress in building a new Pavilion. They improved the existing courts to modern hard court surfaces, and in time, laid two more new courts. Flood lighting has been installed so tennis can be enjoyed day or night, winter or summer, and it is a credit to the committee.

Social:

The Club has become a great social centre in the area during the last number of years, and can boast of many other activities besides Golf and bar facilities. Back in the early years, the committee hired a piano from Piggots in Dublin. It was kept locked away except for special occasions, such as Sunday evening finals of the tennis tournament, which were held on the court in front of the clubhouse. These evenings attracted a huge crowd of young men and women and a 'musical evening' would follow with singers such as John McGoldrick, Stephen Henly, Mrs Violet Healy and Peter Lynch, who was a marvellous tenor, something in the same class as John McCormack.

In 1965 a ballroom was put into full use in the summer months. A new local band called 'The Road Runners' supplied the music. This popular band made an agreement with the Golf Club authorities to accept as payment 50% of the door takings. In which case, if it was a 'good night', the band members went home well rewarded, if it was a 'bad night' well, that was the risk they were prepared to take. As it turned out the dances were a marvellous success but the lifetime and success of this band was short lived, and it appears they broke up in 1967.

Even though the band was only in existence for two short years, its contribution to the dance scene of the swinging sixties made a lasting impression on some locals who still fondly remember those exciting nights over thirty years ago. Soon after that time Phil McLoughlin, one of the members, started his own

'new' band called the 'Trolls', and went from strength to strength in the music world.
The members of the band were Michael and Phil McLoughlin, Leontia and John Somers and Robert Berney. Esmond O'Reilly and Sean Black played with the group on occasions. The manager was Peadar McQuillan.
There was also a Disco held for teenagers on Saturday nights. All the functions ran very smoothly for some years, and generated great revenue.

'Road Runners' left to right - Phil (Berch) McLoughlin, Robert Berney, Leontia Somers, Mick McLoughlin and John Somers

With the introduction of a licensed bar in the club, the opportunity for social evenings became more popular. It became necessary for a sub-committee to be appointed to run these functions and the results can be seen today in the Club.

The building of the new road from Bettystown to Mornington changed the whole area beyond recognition. It opened up housing development, which resulted in full membership in both the Tennis and Golf clubs.[5]

Another of Laytown's favourite sons deserves to be remembered - musical wizard Paddy Farrell, one of Delia and James Farrell's ten children. Paddy's interest in music was apparent from a very young age, when he started playing the piano and piano accordion later progressing to guitar and banjo. While attending the Christian Brothers secondary school in Drogheda he earned a place in the school accordion band. His love for music led him to leave school to pursue a full-time career as a musician.

He joined the 'Arcadian Showband' fronted by Jimmy Smyth, father of country and western singer Gloria. He also played with 'Louis Smyth - Big Band Sound', from Drogheda. Paddy enjoyed success with these bands but his musical career hit the big time when he joined 'Dermot O' Brien and the Clubmen'. With this band he not only travelled around Ireland but also Europe and the United States of America. During his time in the U.S. he was fortunate to meet some of his musical heroes, Jim Reeves and Bing Crosby to mention but two. After the U.S. tours there followed regular weekly appearance on two very popular R.T.E. Television shows, 'Jamboree' and 'Country Style', Paddy also recorded several LP's and singles during these years. Some of his favourite recordings included *'The Blizzard', 'Little Ole You', Waltzing on Top of the World', 'Green Green Grass of Home'* and of course *'Sweet Bettystown'*, which he wrote himself.

The 'Clubmen' eventually split up but some of its members including Paddy reformed and played successfully for about a year under the name 'The Tigermen'. Paddy then teamed up with Cyril Jolly, his good friend from Drogheda, both men enjoyed playing music together, and along with a number of other musicians made an LP 'Live at the Fairways', in Dundalk. Paddy left Ireland at the age of twenty eight to join the love of his life Kate in New York. They were married in 1971, and had two children Marie and James. They never forgot their roots and returned regularly to Laytown and Bettystown over the years. In the States he played with Dubliner Jesse Owens (of Jesse Owens and Ann Byrne duo), for a number of years. Paddy then teamed up with his great friend Noel Kingston, and together they performed and recorded music for the Irish-American market, they were very successful, and enjoyed a comfortable lifestyle from their careers as musicians. It was with great sadness that their partnership was cruelly halted on St. Stephen's Day 1987, with the news that Paddy was diagnosed with terminal cancer. His wife Kate, who came from Carlow, knew how much Paddy loved Laytown and Bettystown, and so moved the family back to Ireland in July 1988. Paddy enjoyed his last few months surrounded and helped by family and his many musical friends who were unrelenting in their support.

Sadly, Paddy passed away on the 24th September 1988, at the age of forty five. R.I.P.[5a]

Paddy Farrell, September 1988.

Laytown Races 1901.
These Races will be held on Monday next on the beautiful strand at Laytown. The capable committee in charge of the fixture have succeeded in securing large entries for the five events on the card; and should the present beautiful weather continue, we have no doubt that the meeting will prove one of the most enjoyable of the season. Apart from the racing attractions altogether a day at Laytown in the summer is one of the most pleasurable experience which one can have. Special facilities are being provided by the Railway Company with cheap special trains from Kells, Navan, and Drogheda, and other places.

LAYTOWN RACES

_____CHARMING DAY AT THE SEASIDE_____

MONDAY AUGUST 12th._____

Splendid Sport._____

A SPECIAL TRAIN
Will leave Kells at 12.15; Calling at intermediate Stations,
arriving at Laytown at 1.40

CHEAP RETURN FARES [6]

The Laytown Races continued to provide a festive fun afternoon/evening not only for the punter, but for all the family, down through the years. Laytown races tomorrow afternoon, this is the only race meeting (barring that at Ballyferriter) where the front runners plaster the cautious with mixture of salt water and sand.
If you are a gambler.... the bookmakers are waiting for you, and so is the tide.
Not present this year in his famous and beloved inn, will be Francie Stafford of Laytown, so well remembered by the eighteenth Battalion in Gormanston.[7]

The following articles written by the Drogheda Independent are brief accounts of just some of the events surrounding the Laytown Races in latter years.

Laytown and its famous strand races were the stars of British breakfast television this week, when a preview of the event was shown on their Tuesday morning show. A Belfast based camera crew led by TV-AM reporter for Ireland, Roisin McAuley caused quite a flurry of excitement when they visited the Meath village on Monday to make the film. This is not the first time the races have featured on overseas television screens. They have previously been filmed by French TV, and Canadian TV, while U.TV did a major documentary on them. The TV-AM crew arrived at Laytown at about noon on Monday and spent most of the day shooting. They opened with a shot of Roisin in bathing costume standing waist high in water, speaking from the tide covered beach race track—the sea was full in at the time, the races are run at low tide.
"This is the first time I have ever had to do a piece of camera work like this, but the sea is nice, it is really worm", said reporter Roisin, emerging from the sea and undoing her clip on the microphone. Later on when the tide went out, the crew took some film of horses doing a practice run along the track, preparing for the following day's races. So what turns British viewers on about racing at Laytown?
"Horsey stories from Ireland go down well among the British animal loving public", said Roisin.
"And Britain doesn't have a strand race like this, infact it is the only one of its kind in Europe".
"Also it is a nice, cheerful, offbeat, light-hearted, summer story, in contrast to a lot of the stories that come out of Ireland".

One of the people who met and assisted the TV-AM crew was local councillor and businessman, Tom Kelly. He described the publicity value of the film to Laytown, as inestimable ——-
"Its great, it must be worth thousands of pounds in advertising to the resort". The races, he said, had helped make Laytown famous all over the world.

Flat out at Laytown, Co. Meath.

The interest in the races stemmed from the fact that they were the only strand or beach race run under Racing rules in the world. He reckoned, however, that a lot more could be done by the authorities here especially Meath Co. Council to develop Laytown as a tourist resort.[8] This unique strand race is certainly a 'one off', a rare event, not only to Ireland but to the whole world. Always among the crowd of people milling around the beach and enclosure will be many tourists and overseas visitors, who are fascinated by this very special evening of Irish sport.

Thanks to the patronage of Woodchester Bank, and the various other sponsors, race meetings at Laytown have been a magnificent success, with a terrific festive atmosphere for many years, and may it continue for many more. Many top trainers frequent this strand meeting, the likes of Mick O'Toole, Kevin Prendergast, and Noel Meade.

During the year 1993 the Laytown race committee lost a very dear friend with the death of Jimmy Lyons, who was the Chairman up until the time of his death.
His son Jimmy has accepted a place on the committee, and will hopefully carry on the honoured family tradition.
Niall Delany of Corballis, Laytown, succeeded as Chairman, he is the grandson of the late Paddy Delany, who revived the Laytown Race Meeting in 1901.[9]

Disaster struck the Laytown Races
Appeals follow tragic events at strand meeting:

A plea not to sound the death knell for Laytown's famous annual race meeting, came from the Secretary/Manager, Joe Collins and one of the mounted stewards, following the tragic happenings at the last drama-filled meeting (6th August '94).
The appeals came in the wake of a day, which saw three horses killed, five jockeys taken to hospital, ten fallers on the beach, a woman spectator who was struck by a loose horse, and a terrified horse which decanted its jockey at Laytown and then took off in the direction of Mornington, and swam across the Boyne river to Baltray.

Mr. Joe Collins, committee secretary felt that the accident during the first race at the meeting, had been 'blown out of all proportion by the media and would do very little for the reputation of the sport'. He said, "unfortunately, when you bring the sport so close to the people, so that they can experience the excitement of racing, you have to be able to take the rough with the smooth, the joy with the sadness. If a horse has the misfortune to get badly injured or breaks a leg, they have to be humanely destroyed".
Nobody wants to see horses injured or mistreated, or any animal for that matter, and it is even more painful to have to see them put down, however humanely performed.

CHAPTER 11
"Railway People".

Dublin/Drogheda Railway:

When the line from Dublin to Drogheda was conceived in 1835, it was the brainchild of Thomas Brodigan of Piltown House. Thomas Brodigan, farmed some three hundred acres of his own land and spent much time and thought on schemes to relieve the lot of the poor, and revitalise the local economy.

At this time the failure of the textile industries of Balbriggan and Drogheda were of great concern to him, and he blamed the poor transport facilities for this state of things. His solution to the problem was the construction of a railway along the coast, and he published a pamphlet (The Establishment of a Northern Railroad 1835), advocating his reasons for this route. It would be the third railway to be started in Ireland and he foresaw the linking of Dublin and Drogheda and the crossing of the Boyne to Belfast.

An opposition group wanted the route to go inland from Dublin, through Ashbourne to Navan and eventually to Armagh. William Cubitt, an eminent engineer of the day, was engaged to survey the district and state which route was preferable. Construction of the line started in 1838, and took six years to complete during which time thousands of men were employed. This was Thomas Brodigan's wish, for employment and prosperity. The line was opened by the Lord Lieutenant who travelled by special train to Drogheda where it he was greeted by "cheering crowds, volleys of guns, and the pealing of Joy-bells".[1]
Note: In 1844, the fares from Amiens St. Station to Laytown were 3s. 6p. first class, 2s. 3p. second class and 1s. 3p. third class. The passenger travelling on to Bettystown would pay 3s. 9p. 2s. 3p. and 1s. 4p. depending on the class chosen.
For Bettystown races on the 15th August 1846, special return fares of 4/- 3/- and 2/- were quoted.[2]

When Bettystown had a Train Station

Laytown train station has been marked on the map since the inceptions of the Dublin and Drogheda Railway which was opened on 15th March 1844 and was one of the seventeen stations opened on the line in that year. One of these stations was also Bettystown, which was nearer to Drogheda, but the passengers would have to walk a mile to the strand. It was opened at the same time as Laytown, but was closed down three years later in 1847.

To some people, especially those living all their lives in Bettystown, it is news to them that there was ever a railway station, yet it was in use for three years and its site is there to be seen today. Bettystown Station was one of the temporary halts along the line. Wooden structures prevailed at these halts, with overall roofs and just big enough for the ticket clerk. It was November 1844, before a waiting room was built. The station was situated on the right hand side of the road, which leads from the present Narrow-way houses to Bettystown strand, at Triton Lodge. This road passes the back entrance to Bettystown House and twists and turns to emerge just before McDonagh's Pub.
The railway entrance is still there, showing a thick twelve inch square wooden gate post, with iron hinge hooks attached. Across from this, the width of a gate are three upright pointed railway sleepers denoting part of the typical fencing of the time, which graced the entrance to a country railway station. It is impossible to travel up the access roadway because of the dense undergrowth and willow trees, but its extent can be seen from a nearby cornfield, as it leads up to what seemed a large triangular shaped space beside 'the permanent way'. This must have been the forecourt at the entrance to the station.

The year the Dublin/Drogheda Railway line opened (1844) was a very good one for the new line, also the following year (1845). By the end of the following year, the novelty was wearing off, and this coupled with the Irish Famine, and the repeal of the Corn Laws in 1846, led to an economic depression, with the result, that Bettystown station was closed down. The closure came at the end of October 1847. During the summer it was used by large crowds but as most passengers were from Drogheda the financial turnover was low.
It seemed that jaunting cars and other conveyances retained much of their former patronage, because of the distance between Drogheda town and its station. Bettystown station was not far from that of Laytown, which was much nearer to the sea.

There was of course an outcry in Drogheda, one letter-writer declaring that "it would appear that the present directors in and around Dublin forget that the Drogheda Railway was projected and originated in Drogheda. There were many other letters of protest, even the local "Drogheda Conservative" in a November editorial suggested that the closure and removal had been undertaken in a rather too hasty manner, and declared that "The Bettystown Station is now partially removed in order to gratify personal pique against an individual".

"This is not the way in which a public company should act. Stations near Dublin, on which little or no traffic takes place, are continued, yet Bettystown Station is pulled down". However, these allegations seemed to be unfounded.

At the annual general meeting of Bettystown Golf Club on the 18th April 1942, the matter of re-opening the station was raised.

In May 1942, (almost one hundred years since the station was closed down) the Drogheda Chamber of Commerce held their annual general meeting, at which there was a discussion on the possibilities of re-opening Bettystown station. But the outcome of much representation to the Railway Company was made known later on in the year. It could not see its way to change running schedules to suit a non-existing railway station and the matter was dropped.

Such is the story of a small wayside station, which served its purpose for a short three years, was then closed down and forgotten. It was suddenly remembered in a time of need and is still partially remembered in the folklore of the area.[3]

The Brodigan Family/Piltown House
Mr. Francis Brodigan

Francis Brodigan was born in 1760. He was married to Mary Mc Evoy, who was a sister of Peter McEvoy, they had five children, two boys and three girls.

Francis Brodigan was a tobacco manufacturer and shopkeeper from the 1780's onward.

After 1800, he became involved in general trading, he manufactured linen, and bought large amounts of market linen, probably for Rodger Hamill. By 1815, he was one of the largest merchants in the town. Between 1800 and 1810, he lent approximately three thousand pounds to landowners, he and his eldest son Thomas, acquired six thousand pounds worth of land in Co. Meath in the 1820's. Francis Brodigan was one of the leaders of the local agitation for Catholic Emancipation from 1810 onwards. He retired from his grocery business in 1817, and concentrated completely on his linen manufacturing business.[4]

Nicholas Whitworth and Francis Brodigan were the founders of the Temperance Society in Drogheda in 1829. He died in 1831.[5]

Colonel Thomas Brodigan

Col. Thomas Brodigan eldest son of Francis, a well established business man before his father died. Piltown House was built in 1833 by a man called Hammond for Thomas Brodigan a gentleman of considerable wealth and property. He farmed his own three hundred acre farm in the 1820's he farmed tobacco, and by all accounts was very successful. He wrote a book on his tobacco growing, a report, as it were, on his progress. He was, as has been already mentioned one of the prime movers for the development of the Dublin-Drogheda railway.

Thomas Brodigan was married twice. By his first wife, he had a daughter Ina, who became an Anglican nun. By his second wife, he had a daughter called Caroline Nellie and a son Francis James.

F.J. Brodigan became a captain in the army, and was one of the three hundred and sixty men from the Drogheda district, who gave their lives in 'The Great War' (1914-1918).

Caroline Nellie (affectionately known as Nellie, after her father's favourite pet dog).

Because Piltown House and estate was entailed, Nellie was next in line to inherit, when her father Thomas Brodigan died.

Nellie married Stanley Robert McClintock from Drumcar, (where the St. John of God's hospital is now) had no children.

Col. McClintock died 16th July 1958 and Nellie (only daughter of Col. Thomas Brodigan) died 26th Jan. 1960. Both are buried in Colpe Cemetery.

In the other Brodigan vault in Colpe, Francis Cheevers father-in-law to Thomas Brodigan is buried.

Francis Cheevers whose brother was married to Ann Sarsfield a sister of Patrick Sarsfield the 'Earl of Lucan'.[6]

When Mrs Nellie McClintock died, Piltown House was inherited by Andy Johnson (a first cousin of Nellie) who lived in Canada. Mr. Johnson lived at Piltown House for a short period of time, but found it too expensive to maintain. He sold it to the Franciscan Brothers (Third order regular) in the early 1960's. The Franciscans used it as a secondary school for young men up to Leaving Certificate standard. It was fee free so many parents had their young sons educated by the Brothers. When the time came for the young men to make their final vows, they left the school, with a free education under their belts! But some young men did stay, took their final vows, and became Franciscan Brothers.

When free education was introduced into the country the pupil attendance at Piltown House was reduced considerably. Eventually the Brothers came to realise they did not need a place as big as Piltown house anymore. In 1970, they sold it to the Christian Brothers, who used it as a home for retired brothers.
A large statue of Our Lady situated in the grounds, carries the inscription "Please pray for the donors...Bellews, 111 West Street, Drogheda, 8th Dec 1961".

During this time a Brother Denis was in charge of the young men working on the farm. When the Christian Brothers decided to sell Piltown House to a Mr. Nevins, Brother Denis went on the missions to Africa.[7]

In July 1978 the Christian Brothers sold three acres to the St. Finian's Trust, who opened a new cemetery 'Reilig Mhuire', for Mornington, Laytown and Bettystown parishes. Reilig Mhuire cemetery was designed in concentric circles by Mr Paul Leech, architect from Navan, and is dedicated to Our Lady. There is a carved stone cross reminiscent of the old Celtic Cross at the north side end of the graveyard. Burials are laid out in sequence, beginning at the north centre point and going towards the east point, and from the north centre to the west point, and so on. Grave space will be reserved for the applicant on the payment of a fee, but will not be allocated until the time of death. The first burial in the new cemetery was Mr. Brian O. Lyons, on the 4th December 1985. To date (1999) there has been approximately one hundred and fifty eight burials in Reilig Mhuire cemetery and a record is kept by Monsignor John Hanly P.P. Laytown.[8]

In 1984 St. Colmcille G.A.A. club bought a further 6.865 acres, adjacent to the cemetery.
The farm yard and forty acres of land were sold to Gerard Toner of Piltown.
In 1996, the Christian Brothers sold the remaining hundred acres to Mr. Charlie Allen, Bettystown House. The stone building opposite the main entrance, known as 'The Gate Lodge' was part of the Piltown House property, was sold to a doctor working in Belfast, shortly after the Christian Brothers bought the entire property.

Piltown House

Piltown House situated about three miles south east of Drogheda. In its glory days, it was a strikingly beautiful mansion set within a park of two hundred acres. Looking at its dilapidated state today, it is hard to imagine it, as it was. But Christine Casey and Allister Rowan in *Houses of North Leinster*, have managed to catch some of the atmosphere, which sadly is lost to most of us living in the vicinity of Piltown House today.

A handsome neo classical house with an odd design. It is a large rectangular two-storey ashlar-faced block, symmetrically arranged, but the entrance of the house is at its north-west angle by a single storey veritable at the back. The front entrance consists of the three side bays of the main block, adjoined by a square single-storey dome vestibule, with a square projected porch and Ionic columns.

Inside the house in the hall of the dome, there was pictorial panels of classical scenes, balustrades were done in trompe l'oeil style, the niches between the pictorial panels held classical statues.[9]

Piltown House, Piltown, Co. Meath.

When the house was the property of Col. McClintock, it held an interesting art and curio collection. Some of the outstanding ones were very fine paintings of the Dutch and Italian schools, reputed to have been conveyed here for safety at the time of the French Revolution. One particular painting was remarkable, it was of the head of an Apostle 9" x 6" on panel, the facial expression was superb.[10]

In the grounds of this great house, there was a beautiful walled-in garden. There were also out-houses and stables, which have since been converted into homes, and are now lived in.

Ogham Stone
At Piltown, Co. Meath

This massive monument, which stands in the grounds of Piltown House, was formerly lying in a field near Seneschalstown House, Painestown, close to the village of Yellow Furze. It was moved to the grounds of Piltown House, (when it was a Franciscan College in the sixties).

The Stone measures 7'4" X 2'6" X 1'1" (maximum dimensions), and the inscription commences at 3'8" from the top, or at exactly half its height, thus allowing the lower portion to be sunk in the ground for up to half of its length without obscuring any of the inscription.

Ogham inscriptions are usually memorial; they are inscribed in the angle of the stone (which provides the stem line), and are read from the bottom upwards. In this case, however, the inscription occurs in two lines on the face of the Stone. No stem lines appear to have been cut to guide the lapidary in setting out his scores, but these may have been painted on.

The inscription is perfectly clear and both the late Professors Rhys and Macalister agree that it reads:-

MAQI - CAIRATINI AVI INEQAGLAS

the last two words being in the second line. Professor Phys who published a reading of this Stone in the (Journal of the Royal Society of Antiquaries of Ireland, Vol. 28. 1898) emphasises that there never was anything after 'glas'; there the surface is smooth and in no way worn into a depression.
The Professor paid particular attention to this point as he had expected a genitive in 'I', 'Inequaglasi', so as to read '(The Stone) of Mac Cairthinn, descendent of Enechglass'. There is no reason to ascribe a gross blunder to the inscriber. Professor Rhys interprets it according to a formula well established elsewhere, 'MacCairthinn's descendent Enechglas'. The inscription seems to be an early one, and is most important as giving us a nominative 'Inequaglas', with the case termination gone, which there are other reasons for regarding as having dropped off at an early date.

The late Mr.H.G.Leask, examining the Stone in its present conveniently upright position, detected traces of Ogham lettering on the Dexter edge of the inscribed face, which would hardly have been visible when it was lying prostrate and half buried in the field at Painestown. Professor Macalister on re-examining it, confirmed that there was in fact an older inscription on the edge specified, which was carried over the top and completed on the Dexter edge of the opposite face.

This had been violently battered away leaving nothing but a few vague traces. This explains why the present inscription is on the face of the Stone as it was the only part, which the destroyer left smooth enough for the later lapidary to work upon.[11]

In short, the inscription on this large headstone appears to be 'MacCairthinn's descendent of Enechglas'. The name Enechglas comes from an ancient Irish Sept family, whose territory was in the Barony of Arklow, Co. Wicklow.
The name Cairatini is also found on a stone in Co. Kerry.
The Ogham Stone at Piltown has since been removed to the museum in Dublin.

It would be impossible to leave Piltown House and its past behind without hearing some of the 'extraordinary and bizarre stories', told by Ted McCormack, whose father, Robert McCormack worked as farm manager among other things at Piltown House for nearly fifties years.
Robert McCormack was born in 1880 and was employed at Piltown House from 1907 until the year he died in 1954, except for a brief period when he worked in Belfast on a similar estate. He was requested to come back and work at Piltown, which he did.
Mickey Brennan also worked there as a gardener for forty seven years.
Robert McCormack was land steward of the Brodigan's estate, in today's terms he would be farm manager. Brodigan's land extended from Piltown House to Beauparc and most of it was rented by tenant farmers.
They owned a house in Drogheda, also town lands on the Cord Rd., Dyer Street, Stockwell Street, and Scarlet Street.
The Family were also merchants, they had seventeen boats coming in and out of Drogheda. They were the biggest wine importers in Ireland.

The Brodigan imported guns from Spain for the 1798 rebellion. They were caught in Annagassan and brought to court, but, because they were merchants, and a very wealthy and influential family in the area, they were not charged!

The Brodigans treated their staff and tenants very well, and regularly organised parties for them.
Being a farm manager Robert.McCormack had twenty men working for him in the garden alone. Every week he would have to visit their tenant farms, to see how they were getting on, and every Sunday he drove to Beauparc to see the tenant farmers there.

It appears the Brodigan family, also, loved the 'good life', and fancy dress and lawn tennis parties were the order of the day for themselves, and their friends.

Col. Brodigan was in the Gorden Highlanders, his 'black man' acted as butler in Piltown House for a period of time.
It was well known that Colonel Brodigan was very good to his animals and it was even thought he pre-

ferred them to humans! In the grounds there is a grave especially for the dogs. There was a plaque made for the grave with the inscription: 'Here Lies the Faithful'. We are told a local farmer that owns the land around Piltown House now, has this plaque in his possession. There was no end to the Brodigan fortune, and in those days when almost everyone else was poor, its hard to digest, however, by all accounts this was one of the 'good' landlords. Well the Brodigan fortune spilled over into Europe, where more houses and property accumulated. Among these properties, was a Villa in France, where Colonel Brodigan spent alot of his time, the reason being he had a mistress living in France.

His mistress died, and the Colonel was so upset, that he had the woman's skeleton brought over to him in Ireland. He hung 'it' up in the front porch of the house, at this time the Colonel's wife was living in the house in Dublin. Every night when he was going to bed he would tap the skeleton on the head and say "good night darling". The skeleton was hung in such a way that when the front door was opened the bones would rattle together (like wind chimes).

Colonel Brodigan died suddenly in 1913, and was buried in the family vault in Colpe cemetery. Mr. McCormack wasn't working at Piltown House at the time of the Colonel's death. When Mr. McCormack resumed work at Piltown, a year later, the first job Miss Brodigan (Nellie) got him to do, was to bury the skeleton in the dog's cemetery, this he did, and put a stone over it, to mark the spot.

World War 1, started in 1914, at this time Nellie was a nurse, she started to run classes in Piltown House associated with the Red Cross. She explained to Mr. McCormack, how useful it would be to have a full sized skeleton to show the people the different bones in the body, and asked him to dig up the skeleton of the French girl, who was buried in the dog's cemetery. After many hours digging the skeleton was no where to be found, so he came to the conclusion it had disintegrated.

In 1954 the night of his father's wake, Ted McCormack told this story. A man in the room listening to this story told Ted he knew what happened to the skeleton. This man worked with Ted's father in Piltown House, and he saw the skeleton being buried in the pet's grave. That night these two jokers dug up the skeleton and painted it white. When the 'lads' were coming home from the pub, feeling no pain, as it were, the plan was to put the skeleton over the wall and shake the day lights out of it in front of them, and see how they reacted! One man from Laytown saw the skeleton, people said, he never was the same again, his hair turned white over night, with the shock. He is supposed to have said to the Laytown station master having told him of his 'experience', he would never set foot in Laytown again, and he never did.
The whereabouts of the skeleton is unknown, perhaps it found it's way back to the dog's cemetery, who knows!

When Ted's father died in 1954, Col. McClintock came to Ted and asked him where his father got the tomato seeds. These seeds were bought from a Fr. Andrews of the Cistercian monks in Collon, so Ted promised to get the Colonel some next time he was getting tomato seeds for himself. Fr. Andrews was from Scotland and his father fought with the Colonel's father in the 1914-1918 war.

In the McClintock's time, the house was always kept in immaculate condition. It was painted every year in May. They had a system that worked very well, the house was so big, the back half was painted one year and the front part the following year. A builder called Jimmy McDonough made sure the place was kept in good condition.
Andy Johnson, was a first cousin of Nellie, he was an engineer and lived in Canada.
When Mrs McClintock (Nellie) became ill, Mrs Johnson came to look after her.

The Staff

The maids slept in the basement of the house. There were two maids that slept in the attic, they were the lady's maids. The staff consisted of a cook, kitchen maid, scullery maid, lamp maid, laundry maids assistant, two parlour maids, two house maids, and a house keeper. Nan McCabe from Donacarney was the cook. Johnny Brennan was the coachman he previously worked as coachman on Coney hall estate in Mornington. Mr. Bolger was the butler, when he retired as butler Mrs McClintock gave him her two thatched cottages in Bettystown.

Nan McCabe was a delightful person, and is still fondly remembered by locals who knew her. Ted remembers with some relish, Nan leaving the bowls out on the window for Ted (when he was a young boy) to lick, when she was finished using them, always making sure to leave a little of the delicious creamed butter and sugar, much to young Ted's delight.

In 1924 Mrs Mc Clintock wanted to build a byre for the cows on Piltown farm, she had to sell one of her diamonds to raise the money to build it. The builder Jimmy McDonough engraved the shape of a diamond on the side of the building when the job was complete, in memory of how the money was raised to pay for it. Electricity came to Piltown House in 1930 and it was supplied by a generator.
Mrs McClintock (Nellie) was very good and kind to her tenants, and looked after all of them very well. At one time Nellie thought that her financial situation was in a bad state. It was only after her death, that Andy Johnson her cousin, who inherited the estate, found out to the contrary.[12]

On a return visit to Ted and Evelyn McCormack's home in Piltown, to clarify a few details, they welcomed me into their home, surrounded by a delightful garden. They had all the time in the world for me, even though it was late and they both were tired. When I was leaving I promised to return another day at an earlier time, in order to take a walk through their beautiful garden.

There was a huge auction at Piltown House, 1st and 2nd June 1960, Hamilton and Hamilton Estates Limited, 17, Dawson Street, Dublin, were the Auctioneers. Piltown House was open to the public for viewing, on the 30th and 31st May. Everything in the main house was on display, and for sale. All the farm machinery and farm implements were on display over an area of several acres, around the front of the house, and in the yard. It was massive by any standards, and I spent one of the days there with my father. I was quite young, but I remember being fascinated by the very large kitchen, and all the saucepans! Upstairs there were shelves of marvellous books, but they were not for sale. My father bought a few small items and a lovely rocking chair for my mother. The auction was held about six months after Nellie's death.

Just an additional piece of information, Piltown House had eleven bedrooms and on the landing there were two black and white Engravings of 'Daniel O'Connell', and 'Henry Grattan'.[13]

CHAPTER 12
"The Murder, at Coney Hall".

How to relate this story or piece together about the horrific events surrounding this appalling forgotten tragedy, presented a daunting and distressful task, in the knowledge that this ferocious crime actually happened and wasn't make believe. All the facts are there in black and white, and definitely would not be material for the faint-hearted!

The quiet village of Mornington awakened Thursday morning 8th January 1880 to the resounding clamour of what had happened in their midst only a few hours earlier. The news of this appalling and outrageous crime had travelled far and fast, and was being received with total disbelief and horror, shaking the very foundations of their lives. After the first shock waves of this monstrous deed subsided, and the dust settled a little, the real truths and details began to emerge. Many of the local people in the surrounding areas, all tenants of Mr. Brabazon would have known something was bound to happen, with such carry on! Like a time bomb just waiting to explode, but they dare not utter a word, their lips were sealed.

The detailed descriptions given by the local newspaper at the time, the Drogheda Argus (January and March 1880) of the hearings in Coney Hall (Mornington House) and the trial in Trim Court House, left no stone unturned and very little to the imagination. The person responsible for this crime was taken into custody, a young woman from Drogheda, (some said she came from Bettystown) by the name of **Margaret Skean.** The scene by all reports was gloomy and depressing, this morose young woman sat in the docks for weeks listening to detailed descriptions about her character and personality, and even more detailed descriptions of the monstrous cruel and outrageous crime she had committed on her fellow human being. This woman remained detached and emotionless, showing no remorse or repentance, baring a face of stone right through and almost to the end of the ordeal, when at last she showed some signs of being human.

On reading the gruesome details of this foul deed committed by this one time very competent housekeeper, the question begs to be asked, how this woman arrived at this seriously depraved state of mind that enabled her to carry out this appalling act in cold blood?

Coney Hall, Mornington

It was the month of January, very cold and dark, the house stood in all its gloom and old fashioned glory. Coney Hall or Mornington House (as it was sometimes called) was no doubt a beautiful place. But the very building itself represented a suppressed and unjust regime, bestowed on the native Irish for hundreds of years. It stood for the unmentionable establishment 'landlordism' that caused deep rooted anger and indignation in the minds and hearts of those people trapped in this system. Therefore, it comes as no surprise this house was steeped in foreboding, misfortunes and tragedies, which ended in the place been burnt down in the 1950s. In order to establish a picture of events surrounding and leading up to this horrific crime, the following is a brief account of the principal people involved and associated with Margaret Skean, and life in general at Coney Hall.

Mr. J. H. Brabazon (J.P.) the last member of this family of landlords to reside at Coney Hall, Mornington, Co. Meath, (see Brabazon family lineage, chapter 5). According to reports he was very unpopular with his tenants, and it appears his reputation in the community left a lot to be desired. He presented himself as some kind of superior being, and looked on his tenants as 'scum and dogs'. He rode rough shod over ordinary people, going about their daily life, cracking his whip at them along the road way.

(The following is just one of the many stories told by local people, which were passed on from people of that generation to their children and their children's children:
John Drew's great grandfather was a tenant of Mr. Brabazon in the mid-nineteenth century. He bought a pony and trap for himself and his family. According to this story Mr. Brabazon asked Mr Drew for the pony and trap, and in those days the tenant had to obey the 'masters' wishes, and duly he handed them over. Some time later they were returned to Mr. Drew in a total 'mess'. This same man built two piers for the purpose of holding a gate into a field from the road, but the piers had to be knocked down because they interfered with the landlord's view!).

Margaret Skean, the woman who committed the murder, not alot is known about this woman except that she came from either Drogheda or Bettystown. She was born in the early 1850's shortly after the famine, grew up and worked in her local town for a few years. In her early twenties she became employed by Mr. Brabazon as the cook and general house-keeper in Coney Hall. She worked there for four/five years. For some reason this woman developed a very poor reputation among the local community. Her dependence on alcohol became apparent during the later months of her employment, and, as a result her conduct and general behaviour at times became a problem and was unacceptable. She was dismissed by Mr. Brabazon's daughter in his absence, on the grounds of her drunken misconduct. A girl by the name of Emma Bouchier from Dublin was engaged by a member of the Brabazon family to take over Margaret Skean's duties. On the 23rd September 1879 Margaret left her place of employment and went to live with her sister Bridget and her sister's husband John Hunt at their home.

John Hunt was also employed by Mr. Brabazon as his coachman and general purpose man around the estate. John was married to Bridget, they had two small children, and lived in the servants quarters in the yard of Coney Hall mansion.

Emma Bouchier a pleasant young woman (by all accounts) aged between twenty six and twenty eight years was brutally murdered in cold blood on 7th January 1880. Was she murdered because of jealousy, as presumed, or was it something much bigger and more sinister and she just happened to be in the wrong place at the wrong time. Not a lot is known about this woman either, apparently she came from Dublin, contrary to some reports that it was Co. Louth. She had lived in America for some years in her past, before returning to Dublin, while she was there, it appears she had to carry a gun for her protection! And as a result became familiar with handling these weapons. She was engaged to take over Margaret Skean's duties as cook and housekeeper by either Mr. Brabazon's daughter or sister in Dublin. She lived and worked in Coney Hall from the 23rd September 1879 until her untimely death on the 7th January 1880.

John Hopely was a very young man of seventeen years, he was hired as a servant, on the 4th September 1879, just three weeks before Margaret Skean was to leave the big house, being replaced by Emma Bouchier. During those three weeks, he lived with the Hunts in the yard. When Margaret moved out, he then moved into the main house, and resided there until he was dismissed on the 5th January 1880. His main duty as a servant was to be in the house with Emma Bouchier at all times, so as to ensure she was never left alone in the house. When John Hopely was dismissed, Mr. Brabazon was in the process of hiring someone else to take his place, unfortunately Emma was murdered before this was achieved.

Bridget Hunt was married to John, coachman to Mr. Brabazon, and sister to Margaret. She lived with her husband and two small children in the servants quarters. She was in a very precarious situation, her husband was employed by the man who was obviously abusing and violating her sister. She had to live with her husband and raise her children, all the time watching her own sister being destroyed, and there was nothing she could do.

The 7th of January 1880 started off like any other day at Coney Hall. That afternoon Mr. Brabazon had arranged to meet a friend in Drogheda at 5 p.m., and his coachman John Hunt took him there. On their return to Coney Hall around midnight they found the place in complete darkness, and were unable to gain entry to the house. Mr. Hunt eventually succeeded in getting through a small scullery window with the aid of Mr. Brabazon who then handed him a lamp. On his way to open the main door for his master he stumbled over some objects on the floor. It was then he became acutely aware of another presence in the kitchen, there, seated by the kitchen table was a ashen faced Margaret Skean, she had a strange look in her eyes, there was blood on her face, and her cloths were covered with flour. Emma Bouchier was no where to be seen! When Mr. Brabazon came into the kitchen, after John Hunt opened the front door, the whole horrific scene became visible to them. The floors, tables and walls were covered with what looked like flour or white meal to conceal what appeared to be blood stains, and both men immediately suspected foul play. Mr. Brabazon then instructed his coachman to summon help from tenants in the immediate vicinity, a James Reynolds and James Byrne (who were accustomed to being called to the main house in the middle of the night), but this time it was different. They were required to stay with Margaret Skean in case she tried to escape, while Mr Brabazon and John Hunt searched the house for Emma, but with no success. The police in Julianstown were contacted, and were at the scene of the crime in record time. The search for Emma Bouchier continued, the police traced blood stains on the floor to a well 15ft deep in the scullery. The body of Emma lay at the bottom of the well, and when it was eventually lifted out, was found to be fearfully mutilated almost beyond recognition. Two doctors who were called to the scene, Dr. Delahope and Dr. Adrian examined the body, and the result of this examination showed thirteen desperate wounds on the body in all. A heavy mallet, a cleaver, two large carving knives, showed signs of having been used in the slaughter. Margaret Skean was arrested for the murder of Emma Bouchier.

The Inquiry
The following day, Thursday 8th January, a magisterial inquiry opened. Hon. Captain Plunkett RM. and Sub-Inspector Raleigh, of Slane were present. The Coroner, Mr. Kelsh, also opened his inquiry. Both were held in Mornington House. The prisoner who was being held in a jail in Drogheda was brought to Mornington House for enquires. She sat during the hearings, listening to the dreadful details quite calmly, more like a disinterested listener rather then the principal in such an outrageous tragedy. Margaret Skean a woman of about thirty years of age with regular features, but the expression on her face was very cold, determined and forbidding.

Five years before, Margaret was hired as the cook at Coney Hall by Mr. J. H. Brabazon. She entered the household then a young woman of good character, what happened during the intervening years? But the evidence given at the trial of this woman, could fill many of the blank spaces. Mr. Brabazon, her employer was a Justice of the Peace, and he was a very wealthy and powerful man in the community. After five years in this service, Margaret Skean was dismissed on the grounds of her drunken and unacceptable behaviour, which was reasonable enough by any standards, if there wasn't so many 'other things' to be considered. She was replaced by another young woman of 'good character' Emma Bouchier from Dublin. Margaret tried on many occasions to get a reference from Mr. Brabazon in order to obtain employment elsewhere, but with no success. She was deeply wounded and outraged at her former employer's callous and cruel treatment of her. She would have liked very much to burn that big house down around his feet, and said so on a few occasions. She was reduced to begging him for money, only to have the door slammed in her face.

Emma's presence in the house presented huge problems for her, it wasn't that she hated this woman, but she had replaced her (Margaret) in her employment, which left her destitute. Emma reminded her of herself five years earlier, when she started work there as a cook, also of amiable nature and good character. But life had dealt Margaret a cruel hand, which turned her very existence into a nightmare. Emma Bouchier became an issue for Margaret, and while she was not the problem very tragically she got in the way.

When Mr. Brabazon and his coachman returned to Coney Hall on that fatal evening, Emma Bouchier had been murdered, and the carnage that confronted them was like something you would read in a horror story. Along with all the other destructions there was a large pool of blood in the hall at the foot of the stairs.

Emma must have suspected something on that night, or was very fearful being left in the house on her own. Having some experience in handling guns, she loaded Mr. Brabazon's gun, which was normally kept unloaded in his bedroom, and placed it beside her bed in her own room. It would appear in Emma's last desperate attempt to escape her murderess and reach the gun, she was finally struck down in the hall. The body was then dragged down the long hall to the kitchen and across into the scullery where there was a 15ft well covered by a trap-lid. The body was thrust into the well and landed at the bottom in an upright position.

Now the terrible deed was done, Margaret Skean was being held prisoner in Drogheda, awaiting trial for the murder of Emma Bouchier. Very soon the town was full of spectators from all walks of life, trying desperately to get a glimpse of the prisoner, and find out every detail of the blood curdling crime because it was no doubt the 'murder of the century'.

Margaret Skean was brought from Drogheda jail to Mornington House to attend the hearings on a side-cart, when passing through the town there was a rush, almost a stampede of people to which ever side of the street Margaret would be facing. It seemed so important to look at this woman's face, and she in turn, took all their curiosity with perfect calm, repaying them with look for look. They did not know anything about Margaret Skean, or her life out at Mornington, she was a nobody, but now she was the principal in this outrageous crime, with blood on her hands!.

The following evidence was taken Thursday evening 8th Jan. before the Hon Mr. Plunkett, RM. John Hunt and his wife Bridget were the first to be questioned.

Mr. Hunt gave details about his employment as coachman to Mr. Brabazon, followed by more details about when he arrived back at midnight to Coney Hall. He was the first on the scene of the murder, followed closely by Mr. Brabazon whom he let into the house through the hall door. When they realised what had happened, he went to his wife where they lived in the yard and told her to take the children away, as he didn't think it was safe to have them near the place. He then followed his masters instructions and contacted the various people including the police at Julianstown. When it became obvious that the body of Emma Bouchier was in the well, one of the policemen present put down a hook and line to draw the body out. Mr. Hunt had to leave as he could not watch the deceased being taken from the well.

Bridget Hunt was the next to be questioned. She explained how the prisoner was her sister, and how she had been living with her since her dismissal from her employment on the 20th September. On the night of the murder she asked her sister to get some milk and bread. Margaret returned with the messages a quarter of an hour later. She went out again almost immediately and did not return for over a half an hour. Bridget asked her where she had been, to which Margaret replied "I was killing Emma" Bridget said, "no, you have not done it", she said "yes I have". Bridget then asked her sister why did she do it and she said, not to be concerned, it had nothing to do with her.

Bridget suddenly remembered that Emma Bouchier was in the main house on her own, as John her husband had gone to Drogheda with Mr. Brabazon, around 5p.m. She said she didn't know Emma very well, except to see her walking through the yard, and the last time she saw her alive was on Wednesday 7th January around 3 p.m. When her sister said she had killed Emma, she did not believe her at first, she had been there all the time with her two small children and heard no noise or shouts of any kind. Then she noticed her sister's hair all tossed and blood on her arms and hands.

After Margaret washed herself and changed her cloths, Bridget noticed the clothes her sister had put on, belonged to the deceased Emma Bouchier, and realised then something terrible had happened. When Margaret left the house it was sometime after 10 p.m. The next time Bridget saw her sister she was a prisoner. Bridget was then asked, if it occurred to her to go to the main house to see if Emma was all right?, Bridget replied "No, it didn't". After what she had heard from her sister, and seen the state she was in, it was very strange she didn't go over to the big house to see if Emma was all right.

Bridget said, the place was silent, there was no shouts or screams, she was afraid to move out of the house and she had two small children to mind, and could not leave them.

She was not aware of any enmity that existed between her sister and the deceased, she never heard her sister make any threatening statements about Emma. As far as she knew they were on speaking terms, Emma never visited her house in the yard, and to her knowledge she didn't go anywhere, except to Chapel.

Avenue to main entrance, Coney Hall, Mornington.

After the body was examined by the doctors the following report was submitted to the inquiry:
There were seven lacerated wounds on the scalp; a wound from a little below the angle of the right ear to about two inches of the left ear at the junction of the spine with the skull. The latter being a clean wound, it must have been caused by a sharp instrument. There was a superficial wound just below the jaw, another wound extending across the neck about three inches long; a severe wound on the left side of the chest penetrating the diaphragm and the abdomen; a wound over the left hip. The wound extending from ear to ear, severed in its course several of the large vessels.

Mr. Brabazon when questioned confirmed all that Mr. Hunt his coachman had said, and added the following statement to it.
When he went to his room, he found someone had been lying on his bed! and also someone had been sick on it, and there was an empty porter bottle thrown on the floor.
When he was endeavouring to secure the prisoner with the help of Mr. Reynolds and Mr. Byrne, she managed to break free she jumped on him (Mr. Brabazon) grabbing him by his beard. When he released himself from her clutches she was locked in a room. Later on some false pretence, she got the door opened, darted along the passage and out into the yard. As they pursued her she lifted a large stone, and as he (Mr. Brabazon) got near her, she went to strike him with it. One of the men managed to grab her hand, but she lifted an iron trough in the yard to strike them with it if they caught her. She got back into the house, turned the key in the door and locked them out. She escaped a second time through a window, and was not captured till the police found her in bed, in her sister's house around 4 a.m (Bridget and the two children had already left the house).

John Hopely who was only employed for a little over three months at Coney Hall, and was dismissed on the 5th January, only two days before the fatal night.
He recalled a day the prisoner came to the house requesting a meeting with Mr. Brabazon, it seemed of the utmost importance to her to speak to him then. He saw the deceased Emma Bouchier bringing mulled porter and toast up to Mr. Brabazon's room, when he went to inform the 'master' that Margaret Skean was downstairs and wanted to speak to him urgently. He found him and Emma in the room alone, his 'master' appeared very drunk.
He (Mr. Brabazon) said he couldn't see her that night, but she appeared desperate and wouldn't wait, and went straight to Mr Brabazon's room; Emma left the room and came down to the kitchen. There was very loud talking going on upstairs. After a short while, the prisoner came down saying "you do well to be in bed with your drunken servant".
Later she (Margaret) confided in young John, with good foundation she believed that Emma would not remain a virtuous woman for very long in that house.

The coroner's jury found a verdict that Emma Bouchier's death resulted from wounds feloniously and maliciously inflicted by Margaret Skean.

The remains of the murdered girl were buried in Mornington graveyard on 10th January 1880 her brother and some of her relatives from Dublin were present.

The hearing continued:
James Reynolds and Laurence Byrne both corroborated with all that had been said by the previous witnesses.
The next witness Constable Kealy who agreed with and confirmed all that had been stated. He then gave proof to finding a loaded revolver in the room that had been occupied by Emma Bouchier, it was loaded in all its six chambers.
Mr. Brabazon identified the revolver as his, and said, on the afternoon of the 7th. January, it was on the mantelpiece in his bedroom unloaded and the ammunition was beside it. He remembered seeing it there before leaving for Drogheda.

The prisoner **Margaret Skean** was then asked if she had any questions to ask him (Mr. Brabazon), she answered - No, Sir.

The Hon. Mr. Plunkett then informed Margaret Skean she was committed to stand trial at the next Trim assizes. He asked her if she wanted to make any statement now that she had heard the charge against her? She said, No Sir, I am innocent!

She then rose, her face flushed, and walked towards the bench the police close behind her, and asked the judge when the trial was going to be held? The Judge could not tell her the exact time.

Margaret placed her hand on the bench for an instant, the hard lines about the mouth and jaw, relaxed, her lips quivered, and for the first time since the inquest begun, her eyes became red and suffused. She thanked the judge, the constable touched her on the shoulder and she immediately withdrew with them. The large tears she fought hard to suppress gathered heavily in her eyes. She was taken back to Trim in the afternoon.

The Trial: Startling evidence:
At the court in Trim before the Right Hon. Lord Chief Justice of the Queen's bench, the trial of Margaret Skean began. She was a domestic servant, accused of murdering Emma Bouchier at Mornington House, Mornington, Co, Meath.
The prisoner pleaded not guilty.

Mr. Gamble QC was acting for the prosecution, and **Mr. C. Molly** was defending the accused.
Mr. Gamble QC in stating the case for the crown, said, Margaret Skean stood accused for the wilful murder of Emma Bouchier, on the 7th January. He gave a statement of the circumstances under which the crime was committed. After a long and detailed deliberation, concluded by saying he hoped the jury understood the enormity of this crime, and would do their duty accordingly.

James Henry Brabazon, J.P., Mornington House, a retired captain in the army, and formerly a grand juror, was the next witness examined.

When cross-examined by **Mr. Molly,** the following were some of the questions:
When the prisoner (Margaret Skean) started employment in Coney Hall, there were two other people living there along with Mr. Brabazon, his sister, and another person.

Q. What happened to them?
A. They left after six months.
Q. How long has Mrs Brabazon been separated from you?
A. About six years.
Q. At certain times was the prisoner and yourself the only occupants in the house?
A. Yes, that was the case for a couple of months.
Q. Did you discharge her?
A. I discharged her for drunkenness.
Q. Did you give her any presents?
A. Never.
Q. When did she show the disposition to drunkenness?
A. In August of last year. I never ill-treated her on any occasion.
Q. Did she ever sleep in your room?
A. Yes.
Q. Did she ever sleep with you?
A. Yes, once or twice.
Q. When the prisoner started employment in your house was she of high and good character?
A. Yes.
Q. Did you often force her to go to your room at night?
A. No.
Q. Did you ever use violence on her?
A. No.
Q. Did you ever strap her down?

A. She was strapped down because of her violent behaviour.
Q. Who strapped her down?
A. A man named Clarke and myself, we put one strap around her waist, another around her shoulder, and around her ankles, and kept her quietly on the ground.
Q. Why?
A. She was too drunk to go anywhere.
Q. Were you drunk?
A. No, I went out for Clarke, who was my gardener, and asked him to assist me in keeping her quiet.
Q. Did not Clarke intercede with you on her behalf?
A. No.
Q. How long did you keep her there?
A. About an hour and a half, until she got sober.
Q. Did you ever get a hammer to break down her bedroom door?
A. Yes. One night a few months ago, I saw a light in her bedroom, and took a hammer from my study, and went up to her room, I could not get an answer from her, I did not break down the door.
Q. Did the woman go out of the house that night in her night-dress?
A. No. Not on any occasion, not to my knowledge.
Q. Why did you strap her down?
A. Because she was extremely violent, and might have done herself harm.
Q. Did the prisoner often refuse to go to your room?
A. Never.
Q. The poor girl told you she was unable to get other employment and needed a proper character letter written.
A. She asked to have the letter written by my daughter.
Q. Had you been taking porter the days the prisoner called to see you?
A. I had porter in my room, Emma Bouchier was at the door when the prisoner arrived up, she was very angry when she saw Emma.
Q. Were you in bed, and Emma Bouchier was coming out of the room?
A. No.
Q. Did you hear what the prisoner said when she was leaving the house that day, "You do well to be in bed with your drunken servant"
A. No. On another occasion I spoke to her outside the door.
Q. What did she want?
A. Money, I did not give her any.

Mr. Dames QC re-examined **Mr. Brabazon** on the occasion just referred to, or any other similar occasion.
Q. Was there any incorrect conduct at any time between you and Emma Bouchier?
A. On my oath, there was not.
Q. Was Emma a perfectly sober girl?
A. Yes, she was a teetotaller.

John Hunt, was next to give evidence, being the first on the scene after the crime was committed.
In cross-examination, Mr. Hunt said the prisoner had a very violent temper. He had seen her on occasion doing very 'queer' things. Last August around 7p.m she was running through the yard in her night dress, bawling and shouting words, like someone demented, she was crying a lot, and looked very frightened.
She said, she had been beaten by Mr. Brabazon, and he tried to choke her on the bed. She looked as if she had been drinking.

Q. Was Mr. Brabazon under the influence of drink?
A. Yes.
Q. What was the cause of the row?

A. It appears the prisoners' work was not to Mr. Brabazon's satisfaction, and she was complaining about pains in her head, her head had been bandaged up for days with a severe headache.

Mrs Hunt, (Bridget) was next for cross-examination, she confirmed what the previous witness said about the prisoner being in the yard in her night-dress, crying and demented. On another occasion the prisoner was unable to comb her hair because of more beating she received. Mr. Brabazon was very annoyed the tea and biscuits were not prepared for him and his friends, there was a terrible crash, followed by Rev. Brabazon's (brother of James Henry) voice saying "Jemmy for God's sake stop beating the girl". After that instance the witness noticed alot of bruises on her sister.

Michael McMahon was then called for the defence. He was employed by Mr. Brabazon for six years since he (Mr. Brabazon) had returned from Australia. He told how he was called to the house to help tie the prisoner down. The prisoner wanted to leave the house, but was not allowed to go until she was sober. When she threatened to break the window to get out, he and the 'master' then tied her down. She was kept in that position for two hours and he (Michael McMahon) stayed with her. The prisoner had done nothing from what he could see, except wanting to leave the house. He also witnessed Mr. Brabazon striking this woman on a few occasions.

Outhouses - possibly the servants quarters in nineteenth century Coney Hall, Mornington.

Mr. Molly then addressed the jury on behalf of the prisoner. He submitted that the crown had not proved the charge of wilful murder, upon which the prisoner was indicted. It was a most painful case (the prisoner Margaret Skean, who, since the beginning of the trial had preserved a calm but observant demeanour, now began to weep silently). The life of his client was in their hands. Having given the legal definition of the crime of wilful murder, in which malice afore thought must be proved. Counsel contended that there was no expressed evidence of malice. No threats or evil intentions against Emma Bouchier was proved against the prisoner.

They were not to jump to conclusion when she said she would like to burn the house down. It was reasonable to assume this threat was meant against her seducer, and not against the deceased. It showed the existence of malice against Mr. Brabazon.

What was the history of the prisoner?, she went into the service of Mr. Brabazon four years ago, with a good character, she left his employment with a damaged reputation, unable to secure alternative employment. When she said Emma Bouchier's character was blighted the moment she entered the house, she was judging Emma's future by the light of her own terrible experience.

She had entered this employment a virtuous girl, and at the end of four years when she realised her desperate situation, she went back to her former employer and said, "Do something for me, for I can't get work in Drogheda or anywhere else". (The prisoner at this time became so overpowered by her feelings that she had to be led out of the dock). At the interview with Mr. Brabazon, the prisoner explained her plight, and asked him for some money! What was the answer of her seducer to this appeal? it was "certainly not, certainly not" then the woman went away. The facts provided in evidence during the trial showed the absence of bad feelings between the prisoner and the deceased, Margaret going to Emma for help and advice when she wasn't well, suffering from severe headaches.

After she had surrendered her virtue to her 'master', one would have thought he would have some consideration for her! But, it was quite the reverse. She was first tied down with straps, beaten regularly, and in the end driven from the house. He (Mr. Molly) did not charge any misconduct upon the part of the deceased (Emma Bouchier). It was enough to say that when the prisoner needed desperately to speak to her former 'master', went upstairs and found the deceased (Emma Bouchier) in the room with Mr. Brabazon, he being in the bed with toast and porter beside him. When she left that room, she was outraged as a woman was never outraged before, she considered all that happened to her, now she believed completely, the deceased was being lured down the same road.

Who loaded the revolver and removed it to Emma's room?, according to the evidence the only person who could have done it was Emma herself, and she had plenty of experience handling them.

It was also the deceased (Emma Bouchier) who had lain on the bed in the 'master's room. It could not have been the prisoner if that was the case there would have been traces of blood left on it. It was now clear that at that time the unfortunate deceased was under the influence of alcohol drink, and while she was in this condition, the prisoner excited by the whiskey she had drank, stole into the big house anxious to get more for herself. While she was there she was confronted by the deceased, what happened then? There was only one living witness, and her lips were shut - the prisoner at the bar.

The appearance presented by the prisoner subsequently showed there had been a conflict between the two women. There were cuts and bruises on her arms and hand, both women were drunk, blows had been given and received by each.

Counsel then suggested the way in which the row may have developed, that brought about the murder of Emma Bouchier. There was a conversation between them, the deceased may have made known her knowledge of the fact that the prisoner was unable to get employment, and may have remarked, "everyone knows what you are!" or, she might have more directly referred to the prisoner's intimate relationship with Mr. Brabazon or, made other observations which were calculated to have outraged the woman, already very excited from the influence of drink. The prisoner may have retorted, "Brabazon seduced me, but it seems very strange coming from you, whom I found in his room the other day". These remarks may have led to a sudden blaze of suppressed anger and indignation, each may have reached for objects, which lay near, and attacked and struck one another. In this struggle Emma Bouchier lost her life.

Counsel then made a powerful appeal for a merciful interpretation of the evidence on the part of the jury, which had been submitted to them. His lordship would direct them upon the law of the case, would show them the distinction between a case of actual deliberate murder and the lesser offence of which designated manslaughter. With the question of facts they had to deal with, and as they themselves would one day be judged before the tribunal of the Eternal Creator and be expecting mercy, he left the case of the life of the prisoner, his client, in their hands.

Mr. Molly, council for the accused, was loudly applauded at the conclusion of his passionate and powerful speech.

Mr. Dames QC replied on behalf of the crown. He contended that there was evidence which proved the prisoner got the idea she had been supplanted by the deceased, and she was jealous of her, in consequence, and that the accused was guilty of the crime of murder.

The Lord Chief Justice charged the jury, who, after a quarter of an hour in consultation, brought in a verdict of manslaughter.

The prisoner (Margaret Skean) displayed no emotion on its announcement.

The Lord Chief Justice in sentencing her, said the jury had taken a very merciful view of the case and returned a verdict of manslaughter. She had killed the unfortunate woman Emma Bouchier with the greatest of brutality, the worst he ever encountered in the course of his experience. Therefore he felt duty bound to impose on the prisoner the severest sentence which the law allowed, that she be kept in penal servitude for life.[1]

There were many applications for discharge submitted on Margaret Skean's behalf to the prison authorities.

The following are two such letters:

Life case   **To His Excellancy**_____

                     the Lord Lieutenant of Ireland:_____

            The Petition of   *B 28 Margaret Skean*

            Humbly Sheweth   *That petitioner was tried at Trim in 1880*

on a charge of Murder and having been found guilty (manslaughter) was sentenced to penal servitude for life.

*   Petitioner feels her sentence has been unusally severe considering the circumstances of the case, her crime which she deeply deplores and shall never cease to regret, was committed when nearly deprived of her senses through injustice, and bad treatment of her master, she then gave herself up completely to intemperance from the effects of which she was suffering, when without the least premeditation she committed this sad crime. Petitioner was servant for four years to a gentleman, from whose service she had been discharged unjustly, he having illtreated her on several occasions and finally took another servant in her place, which exasperated her beyond measure, and the un-fortunate servant named was the victim, when the petitioner left her situation, she still continued to live on the premises with her sister, whose husband was the coachman to her former master.*

*   Petitioner having now served over seven years weary imprisonment most humbly implores your Excellency to be graciously pleased, to take her sad case into your kind consideration, and be pleased to grant her, her liberty, she having to her credit in the Prison a gratuity sufficient to enable her to emigrate, and as the ladies connected with the Prisoner's Aid Society have taken a deep interest in her, and shall arrange to have her provided in a situation, again most earnestly entreats Your Excellency to be pleased to take a favourable view of her very sad case, as she is a good servant and an excellent laundress she has every hope of making up by a good future her shortcomings in the past, and your petitioner as in duty bound will ever pray.*

                                                                      Margaret Skean
                                                                         22 - 4 - 87.

P. S. for Life	**To His Excellency**_____

                the Lord Lieutenant of_____

                The Petition of   <u>B 28 Margaret Skean</u>

                Humbly Sheweth   <u>That petitioner was tried at Trim in</u>

1880 on a charge of 'Murder' and having been found guilty was sentenced to penal servitude for life. Petitioner having spent nearly nine years weary imprisonment, most humbly begs to state the facts of her sad case.

      Petitioner was engaged as cook by J. Brabazon JP the family at the time consisting of two ladies one of whom was Mr. Brabazon's sister and the other his daughter, petitioner lived very happy for some time, but owing to some change in her masters affairs the two ladies left the house also another servant, leaving no person in the house but petitioner, her master, and coachman, who resided on the premises and to whom a sister of petitioners was married. In a short time petitioner discovered her master drank to excess and soon an improper intimacy arose which resulted in her master brutally ill-treating her on several occasions, she frequently threatened to leave the house, but he said that owing to her mother being a tenant of his and her brother-in-law also in his employment he had a claim on her. One evening however she was obliged to fly from his fury and took refuge in her sisters house, she went to him for her discharge but he refused to give her one, consequently could obtain no situation and in this state she continued for three months when she began to drink and on her master engaging another servant she became desperate and while labouring under the effects of drink and blinded by jealousy committed the crime for which she is at present suffering and no sooner done than she regretted from the depths of her heart.

      Petitioner therefore most earnestly entreats Your Excellency to be pleased to take her sad case into your kind consideration and grant her her liberty, she has to her credit in the prison a sum of money sufficient to enable her to emigrate and the ladies in connection with the Prisoners Aid Society have always showed the greatest sympathy for her and she believes would in every way assist her as she is an excellent laundress and in fact could do any work she might get. Petitioner therefore humbly entreats Your Excellency to be pleased to grant her request, and your petitioner as in duty bound will ever pray

                                                Margaret Skean
                                                4 - 10 - 88 [2]

Copy of Chairman's minutes on Memorial of convict Margaret Skean B28.

Submitted:
>For favourable consideration as the prisoner is now at an age when she could find employment and has sufficient gratuity to take her out of the country.

>Her health is good now which prison life may in a few more years impair, having regard to her present age - about thirty seven years. She is I believe thoroughly penitent and is most unlikely ever to fall into crime again.

This case, would in the ordinary course, come up for release in March 1895, as sentence of Death was not recorded, that is in fifteen years from date of sentence. If she had been sentenced to fifteen years, as she would, owing to her good conduct and industry, be entitled to her release on licence to be at large in March 1890.

>At present this woman's mind is disturbed and distressed by the fact of having no definate hope of release.

If therefore, His Excellency does not feel himself able to comply with her memorial at present, I would suggest that some definate time be named for her release, provided her conduct continues good, so as to give her some hope and encouragement to good conduct.

>(Sec.) C. F. Bourke
>5th October 1888.[3]

Local Folklore

In 1938 the school children in primary schools all over Ireland, were asked by their teachers, to collect information from the older members of the community about happenings of some importance in their local area, and write it down in their own words. This exercise proved a huge success, with thousands of essays compiled by the children of the time, now stored in the archives, as a compliment to history and posterity.[4]

The following are some such stories relevant to the murder at Coney Hall.

A Haunted House

In Mornington near Drogheda there stands a house called Coney Hall. It is said that a very rich man lived here, he was in love with two women. While going with the first girl, he used to keep appointments with the second on the quiet and the second girl knew that he was friendly with the first girl. After some time he fell out with the first girl and then the other girl thought he might be keeping dates with the first girl on the quiet. These two girls were working in the house and one day while the man was out, the second girl with spite killed the other girl and put her down a well. The girl was arrested and put in jail for some time. This girl is supposed to come up out of the well and walk about the house during the night. It is a beautiful big house in a wood and people called Smiths live in it at present.

Written by...Christina Bowden,
3, Chord Road,
Drogheda

The above story was told by..............*Mrs Smyth (sixty five years)*
Chord Rd.,
Drogheda.[5]

There was a book written by an English writer called the 'Haunted House' by the Boyne, this story was about a murder committed in a lonely house which the author of the book thinks to be along the Boyne outside the big bridge on the March and which was said by old people to be haunted.
"But the house where the murder was committed is Coney Hall below Morning-town. The Brabazons owned the house and the last of them lived there alone with one servant as house-keeper he spent most of his time in London and Margaret Skean the house-keeper had things mostly to herself.
One day he brought home another maide from England called Emile Boucher a French girl.
Margaret got jealous of Emile and when she got Brabazons away in England the first opportunity she got she killed her with a carving knife and cut up the body with a chopper. These were kept as curios in Coney Hall up to thirty-five years ago and I had them in my hand.
She put the body in a well which used to be under the kitchen floor with a large stone for cover.
The murder was not found out for some time but the police were set on the track to find missing Emile Boucher and found the remains in the well.
Margaret Skean was arrested, found guilty and was sentenced to fifteen years penal sevitude".

Written by.........Anthony McDonnell

The above story was told by : *Mr. Patrick McDonnell*
42, John Street,
Drogheda.[6]

"This is a true story. It happened at Coney Hall on the banks of the River Boyne in Co. Meath. A man in the name of Smith lives there now.
Ema Buchar was the cook in this house, her master was called Brabison and a girl lived in the gate lodge called Margaret Skain.
Margaret Shain was jealous of Ema Buchar because she was the cook and had a good time. One day when Mr. Brabison was out, Ema Buchar was cooking the dinner, Margaret Skain came in unknownst and gave her a blow on the head. While Ema Buchar was trying to defend herself, Skain got a holt of her hair and hit her on the head three or four times. She then cut her head off. Having that done there was a draw well in the yard at the back door. She dragged her out of the house and thrun her in the well. The master when he came home saw the blood from the range to the well. He could not find Ema Buchar. He sent word to the police. They came and after a while they found the body in the well. Margaret Skain was arrested and brought to Trim.

She appeared before three or four courts. A priest pleaded for her and only for the priest she would be excuted, but she was sentenced to life penal servitude. She got out at one of the King's Jubiliees. She lived in James Street, and when I would be coming from work I would see her every night.
After the murder was committed every night when the master would be in the kitchen late, he would see the girl cooking at the range and walking from the kitchen to the well.

That crime was committed about sixty years ago".

Written by.............*Mathew Reilly*
                        11, Old Hill,
                        Drogheda.
The above story was told by.........*Mary Meehan,*
                                    Sampson's Lane,
                                    Drogheda.[7]

To conclude this very sad and indeed terrifying episode in the lives of the people of Mornington.

Margaret Skean spent from the time of the murder 7th January 1880 until the 8th March 1880 in Trim jail, and, from 8th March 1880 until the 5th June 1883 in Mountjoy prison, and, from 5th June 1883 until 3rd March 1890 in Grangegorman prison, when she was discharged on licence (parole).[8]

On her release, she returned to her relations in Co. Meath, with the intention of perhaps going to other relations in America later on, depending on how her parole went.

But according to local stories, when Margaret Skean returned to Mornington she lived with some neighbours for a period of time. It is not known for certain if she did actually make it to America.[9]

On her return to Mornington after her release from prison, Margaret got a lift in a horse and cart by a local man called Jack Brodigan. The conversation between the two went as follows: "You don't know who I am, do you?" enquired Margaret Skean, "No" replied Jack, "Well" said Margaret, "I am the Coney Hall murderer". Nobody knows how Jack reacted to the above statement!. But according to Vincie Mullen this is a true story, because he heard it from Jack Brodigan's son, whom he went to school with.[10]

James Henry Brabazon may have died on 28th June 1913, but he did not die in Ireland or England on that date.

CHAPTER 13
"New Century, New State, New Churches".

The outbreak of World War 1, in 1914, put the Irish question of home rule in the background, but the build up of pressure that was brought to bear by the Irish, over previous decades regarding this question, was not about to be discarded.

In 1914, Ireland contained five armies. The official forces, which according to reports could not be relied on to ensure a home rule settlement for all Ireland.

Then there was the private armies - the Ulster Volunteers, the Irish Volunteers, the Citizen Army, and the I. R. B.

The Irish Volunteers split, when John Redmond pledged support to England in the war, for the defence of 'small nations'.

After the outbreak of the war, the I.R.B. whose members held strong positions in the Irish Volunteers decided on an Insurrection, to take place before the ending of the war. They secured the co-operation of Connolly's Citizen Army, which was also planning on a Rising. The outcome was the Easter Rising in Dublin, April 1916. The aftermath of the Easter Rising, resulted in a complete change of attitude by the Irish people. Ninety rebels were condemned to death for their part in the Insurrection, despite a mounting volume of protest, fifteen were executed on the 3rd May, and the remainder spread over the following days, ending on the 12th May. There was a huge outcry, the Government appeared to panic, and martial law was imposed.

The Irish parliamentary party blundered and lost the initiative, everything that happened in the following months played straight into the hands of Sinn Fein.

In the general election December 1918 Sinn Fein won seventy three seats, the unionists twenty six, and the parliamentary party six seats.

The victorious Sinn Fein constituted itself as Dail Eireann, headed by Eamon de Valera, with Arthur Griffith as his deputy, and Michael Collins as the ruthlessly efficient organiser of the military resistance against any British attempts to bring down Sinn Fein.

The Anglo-Irish war or 'troubles' was firmly set in place from early 1919 until July 1921, when a truce was called, due to public outcry in Britain and America. The following December 1921, a treaty was signed by the British and Irish representatives.[1]

Who were the 'Black-and-Tans'?
The following is one local man's description of them: The 'black-and-tans' were Auxiliaries of the British. It appears these 'auxiliaries' were prisoners (criminals etc.) let out of the British prisons, sent to Ireland by the British government, to try to force the Irish to conform and adhere to British rule. This so called army of untrained personnel were ruthless and cruel. They were called 'black-and-tans' because of their uniform, which was black trousers, tan tunic and black berets. They were stationed in military camps all over Ireland, the local one was Gormanston military camp. Along with many other awful atrocities, they were responsible for the shooting in cold blood, of two local men on the Marsh road near Drogheda, Mr. Thomas Halpin and Mr. Sean Moran. A monument now stands at the place where these two men died.[2]

Events of Easter 1916 in Drogheda.
The Rising commenced in Dublin on Easter Monday 24th April 1916 and concluded on the following Saturday 29th April with the surrender to prevent 'innocent bloodshed'. On Friday 28th the battle of Ashbourne commenced with an attack on Kilmoon Barracks by a force of insurgents 'estimated at between one hundred and thirty and four hundred'. The seven policemen eventually surrendered.

There was another attack at Rath Cross, this battle lasted six hours, during which time nine lives were lost and fourteen seriously injured. During the following week arrests were carried out on a wide scale.

Meath County Surveyor Arrested.
" On Tuesday evening Mr. James Quigley, the Meath County Surveyor, was arrested in Dunboyne on a charge not publicly specified. His home was subsequently searched and a seizure made. He has, it is stated, been conveyed to England".

"Mr. J. Hastings, an agent in the Singer's Machine Co., was also arrested towards the end of last week, and has since been detained in custody".

Arrests at Drogheda
A large number of arrests were made of suspected parties in Drogheda, Ardee and Dunleer, by the police authorities in Drogheda. The following are the names of those taken into custody:
William McQuillan, Fair Street, John Philip Monaghan, Chord Rd., Michael Harkin, North Strand, J. O' Kiely, Chord Rd., Joseph Carr, Black Bull, Michael J. Keenan, Beamore Rd., Thos Burke, Duleek Street, Thos Halpin, Stockwell Lane and Tom Gavin, Duleek Street.
At Ardee, P. J. Mc Mahon, Mr. Wrenn, James Farrelly, and Thos Matthew.
At Dunleer, J. Lang, Thos Kelly, James Butterly, John Butterly and Michael Reynolds.
The above men were kept in various places of detention in England for periods varying from weeks to eight months, with the exception of William McQuillan who was released within a week of his arrest, and proceeded to bring an action for ' wrongful arrest' against DI Carbery RIC.

After Thomas Halpin's release, he was returned as a Sinn Fein Alderman for West Gate Ward in the local Election of 1919-20. On the 12th February 1921, he was taken from his bed in George's Street by the 'black-and-tans' and shot in the back on the Mornington Rd..
The rest of the people involved suffered greatly from their experience, but managed to eke out a life for themselves, with some being more successful then others.[3]

An Interesting connection:
The Officer in charge of the party who shot Sean Moran and Thomas Halpin was from Enniscorthy, as was Sean Moran.
In the 1930's, the Officer's widow, Dr. Marie Lea-Wilson presented the picture " The Taking of Christ" to the Jesuit Fathers, House of Studies, Leeson Street, Dublin, some time before she died. Many years later, it was discovered to be a work by Carravagio, and was considered 'priceless'. The Jesuit Fathers presented the 'painting' to the National Gallery on a long-term 'loan' agreement in 1993.[4]
Having gone through the pages of history over the last twenty to thirty years, and reading about the extraordinary events that took place during that very exciting period in Irish history, one would almost imagine that Ireland stood still with bated breath, awaiting the dawning of a new independent Ireland. But the reality was the small local villages and town of Ireland that made up the national picture were already busy building up their communities and endeavouring to meet the needs of their ever increasing populations.
The following gives an account of the history of the Schools, Churches, Lifeboat services and the general growth of these small fishing villages; Laytown, Bettystown, Mornington, Colpe, Donacarney and Piltown, which didn't start with the passing of the Home Rule Law or the 1916 Rising. But were firmly established during the nineteenth century, and attempted to flourish and grow in a free Ireland of the twentieth century.

Churches and Graveyards
Mornington (Marinerstown) and Colpe constituted the medieval parish of Colpe-cum-Mornington, and was a separate parish in its own right, prior to the Norman invasion.[5]

In 1182, Colpe/ Mornington (Monastery of Augustinians) became subject to the Priory of St. Cianan in Duleek and cell of Llanthony in Wales, by gift of Hugh de Lacy.
During the middle ages the rural parish church was 'very poor' due to lack of funds and proper security, St. Columba's in Colpe/Mornington and other churches went into a state of dilapidation. The Carmelites, it seems attended to the urban part of the parish, and St. Mary's in Drogheda prospered.
After 1541, the chaos of the Reformation then set in, the dissolution of the monasteries followed by the penal laws, took their toll. In July 1704, at the second Tholsel of Drogheda, Rev Thomas Reilly was registered as Parish Priest of St. Mary's Drogheda, Colpe and Mornington. The Church of Ireland parishes of Colpe and Kilsharvin were united in 1793.[6]

St. Columba, Church of Ireland, Colpe, Co. Meath (1809-1996)

Colpe: Church of Ireland (St. Columba) and Graveyard
The present church was built in (1809) on the original site of the Augustinian Priory (1182). It was erected mainly by the aid of a grant from Board of First Fruits.
St. Columba 's church has since been united with St.Marys, Drogheda, and St. Mary's, Julianstown, Co. Meath. The Rev. A. James Nelson was the incumbent clergyman until recently, he has now retired due to ill health, and has been replaced by the Venerable Patrick Laurence B.A., who was installed on the 21st July, 1998.
In 1996, the doors of this old church closed forever as a place of worship.

Colpe Graveyard
Colpe graveyard is situated on the right of the church, it is dominated by a large enclosed over-ground monument to the Brodigans of Piltown (see Brodigan family - Chapter 14).
The inscriptions, which were written down by Jim Garry in 1985/86 are from seventy nine stones above the ground. There were eighty seven different surnames, the most common are as follows: Durnin, Reilly, Murphy, Kelly, Kane, Hughes, Callaghan, Matthew and Proudfoot. The earliest inscription is Bellew 1733.

List of Inscriptions:
Allen
Margretta Susanna Allen, Whitefields, 17 March 1943. Her sisters, Marie, 8 June 1946. Hennrietta Anna McDowell, 18 July 1945.
Bellew
Here lies the Body of Col. Thomas Bellew who departed this life 23rd day of December 1733 aged 72 years.
Black
Erected by Michael Black in memory of his two sons Tom and Dan, who died young.

Branigan
Erected by Annie the beloved wife of Andrew Branigan who departed this life the 17th of March 1842 aged 33 years. Also Anne the only child of the above Andrew Branigan 20th Jan. 1844 aged 3 years. Margaret Ward, 7th Jan. 1891. Her husband Patrick, 14th March 1928 aged 81 years.

Brodigan
See McClintock.

Byrne
Erected Anno Domini 1793 by John Byrne, late of Sheephouse who departed this life the 22nd of July 1788 aged 77 years. His wife Ann Byrne, alias Conley who died 23rd of December 1797 aged 84 years.

Byrne
See Fitzpatrick.

Callaghan
Erected AD 1800 by Patrick Callaghan, Duleek Gate, Drogheda. Weaver, for him and his Posterity.

Callaghan
Erected A.D. 1803 by Patrick Callaghan, of Magdalene Street, Drogheda. Weaver, for him and his Posterity. Here lieth five of his children who died young.

Campbell
Michael Campbell, Black Bull, 19 Dec. 1863. His wife Mary, 18 Dec. 1909 and their sons, Patrick and Thomas and their daughter Margaret, 22nd March 1944.

Cannfield
See O'Byrne.

Carolan
Erected by John Carolan, Barrack Lane, in memory of his wife Margaret Carolan who died Nov. 9th 1900.

Carr
Erected by Joseph Carr, Black Bull, in memory of his father Thomas, 12 Oct. 1917. His mother Margaret, 1 Nov. 1922. Mrs. Annie J. Carr, Feb. 13th 1929. Also the above Joseph Carr, 22 Feb. 1968. Their infant Grand daughter Fiona Bernadette Smith died 9 March 1970. "Safe in the arms of Jesus".

Chatham
Arther. May 3rd. 1976.

Clarke
Erected by Anne M. Clarke, Black Bull in memory of her father, mother, sisters and brothers.

Conley
See Byrne.

Courtney
Erected by Richard Courtney of Beamore in memory of his beloved wife Annie Courtney. She died 28 April 1867, aged 49 years. Also of his father and mother James and Mary and two of his children.

Coyle
Erected by Stephen Coyle, Bryanstown in memory of his father Richard, 20 Nov. 1871. His sister Margaret, 3 Dec. 1910. And his brothers - Thomas, 12 May 1903. Richard, 9 April 1914. Patrick, 4 Dec. 1945. The above Stephen Coyle, 18 May 1951.

Crolly
See Hamill.

Crosbey
Erected by Thomas Crosbey, senior of the Fortyachres, in memory........(rest of inscription buried deeply)

Cunningham
Erected by Thomas Cunningham in memory of his son Bernard Cunningham, 20th Dec. 1827 aged 38 years.

Divine
Momento Morti. Erected by Laure Divine, Meason, (mason?) in memory of his beloved wife Molly Divine alias Potts who died Jan. the 20th 1813 aged 56.

Druitt
The Rev. Joseph Druitt for 29 years Vicar of the Parish of Colpe, 25th Oct. 1869 aged 57 years.

Dunne
Patrick Dunne, Black Bull, 16th May 1922. His daughter Margaret 10th March 1910 aged 9months. His wife Elizabeth, 22 April 1970, aged 85.

Durnen
Erected A.D. 1821 by Peter Durnen of Baymore in memory of his fatherThos. Durnen aged 81 years. Also of his mother Bridget Durnen aged 41 years. Also of his Brother and Brother's son, also the said Peter Durnen, Feb. 19th 1848 aged 84 years. Also his wife Anne, Dec. 19th 1840 aged 65 years. And John Durnin 30th Nov. 1941, aged 82 years.

Durnin
John Durnin, 30th Nov. 1941 aged 82 yrs. His wife Alice, 21 May 1944 aged 71 yrs. Their son James, 14 May 1954 aged 56 yrs. Also Mary Agnes Stafford, 20 March 1938 aged 66 yrs. Also Peter, 27 Feb. 1969 aged 72 yrs. Alice Durnin, 27 Dec. 1977 aged 70 yrs. and Annie, 23 Nov. 1979 aged 74 yrs.

Durnin
Erected 1865 by Matthew Durnin, Beamore in memory of his brother Michael 23rd Oct 1862 aged 47 years. Also his wife Catherine and two of their children, Peter and Michael who died young. Also of his sister Anne Long, May 1856 and his brother Bernard, 30th Sept. 1862. Also Peter son of the above Matthew Durnin, 2 Jan. 1865 aged 2 years. Also the above Matthew Durnin, 5th of June 1877 aged 52 years. His daughter Mary Anne Durnin, 31st of March 1869 aged 15 years. And Anne Durnin daughter of the above Michael Durnin, 17th April 1879 in the 21st year of his age.

Durnin
See Durnen

Ennis
This Burial Place belongth to David Ennis of Drogheda.

Eustace
James Eustace, Kiltrough 27th May 1985 aged 73 years. Michael Murphy, 14th Jan. 1942. His wife Catherine, 10th March 1968.

Farrell
Patrick Farrell, Black Bull 14th May 1921. His son John, 18th April 1956. His daughter Elizabeth, 19th Jan. 1964. Mary Josephine wife of John, 11th Nov. 1983.

Faulkner
Peter Faulkner, Colpe 27 May 1912 aged 27 years. His father John Faulkner, 13th Jan. 1915 aged 72 yrs. His mother Mary Faulkner 18th July 1918 aged 73 years.

Fawcett
See Garvey

Fitzpatrick
Mary Fitzpatrick for over forty years the faithful servant and friend of Mr. William Parr, of Drogheda and his family. Near this grave are also interred her father and mother, Peter and Mary, her brother John. Her sister Margaret Byrne and her niece Kate Byrne.

Flinn
This Stone was put here by Thomas Flinn of Greenhills near Drogheda in memory of his wife Elizabeth Flinn who died the 20th Oct. 1795 in the 40th year of her age. Also of Patrick Thornton and Bridget his wife and his Father and Mother.

Flood
See Moore.

Garvey
Henry Garvey of Donecarney Cottage, March 10th 1876 aged 68 years. And his son Henry Charles - Feb. 1854 aged 9 years. His brother-in-law Charles Fawcett, formerly of Mornington, March 22nd 1871 aged 60 years. Also Anne wife of the above Henry Garvey, September 8th, 1884 aged 80 years.

Graham
In memory of Christopher Graham 26th October 1955 aged 16 months.

Gray
John Gray, Blackbull, 28th August 1976.

Hacket
Erected by Michael Hacket in memory of his son - 11 June 1818, aged 12 years.

Halligan
Erected by Alice Halligan, Chicago. U.S.A. in memory of her father Bernard halligan, 13 Nov. 1893. Also her mother Anne Halligan. 16Oct. 1899.

Halpenny
Erected by John Halpenny in memory of his Ancestors. Also for him and Posterity.

Hamill
This Monument was erected by Mr. Roger Hamill, Merchant, Drogheda to the memory of his beloved wife Margaret Hamill who departed this life the 12th of September 1795 aged 22 years. And the bodys of Thomas Hamill and Margaret Hamill, their children who died infants and the above named Roger Hamill who departed this life on the 10th of May 1842. Also the body of Mrs Crolly of Shallon wife to Mr. George Crolly, sister to the above Roger Hamill who died Sept 14th 1848.

Harford
See McEvoy.

Hoey
This Monument is erected by Mrs Eliza Hoey of Drogheda to the memory of her parents who are interred. Mrs Margaret Pentony departed this life the 6th of August 1808 aged 57 years. Mr Patrick Pentony of Drogheda, Builder, died 23rd of Oct 1808 aged 56 years. And the above Eliza Hoey, their affectionate daughter who died the 31st of Dec. 1959 aged 71 years.

Hughes
See Kevelin.

Hunter
In memory of our beloved Aunt Dolly Hunter who passed into rest 1st April 1958, Peace, Perfect, Peace.

Jones
This Stone was erected by Nicholas Jones of Georges Hill Dublin in Memory of his father Thomas Jones. Margaret his mother and Patrick Jones his brother.

Kane
James Kane, 2 May 1883 aged 69 years. His son Alexander, 21 Nov. 1875 aged 22 years. His daughters, Jane, 26 June 1874 aged 18 years. Anna Maria, 2 Dec. 1881 aged 20 years. "I am the Resurrection and the life" John. 11. 25. Jane Kane wife of the above named James Kane 15 Feb. 1899 aged 64 years. Also their sons, James, 2 Oct. 1923 aged 66 years. John, 9 Dec. 1929 aged 70 years. Their daughter Margaret Alice, Dec. 1940. William Andrew Kane. Jan, 1941. Thomas, Dec. 1942. 1942. His wife Mary, Nov. 1948.

Kelly
Sacred to the memory of Mr Joseph Kelly late of Drogheda, Coach-Builder, 2nd Aug. 1838 aged 59 years.

Kelly
This Tomb is erected in memory of Micheal Kelly late of Piltown who departed this life the 3rd of Sept 1835 in the 73rd year of his age. His wife Anne Kelly, 17th Jan 1830 aged 77 years. His son William who died 22nd May 1860 and his wife Catherine 7th May 1877. Their daughter Mary Jane, 22nd Jan. 1910. Katie 9th May 1911, his son William, 7th October 1913 aged 71 years.

Kevelin
Erected by Owen Kevelin, Drogheda in memory of his two children who died young. And the above Owen Kevelin 4th May 1831 aged 58 years. And his son Owen, 15th Dec 1844 aged 26 years. Also his wife Elizabeth Dec. 1847 aged 80 years. And his daughter Mary A. Hughes, Dec 21st 1883 aged 77 years. Also Richard, John and Owen Hughes sons of Mary A. Jughes who are interred here and Patrick Kevelin son of the above Owen 1887. Also Peter Hughes son of the above Mary A. Hughes, Oct. 17th 1906. And also his three children and his wife Margaret Hughes 27th Jan,.1944 and their son William Hughes iith Dec. 1945. Their daughter Elizabeth 23rd Dec. 1973.

Kirwan
Bridget Kirwan, Kiltrough 18th Sept. 1976. Her daughter Vera 31st Aug. 1983.

Long
 See Durnin.

Lyons
See Slevin.

Mackenzie
Colonel Thomas Campbell Mackenzie. D.S.O. Royal Army Medical Corps. Born 26 July 1872. Died 20 August1968. His wife Elsie Georgina, Born 22 May 1872. Died 22 June 1955.

Mackin
See Murphy.

Maguire
Margaret Maguire, Colpe 26th Nov. 1961. Her mother-in-law, Mary 11th July 1934. Her father-in-law, John, Nov. 1952. Her husband John 28 July 1980.

Mathews
Erected by Peter Mathews, Beabeg in memory of his daughter Kathleen, 12 Oct 1916 and his infant children Thomas and Josephine. Also his wife Mary. 29 April 1944 and Margaret Matthews, 7 April 1964 aged 59 years.

Mathews
Erected by Peter Mathews, Black Bull in memory of his wife Mary Ann, 7 July 1941. The above Peter Mathews. 2 July 1971 and Elizabeth Mathews, 24 Sept 1984.

Moiles
Erected by John Moiles in memory of his father Richard Moiles Dec. the 2nd. 1783 aged 79 years.

Moore
This Stone was erected by Luke Moore in memory of his mother Bridget Moore, alias Flood who departed this life April 22nd 1769 aged 39. Also Mary, sister to the above Luke Moore...(rest of the stone buried deep)

Mullen
Patrick (Paddy) Mullen, "Riverside" Mornington, 12th Aug. 1983 aged 69 years.

Murphey
This Stone was erected by Richard Murphey of Dunnegarney for him and his Posterity. Here lieth the Body of his father Patk. Murphey and his mother Nealy Murphey and his son Patk Murphey 17 August 1774.

Murphy
Here lyeth the body of Felix Murphy who departed this life the 27th of May 1746 aged 69 years. Also seven of his grand-children. This Stone was resculptored by Michael Mackin of Drogheda in memory of two of his children who died young. Also M. Wiseman.

Murphy
See Eustace.

Murray
Erected by James Murray, Black Bull in memory of his wife Annie 3 Sept. 1910 aged 29 yrs. Also the above named James Murray, 19 July 1944.

McArdle
MARIANNE McARDLE, Beabeg, 2Dec. 1935. Bridget McCullen 27 April 1954. Her son Jack McCullen died 30th August 1986.

Mc Clintock
Loving memory of Stanley Robert McClintock of Piltown House. Born, May 17th 1882. Died, July 16 1958. And his wife Caroline Nellie. Born. July 10 1881. Died Jan 26 1960. Youngest daughter of Colonel Francis Brodigan.

McCullen
See McArdle.

McDowell
See Allen.

McEvoy
This Stone was erected by Owen McEvoy, Beamore, Carpenter in memory of his wife Mary McEvoy, otherwise Harford, who departed this life 22nd of July 1794 aged 47 years. And the above Owen McEvoy 19 June 1808 aged 56 years.

McGlew
Erected by John McGlew in memory of his brother Patrick McGlew and his nephew James McGlew.

McLoughlin
Annie, youngest daughter of John McLoughlin, March 13th 1873. The above named John McLoughlin of Kiltrough, 24th March 1886. His wife Mary, 26 March 1880. Also his son Christopher, 17th May 1893. His daughter Julia, 5th Feb. 1912.

McNally
Erected by Patrick McNally o.....in memory of his father .....who died 1st....aged 70 years.

O'Byrne
Here lieth the body of Mr. Patk O'Byrne of Bellewstown. He died 20th April 1817 aged 39 years. Ann Cannfield alias Reed who departed this life August the 2nd 1767 aged 39 years. Also her brother Patrick Reed aged 3 years.

Parr
See Fitzpatrick.

Pentony
This Stone was erected by Patrick Pentony, Carpenter of Drogheda where lieth the body of his father Christopher Pentony who departed this life 20th of August 1761 aged 54 yrs. Also 4 of his children.
Pentony
See Hoey.
Potts
See Divine.
Proudfoot
Erected by Peter Proudfoot in memory of his Posterity. Here lieth the Body of his mother Margaret Proudfoot who departed this life May 28th 1810 aged 58 years. Here also lieth the body of his father George Proudfoot who departed this life the 2nd Feb 1812 aged 60 years. Also 6 of their children.
Quinn
Patrick Quinn, 22nd May 1954, aged 73 years. Also his mother Margaret Quinn and sister Juliann Quinn. Also John Quinn, 8th May 1957. Erected by Ted Quinn.
Reilly
Erected by Patrick Reilly of Bettystown in memory of his brother John Reilly. Also his father James Reilly. Also two of his children who died young. His son - Reilly, 29 July 1819 aged 21 years. Also said Patrick Reilly, June 10th 1841. His daughter Catherine, Jan 9th 1848. His wife Mary Reilly, Sept. 25 1850. His daughter Margaret J. Kelly, 1854 aged 20 years. Anne Kelly. 1856 aged 23 years. Patrick Kelly, Feb 25 1874 aged 33 years. James Kelly, April 17th 1878 aged 39 years, children of the above. Anne Reilly daughter of the above PatrickReilly, 17th March 1899 aged 98 years.
Reilly
John and Mary Reilly, Minnistown, their son Patrick and their daughter Kate.
Reed
See O'Byrne.
Shepheard
William Shepheard of Bettystown in this Paris. Esq. 29th of Nov. 1830 aged 74 years and of Robert Shepheard, son of the above who died ay Bettystown the 14th day of April 1867. Also of Mary Jane beloved wife of the above, 11th day of February 1888.
Slevin
John Slevin, Fair St. Drogheda, 7 Sep. 1898 aged 68 years. His wife Anne, 3 Jan. 1903 aged 64 years. And their two infant children. James Francis and Elizabeth. Also his father and mother Peter and Elizabeth and his brother Owen, 21 Jan. 1881. Also their son-in-law, Capt. James Lyons, 21 July 1933 and their daughter Mary Lyons, 6 Oct. 1947 and their son James J. Lyons, "Lis-Maura", 12 Nov. 1958.
Smyth
John Smyth, Mary St. 9th March 1892. His sons Patrick, 29 Feb. 1912. James and John who died young.
Stafford
See Durnin.
Stephens
Erected A.D. 1818 by James Stephens of Pilltown in memory of his wife Margaret Stephens, 27th December 1817 aged 47 years. His daughter Margaret, 11 Novr 1820 aged 15 years. Here also lies the body of the above James Stephens, 23rd March 1825 aged 62 years.
Thornton
This Stone and Burial Place belongeth to Rich. Thornton of Drogheda, Taylor, where lieth ye body of his father Henery and Mary his mother.
Thornton
See Flinn.
Tiernan
Erected by John Tiernan of Bettystown for him and his Posterity. Here lieth the body of his beloved wife Mary Tiernan, 19 June 1802 aged 67 years.
Tuite
This Stone was erected by John Tuite for him and his Prosterity.
Ward
See Branigan.

Whearty
Here lies the body of Thomas Whearty late of Bettystown who departed this life the 17th of April 1803 aged 68 years. Also his wife Bridget who died 21st Oct, 1791 aged 61 years. Also his daughter Catherine, 3rd Feb. 1793 aged 21 years.

White
Anno Domini 1765. This Stone was erected by James White of Coalp in memory of his father, mother and relations here interred. Here lieth the body of Henry White who departed this life the 27th day of Feb. 1746 aged 52 years.

Wilde
Charles Edwin Wilde. Born 1899. Died 1980. "I know that my Redeemer lived"

Williams
Jennie Williams. 22 April 1962.

Wiseman
See Murphy.[7]

****

During and after the Reformation, many ancient and very valuable manuscripts, became lost to Meath, among which was the Mornington missal.

In the confusion following the dissolution of the monasteries, these valuable documents became the property of Henry Draycott, and were kept in his library in the castle at Mornington. Among this collection was the Black Book of Llanthony, and a fine manuscript missal once the property of the church at Mornington, and undoubtedly many more.

In 1642 Draycott's castle at Mornington was burnt by troops of the English Garrison at Drogheda, fortunately several of these ancient manuscripts were rescued, including the Mornington missal. Nicholas Bernard, dean of Ardagh, described it as 'a very fair large parchment manuscript of an old missal, dedicated to the church of Mornington'.[8]

The ruins of this ancient church can be found in the old Mornington cemetery attached to the former Star of the Sea, R.C. Church. A slab in the wall of the ruins record that in 1794, James Brabazon of Mornington appropriated a plot of ground there for his burial place.[9]

Traditions tell us this church was dedicated to 'St. Columba', and was connected to the monastery at Colpe. At the time of the reformation and the reign of Elizabeth 1, the Catholic churches were taken over by the 'established church', and Catholic worship was outlawed. The local parish church was abandoned and neglected eventually falling into ruin. St Columba's of Mornington suffered the same fate.

In the early eighteenth century the Penal laws made religious practice very difficult for Catholics. By the end of the eighteenth century, a measure of freedom to practice was restored. A wooden church with straw roof and cross was erected in the old cemetery beside the pre-reformation church.[10]

In 1841, the third church 'Star of the Sea' was built in Mornington, when Fr. Donnellan was parish priest of St. Mary's Drogheda.[11]

Fr. Tom Mathews (son of Patrick Mathews and Miss Duff of Colpe farm), was also involved in the building of the church at Mornington, when he was a curate at St. Mary's, before he became the parish priest in 1847.[12]

Description
Star of the Sea Church Mornington, a chapel of ease to St. Mary's Church in Drogheda. A simple four-bay cement rendered lancet hall, with a Gothic frontpiece of coursed rubble and limestone trim. Advanced central-bay with pointed arch, flanked by blind outer bays with corner quoins and pinnacles.[13] Because this church was built close to the famine period, it was known as the famine church. In 1953, extensive renovations were carried out on the church, which eliminated the serious problem of dampness.

Laytown Bettystown Parish

The new parish of Laytown/Bettystown was established by Most Rev. John McCormack, Bishop of Meath, on the 1st September 1986. The parish of St. Mary's Drogheda was divided, and from its territory the new parishes of Drogheda- Holy Family and Laytown- Mornington were formed, leaving a significantly reduced St. Mary's parish.

Rev. Joseph Gleeson, formally C.C. in the Laytown section of Drogheda parish.
After spending eleven years in Laytown in 1987, he was appointed P. P. of Skryne.
Monsignor John Hanly, Rector of the Irish College in Rome, was appointed first P.P., of the Laytown-Mornington parish in 1987. A scholar in Ecclesiastical History. In 1979 he published, with translation and commentary, The Letters of St. Oliver Plunkett.

The boundaries of the new parish on the coast were determined by the line of the estuary, the coast itself and the railway line running from Laytown to Drogheda. West of the railway line all of the dwellings opening onto the Colpe road and the Piltown road are incorporated into the new parish, as are the buildings on the Ministown road, north of the stream. In 1983 the population of the new parish of Laytown-Bettystown was approximately 4,250 Catholics, with 1,100 families, 660 of which were in the Laytown end of the parish. There were 112 of other religious persuasions. The two areas, each having its own church in the parish, are Star of the Sea in Mornington, and Sacred Heart in Laytown.
In 1986, when Laytown/Mornington new parish was established, it was decided then to build a new church and priest's house in Mornington. In 1987 a three acre site was donated by Joseph and Rhona Connolly. Mr. Turlough McKevitt from Drogheda was the architect and Mr. Frank Duffy from Dundalk was the builder.
The total cost of building the church, the curate's residence and the car park came to 480,000 pounds.
Rev. Patrick Dillon, C.C., St.Mary's Drogheda, was appointed first curate of the new parish. In 1991, he was appointed P.P., Kilcloon.
In 1991, Rev. Terence Toner, a native of Donaghmore (then part of Curragha parish), was appointed C.C. in Mornington.
The church has a capacity to seat over five hundred people. The name of the new church remained dedicated to Mary, Star of the Sea. It has a number of interesting features, the stain glass windows from the old church were preserved on the north wall, other new windows were designed by Eoin Butler. The new church was formally opened on 27th August 1989, and blessed by Most Rev. Michael Smith, Bishop of Meath.[14]

Mornington Graveyard Inscriptions :
A survey of this graveyard in 1987/88 showed one hundred and ninety eight stones of which only one hundred and sixty eight had inscriptions. The other thirty are of different material and have no identification whatsoever.
There are one hundred and thirty different surnames, the most common are as follows: Campbell, Kelly, Lynch, Matthew, Reynolds, Boylan, Long, Stafford, Smith, McCann. Verdon, King, Heaney and Brodigan.
Occupations recorded include ten Ship's Captains, a Seaman, a Servant, a Merchant, a Baker, a Knight, a Surgeon and a worker in Coca-Cola (1985).

Earliest Inscriptions:
Cullin. (1717 Bellew. (1738) Boylan. (1761)
Raffter. (1766) Campbell.(1772) Boyle. (1785)
Brabazon. (1794) Duff. (1794) Ryan. (1794) Read. (1799)

List of Inscriptions:
Bellew
Here lieth the Body of James Bellew who departed this life the 7th day of Dec. 1738 aged 64 years. Also the Body of his wife Catherine who died the 10th of Aug. 1754 aged 79 years. 1759

Bird
In loving memory of Patrick Bird, Pearse Park 2 Dec. 1962 aged 67 years. His daughter Angela 29 Oct. 1926 aged 4 years. Mary Agnes. Died 26 Dec. 1926.

Bowen
Monemto Morti. Erected Anno Domini 1803 by William Bowen in Memory of his father and mother also Mary and Catherine Bowen, his pistertyes.

Boylan
Erected by Capt. Boylan of Baltray in memory of his father Capt. William Boylan who departed this life the 5th of August 1832 aged 30 years. Also the Memory of his niece Kate Boylan who died January 28th 1860 aged 1 Month. And also the memory of his sister Catherine Freemen who departed this life the 23rd of March 1861 aged 28 years. William Joseph Boylan died 1st July 1869 aged 7 years and 10 months. Capt. William Boylan, brother of the above Peter died January 16 1879. Also Capt. John Boylan who died 23 Oct. 1945 aged 81 years. Mary Catherine Boylan, daughter of the above who died 1 March 1982 and her brother John Francis Boylan who died 14 May 1984 aged 75 years. May they rest in peace.

Boylan
Erected by Thomas Boylan of Baltray in memory of his wife Margaret Boylan, alias Tallon, who departed this life 24th Nov. 1810 aged 58 years. Also his son Christopher Boylan who died the 6th Sept. 1809 aged 19 years. Also James Boylan, son of the above Thomas Boylan who departed this life the 19th Oct. 1958 aged 72 years.

Boylan
This stone and Burial place belongeth to Patrick Boylan and Posterity. 1761.

Boylan
This stone and Burial place belongeth to Patrick Boylan and Posterity. 1761.

Boylan
Sacred to the memory of Eva the beloved wife of Nicholas Boylan of Drogheda who departed this life the 17th June 1840 aged 22years. Also their infant daughter Mary Anne.

Boylan
See Reddy.

Boyle
This Stone and Burial Place belongeth to William Boyle of Dunecarney and his Posterity. (1785). Here lieth the remains of Patrick Boyle of Whitefields and Alice his beloved wife. She departed this life the 5th of Dec. 1810.

Brabazon
The Burial Ground of James Branazon of Mornington. Esq. Chosen by him Jany 1794. Allied by the male line to the Earls of Meath and by the Female line to the Earls of Mornington. (Plaque on the north side of ruined gable).

Branagan
Erected by James Branagan of bettystown in memory of lhis daughter Margaret who died 3rd april 1832 aged 18 years. Also his son Peter who died 5th March 1833 aged 15 years.

Branagan
See Mackin.

Bray
In loving memory of Peter and Elizabeth Bray. His son James., His brother Michael and his sister Mary. His daughter Kathleen M. Vallely, died 22nd Oct 1966.

Brodigan
In loving memory of Patrick Brodigan, died 30th June 1965. His daughters Anne, 3rd Sept. 1944 and Patricia, 2nd Jane 1944. His parents Thomas and Jane and brother Thomas. Also the Kelly family who are interred here.

Brodigan
In loving memory of Patrick Brodigan, died 21st March 1978 aged 63 years. His parents John 14th Jan 1944 and Kate 2nd Sept. 1967.

Butler
Erected by Catherine Butler of Mornington in memory of her husband Michail Butler who died 29th Oct. 1874 aged 78 years.

Burke
See Matthews.

Byrne
In loving memory of James Byrne died 26th Jan. 1970 aged 92. His wife Margaret, died 16 Nov. 1968 aged 82. And his daughter Josie Halpenny 15th April 1979.

Caffrey
See McEvoy.

Campbell
Erected by Thomas Campbell, Bettystown, in memory of his father Patrick Campbell who died Oct. 18760 aged 60 years. And his motherEliza Campbell 2nd Feb. 1870 aged 64 years. Also his sister Bridget who died young.

Campbell
Erected by Larry Campbell, Mornington in memory of his father and mother, James and Margaret, his brothers James and Patrick and his three daughters. The above Larry died 15th Sept. 1944. His wife Catherine died 17th April 1953. His son James and his grandsons Tony and Thomas Felix Campbell died 27 Oct. 1976. Laurence Campbell died 21st Oct. 1980 and Agnes Campbell 6th Aug. 1981.

Campbell
Here lies the body of Michael Campbell who departed this life April 15th 1772 aged 83 years. Also his wife Jane Campbell who departed this life August 17th 1775 aged 80 years. His son James Campbell of Bettystown.

Campbell
In loving memory of Rose A nne Campbell, Mornington, died 23rd Jan. 1976 aged 76 years. Her husband Patrick, 27th Oct. 1979 aged 85 years.

Carr
In memory of Patrick Carr, Mornington, died 26th July 1905 aged 87years.

Carroll
In loving memory of Eliza Carroll, 9th April 1939. Her son Michael 17th Feb. 1956.

Cassidy
See Doolan.

Clinch
Pray for the soul of Lucie C. beloved wife of Thomas H. Clancy. "Drogheda Independent" died 21st May 1898 aged 27 years. The above named Thomas H. died 25th Dec. 1912 aged 48 years. And their daughter Helen Ursula Jones died 23rd June 1944 aged 47 years. And her husband Thomas F. died 28th Sept. 1960. (The newspaper title is written like its early mast head).

Clinch
In loving memory of my dear wife Maisie Clinch 23rd august 1971 aged 56 years. Her husband Patrick (Paddy) 2nd June, 1983 aged 69 years.

Clinton
See Lynch.

Cogan
In loving memory of Julia Cogan, Donacarney died July 1942. Also her dear husband Matthew, died Sept. 1958. R.I.P.

Collier
Double grave with white wooden cross, no inscription. Surname on flower pot.

Connor
Erected by John Connor of Mornington in memory of his only daughter Anne who died on the 2nd day of January 1873 aged 17 years. Also his son John Connor who died young.

Connor
Have mercy on the soul of Joseph Connor, late of John St. Drogheda who died May 6th 1878 aged 79 years.

Corrigan
Erected by Edward Corrigan of Mornington in memory of his wife Anne who died Sept. 18th 1938 aged 60 years.

Coyle
Erected by Patrick Coyle in memory of his father who departed this life Dec. 1832 aged 81 years. Here also lies the body of the above Patrick Coyle who departed this life 29th July 1857 aged 53. Marann Coyle died 26th Sept. 1872. Also John Coyle who was lost on sea. His daughter Julia Owens who died 14th July 1884. Also his wife Bridget, who died 17th Dec. 1892.

Cullin
Erected by John Cullin for Catherine his wife who departed this life 11th Nov. 1717.

Cusack
Jimmy Cusack, Mornington, who died 16th Feb. 1974 aged 21 years. Following an accident. His nephew Conor. His father James, 6th May 1987.

Crilly
In loving memory of Francis Crilly, Mornington who died 27th March 1916. R.I.P. (An Iron Cross).

Cunningham
See Sherlock.

Day
This stone was erected by Thomas Day of Morinington where lies his stepson, James Harlin. 1781.

Deery
Small Modern stone with one word and R.I.P. (Recently added) Patrick Traynor, Donacarney 14th May 1986.

Deery
See Keegan.

Didmond
Erected by Emily Didmond, Mell in memory of her mother Alice who died March 1898. Her brother Robert died May 1903 and Thomas Nov, 1908.

Donegan
Erected by John Donegan, Stameen in memory of his father William Donegan, died March 31st 1894 aged 75 years. Also his sister Margeret died Oct. 22nd 1869 aged 16 years. The above John Donegan 27th Nov. 1942 aged 72 years and his wife Margaret 20th May 1954 aged 77 years. Great Grand Daughter Jacinta McArdle 14th Feb. 1976 aged 4 years. Their son William 2nd Nov. 1976.

Doolan
In loving memory of James Doolan, 27th March 1931. His wife Catherine, 26th Dec. 1965. Their daughters Alice 7th Sept. 1923. Mary Cassidy 18th July 1942. Their Son-in-law Richard Cassidy 16 Jan 1973. Their daughter-in-law Bridget 23rd may 1977.

Doolin
Erected by Edward Doolin, Mornington in memory of his father John who died Nov 1894 and his mother Mary Ann who died March 1918.

Duff
This is the Burial Place of Patrick Duff of Beatystown and his Family 1794. Here lieth the Body of the above Patrick Duff who departed this life the 4th of May 1796 aged 76 years. Also the Body of his wife Elizabeth Duff who departed this life the 3rd of February 1817 aged 93 years.

Duggan
William Duggan, 28 Glenview, Drogheda, 23rd Sept. 1962. His wife Bridget, 24th Oct. 1968. Their son William who died young.

Fanning
Erected by Thomas Fanning, Ninch, Laytown, in of his father and mother James and Annie Fanning and his brothers John and James. Also his uncle John Ò Also his brother Hugh who died 5th July 1922. And his wife Anne, 26th Nov. 1926. His son William, 4th March 1948.

Farren
Erected A.D. 1821 by Mrs. Jane Farren for her husband Thomas Farren Ò (badly flaked stone).

Finegan
See Verdon.

Finegan
See Owens.

Fleming
Erected by Peter Fleming, Stagreenan in memory of his father and mother, his sisters and brothers.

Floody
Patrick Floody, 4th Nov. 1964 aged 77 years. His wife Dora, 29th Jan. 1987 aged 92 years. Their daughter Mary, 1932, aged 9 years.
Fox
Erected by Peter Fox in memory of his wife Catherine Fox who departed this life 23rd Nov. 1850 aged 56 years. Also his daughter Rose 21st May 1828 aged 26 years.
Freeman
See Boylan.
Garvey
In loving memory of John H. Garvey, Harbour House, Howth, lost at sea 5th March 1943. His father Patrick 26th Sept 1953. His mother Mary Hilda, 16th April 1971. Sweet jusus have mercy on them.
Garvey
In fond and loving memory of John Garvey, Mornington who died 1st Nov 1907 aged 27 years.
Gorman
In loving memory of Mona Gorman, Clogherhead, died 9th July 1950 aged 53 years.
Gough
Erected by James Gough, Mornington, in memory of his Mother Mary Gough who died Jan. 28th 1869. Also his father John Gough who died Oct 24th 1885. And his two brothers, John and Patrick. The above James died 11th Dec. 1919.
Greene
In loving memory of Mary Greene, Donacarney who died 27th Oct. 1973.
Halfpenny
See Byrne.
Halpin
In memory of the Halpin Family, Narrow Way. R.I.P.
Hammond
Sacred to the memory of James Hammond son of Thomas Hammond of Drogheda who departed this life the 5th of April 1848 in the 20th year of his age. (Large slab on four legs just inside the ruined gable).
Hammond
In loving memory of Anna E. Hammond, Mornington, died 22nd Nov. 1946. Her husband Henry died 19 Dec. 1949.
Hammond
21ST April 1831. It pleased Almighty God to take unto himself, Mary, the beloved wife of Thomas Hammond of Drogheda in the 34th year of her age.
Harlin
See Day.
Harris
Erected by Nicholas Harris and his wife Alice, Scarlet Street, Drogheda, in memory of his father Nicholas Harris, 2nd May 1882. And his mother Ellen, Feb. 1894 and their daughter Bridget Josephine, 10th Dec 1885 aged 15 years.
Heaney
This Stone was Placed here by Mrs Jane Heaney in memory of her beloved husband Mr Philip Heaney who died 2nd Jan.1876. Also of their children who died young. Here also lies the remains of the above named Jane Heaney who departed this life October the 29th 1884 aged 79 years.
(This stone, along with numbers 154,155 and 156 are all together, lying flat, enclosed by an Iron Railing).
Heaney
Erected by James Heany of Mornington in memory of his two children Michael and John, the former departed this life October the 10th 1825 aged 29 years, the latter Aug. 16th 1817 aged 30 years. Here also is interred his daughter Bridget who departed this life the 15th Aug. 1841 aged 46 years. And his wife Anne who died 15th of May 1815 aged 97 years. The above Mr James Heany who died 10th of March 1852 aged 99 years. Also Miss Rose Heany who died 15th of May 1884 aged 90 years.
Houghes
See Mackin.

Irwin

Erected by James Irwin in memory of his father and mother Henry and Bridget Irwin. And his son Henry 1st June 1889 aged 9 years. Also his sister Annie and the Above named James, and his wife Elizabeth, and their sons, Patrick 4th May 1945 and James, 27th Sept. 1948. The stone is signed by F. Whyte, Chord, Drogheda.

Johnson

Erected in memory of Francis Johnson of Colpe who died 20 Dec. 1899 aged 52 years. Faithful Servant at the Glen for over 30 years

Jorden

See Lyons.

Jones

See Clancy.

Kavanagh

Eileen Havanagh who died on April 27th 1948 aged 38 years.

Keegan

Mary Keegan (nee Deery) North Road, Drogheda, 22nd Sept. 1981 aged 72 years. Her husband James, 26th Nov. 1981 aged 74 years.

Kelly

Erected by Mary Kelly, Freeschool lane, Drogheda to the memory of her son Thomas Kelly, 14th Feb. 1891 aged 38 years. The above named Mary Kelly, 26th Jan. 1899 aged 84 years.

Kelly

Erected in 1805 by Nicholas Kelly of Painstown in memory of his father-in-law Patrick Kelly and his Posterity. Also his son Michael Kelly, Seaman, who departed this life, Oct. 1836 aged 26 years. Also Patrick Kelly, son to the above who died 11th August 1847 aged 52 years. This tribute to his memory by his brother Mathew Kelly.

Kelly

Erected by Michael Kelly, Baker, of James Street, Drogheda to the memory of his father Laurence Kelly who died the 16th March 1852 aged 60 years. Also his daughter Mary Kelly who died the 7th of June 1862 aged 26 years and his son Laurence who died young.

Kelly

See Brodigan.

Kelly

See Souhan.

Kelly

See McKone.

Keenan

See Rooney:

Kennedy

James Kennedy, Bettystown, 16thOct. 1938.

King

Erected to the memory of George King, Sea Side, who died 28 Jan. 1907. His wife Catherine 23rd Nov. 1908 and their son James 5th April 1907. Also their son-in-law Michael Mackin, 31st Dec. 1933.

King

In loving memory of John King who died on May 16th 1930 aged 84 years. Also his son Laurence who died Nov. 26th 1914 aged 23 years. Also Margaret King who died 18th April 1941 and her son James King, 6th Jan. 1943.

King

In loving memory of John King. Kings Square, Laytown, 23rd Dec. 1951 and his wife Jane, 22nd Jan. 1965. Also their daughter Mary Bridget, 12th Nov. 1943 and their son Christopher, 16th Sept. 1969.

Long

This Stone was erected by Patrick Long of Drogheda 1780.

Long

Erected to the Memory of Bridget the beloved wife of Captain Patrick Long of Mornington who departed this life the 15th July 1830 aged 50.

Long

This Stone was erected by James and Michael Long in memory of their father and mother with a 11 of their children. 1781.

Lynch
Erected by Joseph Lynch, Coney Hall Road, in loving memory of his parents John and Mary Ann Lynch. Also his brothers Richard, John, James, Michael and Peter.

Lynch
Erected by Bernard Lynch, Mornington in memory of his father Bryan Lynch, died 1851 and his mother Elizabeth, April 17th 1887. Also his wife Helena, 21st May 1898 aged 33 years. And his sons William, 24th March 1911 aged 21 years. And Patrick Joseph, 6th March 1929 aged 37 years. And Kevin, 12th August 1930 and John 20th Jan. 1934 and Brendan who died young. The above named Bernard Lynch died 18th June 1932 aged 88 years. And his wife Margaret 15th Aug. 1953. Their daughter Norah Clinton, 23rd April 1969. James J. Maguire, 10th Sept. 1978.

Lynch
Cherished Memories of our dear Mam and Dad, Mary Lynch "St. Josephs", Mornington, who died 30th April 1957. And Christopher Lynch who died 15th Feb. 1968. Their baby daughter Enda who died in infancy. His sister Polly Lynch who died 16th Jun 1975.

Lyons
In loving memory of Mary Ann, daughter of the late Capt. James Lyons of Newfoundwell, Drogheda who died 4th Feb. 1927 aged 73 years. And her brothers, Capt. Denis Lyons who died 14th June 1938 aged 80 years. Also Capt. Joseph Lyons died 16th Jan. 1945 aged 80 years. Their niece Anne Jordan. 23rd Jan. 1978. "The Anchorage".

Mackin
Erected A.D. 1859 by Thomas Mackin of Liverpool in memory of his beloved father and mother Matthew and Margaret Mackin. Also his brothers and sisters who lie underneath awaiting Joyful Resurrection. Also his sister Margaret Branigan who died 9th April 1868. Also his brother-in-law Luke Branigan, 28th Feb. 1893. And also his niece Bridget Hughes who died 3rd July 1897. And Julia Woods who died 22nd Sept 1907, Newfoundwell. May they rest in peace, Amen.

Mackin
Pray for the soul of Thomas Mackin who died 18th Dec. 1871 and of his brother Matthew Mackin who died 25th Dec. 1891. Also his sister Julia Mackin who died 13th October 1895 and also of his nephew John Branigan who died 5th December 1897.

Mackin
See King.

Magill
Erected by Bryan Magill of Drogheda in memory of his beloved wife Mary Magill, alias Wild, who departed this life 19th Sept 1819 aged 33 years. Also two of his Children who died young.

Magrane
I.H.S. in memory of Christopher Magrane, died 1901. R.I.P. (An iron cross similar to number 45, with no Star and Crescent).

Maguire
See Lynch.

Mathews
Erected by Bridget Mathews of Mullaghard in memory of her husband Michael Mathews who departed this life the 19th June 1809 aged 76 years. Also of her son James Mathews who died 19thAugust 1809 aged 38 years. (Inscription built into the East ruined gable wall).

Mathews
In memory of James Mathews, Mornington who died April 3rd 1886 aged 68 years. And his wife Margaret who died June 4th 1881. His brother Patrick who died in America. Also his father John and his mother Catherine and his brother Edward and two children, Julia and John who died young.

Mathews
This Monument was erected by Patrick Mathews of Colpe for him and his Posterity where underneath lieth two of his children. Anne an infant and Philip who died 5th Feb. 1811 aged 9 years. Here also lieth the body of the above Patrick, died 27th Oct. 1816 aged 81. Also James Mathews of Mount Hanover died 29th Oct. 1873 Peter, 26th Aug. 1882. The sons of James, James Duff of Mount Hanover died 9th June 1879. Patrick died 9th Dec. 1895. Thomas Michael of Annagor, 10th March 1895. Helena, daughter of James died 18th Nov. 1907. Elizabeth, wife of Patrick of Mount Hanover died 10th Feb. 1930. Also Elizabeth Mary, daughter of Patrick and Elizabeth and wife of Sir Gerald Burke, Bart. 27th June 1918.

Moran
Erected by John Moran of Drogheda in memory of his father Patrick Moran who died on the 20th of Sept 1830 aged 79 years. Also his mother Jane Moran, 14th of July 1832 aged 67 years. And his wife Catherine who died 29th May 1859 aged 56 years. The above named John Moran died 10th March 1880 aged 87 years. His grandson Francis Joseph Moran, Mornington, died 8th June 1928 aged 47 years. Also Margaret, wife of Francis J. Moran died 12th Jan. 1960. Their son Frank, 1st Sept. 1983.

Mullen
In loving memory of Jack Mullen who died on 10th Dec. 1945 aged 78.

Mullin
Erected by Thomas Mullin of Borough of Mornington to the memory of his father John Mullin who died 27th Dec 1843 aged 87 years.

Mullin
To the memory of Mr Cornellius Mullins of Whitefields, who dying on the 10th day of July 1888, left the Parish of St. Mary's, heir to his Possessions. Also his wife Ellen who followed him to the grave after an interval of one month.

Murphy
Sacred Heart of Jesus have mercy on the soul of Patrick J. A. Murphy died 24th Nov. 1906 aged 29 years. Also his father Patrick Murphy died on Holy Thursday 4th April 1912 aged 72 years. And his mother Ellen Murphy, 30thSept.1924 aged 80 years. His sisters, Mary Josephine Murphy, July 29th 1951 and Genevieve Murphy Reid, August 13th 1953.

Murphy
The Murphy Family, Mornington.

Murtagh
In memory of John Murtagh, died 31st Oct 1972 aged 65. Erected by his wife Kathleen.

McArdle
See Donegan.

McCabe
In loving memory of Hugh McCabe, Donacarney who died 20th Feb. 1974 and his wife Anne (Nan) died 31st Jan 1984 aged 89. Also his father Hugh and his mother Elizabeth, of Donacarney. May they rest in peace.

McCann
Erected by Thomas McCann, Bettystoown in memory of his father Joseph who died 24th Jan 1888. His mother Jane who died 6th Aril 1881 and his son Christopher who died 29th Sept. 1913. The above Thomas died 14th Nov. 1944 and his daughter Annie, 17th March 1948. His wife Kate, 30th Nov. 1948. His son Joseph, 1st Dec. 1957. Thomas, 4th July 1965. His daughter Mary Jane, 8th Oct 1973 and Margaret wife of Joseph, 3rd Dec. 1974.

McCann
Erected by Thomas McCann, Bettystown in memory of his father Patrick who departed this life Nov. 1811 aged 35 years. His beloved mother who departed this life August 1834 aged 50 years. The above Thomas McCann died 12th July 1893 and his wife Mary McCann who died 6th June 1895.

McCloskey
In loving memory of Ita McCluskey, Mornington who died 7th may 1959 aged 8 years.

McCullagh
Erected by James McCullough of the Marsh, Drogheda in memory of his beloved father Thomas McCullough who departed this life 7th December 1853 aged 60 years. Also his mother Margaret who departed this life 21st August 1860 aged 62 years. Also the above named James, 1st January 1874 aged 42 years.

McCullagh
In loving memory of the McCullough Family, Mornington. R.I.P.

McDonald
See Stafford.

McDonough
Charles McDonough, Donacarney, 21st Jan. 1959. His wife Bridget, 12th April 1966. Their daughter Rita died in infancy.

McEntegart
Erected by Elizabeth McEntegart, Newtown in memory of her husband Thomas who died the 7th of Nov. 1860 aged 59 years. Also her son Patrick McEntegart, 24th February 1864 aged 26 years. Of your Charity pray for the soul of the above Elizabeth McEntegart who died on the 14th July 1879 aged 70 years.

McEvoy
In loving memory of James McEvoy, died 2nd Aug. 1953. His daughter, Dolly Caffrey, died 19th Jan 1963. His wife Margaret McEvoy died 18th Feb. 1975.

McEvoy
Bridget McEvoy, 18-7-1943. Her Husband Joseph, 28-7-1982.

McKenna
In loving memory of John McKenna, Mornington who died 7th Sept, 1925. His wife Bridget, 30th March 1926. Their son James 13th Sept, 1900. Their daughter Lizzie who died 11th Jan. 1906. Bridget, 19th March 1946 and their son John, 4th Nov. 1941.

McKone
Father and mother Michael and Julia McKone. Also his children, namely, Richard, Thomas, Patrick, Joseph, Maryann, Eliza and Julia Kelly. Also his beloved wife Mary Kelly who departed this life Nov. 9th 1879 and the above named Michael Kelly who died Sept. 5th 1885 and his son John, 4th Jan. 1923. His wife Rosanna, 31st Jan 1935.

McMahon
In loving memory of Peter McMahon who died 25th December 1907 aged 23 years. Also Patrick McMahon who died 16th November 1909 aged 32 years. (A broken Iron Cross lying in the grass).

McMahon
Margaret McMahon, Tower Road, Mornington, 18th Aug. 1943. Her husband Bernard, 28th Jan. 1951. Their son Michael (Mixie) 18th Oct. 1986. Also Bridge McMahon.

McTegat
Erected by Own McTegat for him and his Posterity. Her lie the remains of his wife Catherine who departed this life 19th of December 1807 aged 78 years. Also his brother John died 10th of Jan. 1809 aged 64 years. His son Thomas, 27th November 1857 aged 54 years. Also James who died 6th March 1839 aged 19 years. Also Peter Jan. 1849 aged 39 years. Also Margaret wife of said Thomas who died April 1853 aged 77 years and Patrick, 31st Jan. 1867, aged 60 years.

McQuillan
Peter McQuillan, Piltown, 2nd May, 1967. His wife Mary, 10th Aug. 1977.

McQuillan
I.H.S. In memory of Patrick McQuillan died 1898 R.I.P. (An Iron Cross same as number 45 but has no Star and Crescent).

Owens
This Tomb is erected by Mr John Owens of Drogheda in memory of his beloved wife Mary who departed this life the 11th of August 1824 aged 31 years. Underneath are deposited the remains of Captain John Owens the above named, who departed this life the 14th of March 1839 and his affectionate daughter Mrs Marianne Verdon of Dundalk, who departed this life the 9th of January 1846. Also his son Captain Richard Owens who departed this life the 20th of February 1856 and his daughter Mrs Catherine Finigan who died 9th March 1859.

Owens
See Coyle.

Plunket
Erected by Thomas Plunket of Bettystown in memory of his son John who departed this life 26th Aug. 1822 aged 16 years.

Plunket
Erected by Joseph Plunket in memory of his father Peter Plunket, Mosney who died March 25th 1892. Also his sister Bridget who died Sept. 1877 and his mother Margaret Plunket who died may 6th 1902. Also the above Joseph Plunket who died May 11th 1910 and baby Noel.

Raffter
Here lies the body of Lawrence Raffter who departed this life 27th Jan. 1766 aged 65 years.

Read
Erecred by .....Read in memory of her husband Edward Read who departed this life 1st June 1799.

Reddy
Erected by Anne Reddy of Mountgranville in memory of her father Patrick Boylan who died 13th September 1839 aged 69 years. Of her husband Patrick Reddy who died 6th august 1849 aged 30 years. Her mother Agnes Boylan, 17th November 1878 aged 90 years. And the above named Anne Reddy who died 1st of October 1883 aged 66 years. Anne Maria Reddy, 17th March 1935 aged 44 years.
Reddy
Erected by Bridget Reddy in memory of her husband Patrick Reddy, Mell, Drogheda, who died July 12th 1898 aged 48 years. Also Bridget, relict of the above Patrick Reddy who died in Dublin, Dec. 30th 1924 aged 66. James, 4th son of the late Patrick and Bridget Reddy who died in Dublin, 30th Jan. 1925 aged 35 years.
Reid
See Murphy.
Reilly
In loving memory of our dear parents James Reilly, Mornington who died 22nd March 1962 agerd 74 years. Alice died 7th March 1976 aged 81 years. R.I.P.
Reynolds
In loving memory of John Reynolds, Mornington died 26th Nov. 1958. His wife died, 7th Dec. 1965. Their daughter, Gabrielle, died 24th July 1943. Their son Gerard, died 24th April 1944.
Reynolds
I.H.S. In memory of Owen Reynolds, died 1897 R.I.P. (An Iron Cross the same design as number 45, with no Star and Crescent).
Reynolds
In memory of Patrick Reynolds , died 1902. R.I.P. (An Iron Cross same design as number 45, with no Star and Crescent).
Reynolds
Sacred to the memory of Mary Reynolds who died 6 July 1906 aged 11 years. And her sister Martha, who died 21 April 1907 aged 22 years. Sadie Reynolds, died 15 January 1978 aged 80 years. Her husband John L. Reynolds died 7 Oct 1979 aged 76 years.
Reynolds
IN LOVING MEMORY OF Margaret Reynolds died 27th Nov. 1923. Her son James died 24th Jan. 1908. Her daughter Kathleen, died 24th Jan. 1944.
Reynolds
Erected by John Reynolds in memory of his mother Margaret who died 12 Feb. 1915 aged 80 years.
Reynolds
In loving memory of Mary Reynolds who died 7th Jan. 1954.
Reynolds
In memory of Christina Reynolds, New Road, 13th April 1971.
Reynolds
Cherished Memories of our dear daughter, Julie Reynolds, who died 31st may 1984 aged 11 years.
Reynolds
In loving memory of Margaret, 21 September 1985 aged 55 years.
Roche
Pray for the soul of Elizabeth Roche of Tulllyallen, who died august 24th 1893 aged 62 years. Erected by her son Luke.
Roe
R.d. Roe (These are the only words on this badly weathered stone).
Roe
Erected by Simon Roe of Duleek Gate, Drogheda in memory of his father and mother John and Margaret
Roe
Also his son John who departed this life 17th of Oct. 1828 in the 18th year of his age. Also the above named Simon Roe who died 22 June 1850 aged 50 years. And his sister Jane Roe, and his wife Rose and his son Thomas who are interred here.
Rooney
Thomas and Ann Rooney and family late of Bettystown Cross. Their son-in-law James Keenan, 17th March 1907.

Russell
Pray for the souls of Jane Russell, Donecarney who died Jan. 17th 1900 aged 18. And her mother Jane who died Nov. 15th 1911 aged 70.

Ryan
In loving memory of Una Ryan died 10th Aug. 1976 R.I.P.

Ryan
This Stone was Erected by Thomas Ryan of Mornington in Memory of himself and his Posterity. 1794.

Sheehy
Sacred to the memory of Patrick Sheehy, Stameen, 11 Jan. 1908 aged 62 years. His wife Margaret, 25 Jan. 1948. Their daughter Mary, 5 June 1969.

Sheeran
James sheeran, 20th May 1979. His wife Catherine, 18th Aug. 1969. His father Joseph, 10th Dec. 1924. His mother Bridget, 17th March 1935. His son Peter, 17th Oct. 1985. (Small Plaque) Peter from his work-mates at Coca-Cola.

Sherlock
Erected by Thomas Sherlock of Stameen House in memory of his Grandfather and Grandmother. Thomas and Margaret Cunningham and of his uncles James and John Cunningham, all of said place. Here also lies the Body of Kate, the beloved wife of Thomas Sherlock. Esq. Of Stameen House. Drogheda, who died 9th Feb. 1861. Here also lie the mortal remains of the above named Thomas Sherlock who departed this life 14th February 1868 aged 81 years.

Souhan
In loving memory of Christopher Souhan, Painstown died 10th August 1975. James Souhan. 1931. John Kelly. 1927. Roseanna Kelly. 1935. R.I.P

Smith
Erected by James Smith. Mornington in memory of his father Patrick who died Jan. 6th 1856 aged 67 yers. And his mother Rose who died Feb. 18th 1859 aged 63 years. Also his sister Eliza, who died April 3rd 1894 aged 60 years and his wife Kate who died 12th August 1904 aged 64 years. Also her husband the above James Smith who died 9th April 1906 aged 74 years and his grand child Marie Smith. 18th March 1942 aged 19 years. His son Patrick, 3rd March 1953 aged 83 years. Bridget, wife of the above Patrick. 7th June 1973 and their daughter Catherine, 3rd Sept. 1980

Smith
Edward Smith, Bettystown, 11th July 1963 age 71 years. Erected by his wife Annie.

Smith
In loving memory of Eugene Smith, High St. Mornington 1st Nov. 1972 aged 6 years.

Smith
In loving memory of Elizebeth (Lilly) Smith, Mornington who died 26th Dec. 1983 aged 68 yrs.

Stafford
In loving memory of Patrick Stafford who died Jan. 20th 1873 and his wife Bridget who died March 17th 1880. His son, Thomas, Oct 30th 1893. His children Elizabeth and William who died young. Also his daughter Bridget McDonald, Feb 10th 1917.

Stafford
Erected in memory of Catherine Stafford, Laytown died 24th Feb. 1943. Her daughter Kitty Stafford died 26th Nov 1926. Her daughters, Rita Stafford. 10th Jan 1911. Annie died 11th March 1952. Her husband James, 30th April 1950. Her sons Michael, 3rd Aug 1954. Francis, 2nd March 1976. Her daughter Susan, 4th July 1981. (Stone by W. Gogarty, Donore Road).

Stafford
In loving memory of James Stafford, Donacarney, died 8th Sep. 1964 aged 65. His wife Margaret died 10th Nov. 1977 aged 73 years.

Sweeney
Our darling daughter Nicola Sweeney, 12 St. Nicholas Village, 20th July 1987 aged 10 years.

Taaffe
In loving monory of Patrick Taaffe died 21st March 1963. His Wife Nora died 26th Jan. 1961. His father, mother and brothers, Michael and John.

Taaffe
In memory of Aiden Taaffe, 5th Oct. 1948 aged 3 1/2 years.

Tallon
See Boylan.

Tracy
Large Kerbed plot with one stone and name.
Traynor
Patrick Traynor, Donacarney, 14th May 1986.
Traynor
See Deery.
Tuite
In loving memory of William Tuite, died 8th Dec. 1970. His wife Molly, 9th April 1982.
Teeling
Erected by John Teeling, D.M.P. in memory of his father Thomas who died 16th Feb. 1898 aged 59 years. His Mother Alice who died 27th June 1921 aged 85 years, and his brother Patrickwho died 2nd March 1935 aged 58 years.
Vallely
See Bray.
Verdon
Beneath this stone are interred the Children of Peter Verdon of Drogheda. John, died an infant, 30th Jan.1837. William John, an infant, 8th April 1838. Also James, 12 years. Peter, 9 years. Ann Catherine, 8 years. Maria Sophia, 7 years. Emily, 2 years and 8 months who died of Scarlatina, December 1841. And Bernard James Finegan, Esq. Assistant Surgeon, 2nd Queens Own, who died January the 4th 1868. Also Kate the beloved wife of the above Peter Verdon Esq. J.P. who died 19th June, 1875.
Verdon
Of your Charity pray for the soul of Peter J. Verdon who departed this life October 25th 1879 in the 34th year of his age. And of Michael J.Verdon, his brother, who departed this life May 19th 1881 aged 41 years. Pray of the soul of Clara beloved wife of Peter J. Verdon, died April 11th 1896.
Verdon
See Owens.
Walsh
Mary Walsh died 1st May 1909 aged 81 years.
Ward
In loving memory of Laurence Ward, Mornington, 26th Jan. 1938. His wife Kathleen, 22nd Feb. 1976. His mother Mary, 26th Feb. 1935. His grand daughter Joan died in infancy. Also baby Daniel Ward.
Ward
In loving memory of Michael Ward, died 29th Nov. 1951 aged 73 yrs. His wife Margaret, 23rd Aug 1973. Their infant daughter Concepta.
Wardick
See Young.
Watters
In loving memory of Bridget Watters, died 22nd May 1961. Her husband Thomas. 7th Nov. 1966. Also their infant daughter Alice. R.I.P.
Weir
Three wooden crosses on concrete bases. Belonging to the Weir Family.
Whearty
I.H.S. In memory of Patrick Whearty, died Sept. 1879. R.I.P.(An Iron Cross like number 45 with "Drogheda Ironworks" and Star and Crescent on the back).
Whearty
In memory of Patrick Whearty, The Garra, Mornington, 1875-1952 and his wife Margaret, 1885-1957. Requiescant in pace.
Whearty
Margaret Whearty, 1885-1957. R.I.P.
Whearty
In loving memory of Thomas Whearty, Colpe East, died 13 Feb. 1966aged 67 years. R.I.P.
Wild
See magill.
Williamson
Sacred Heart of Jesus have mercy on the soul of Robert Williamson who died 5th Nov. 1918 aged 27 years. A devoted son dearly loved.

Woods
See Mackin.
Young
Erected in loving memory of Francis Young who died 11th May 1930 aged 73 years. Also Margaret Wardick who died 24th May 1930 aged 73 years. Also Margaret Wardick who died 24th May 1925, aged 32 years. R.I.P.

Laytown Church (1876-1979)
In 1866 a temporary church was opened at Bettystown on a site provided by Mr. Simcocks of the Neptune Hotel. In 1976, when asked, the local residents said, that the temporary chapel was on the site then (1976) occupied by Ryan's Caravan site.

Prior to that, residents and visitors attended Mass in the Star of the Sea church at Mornington, which was built in 1841. During the holiday season, Mass was occasionally celebrated in some private houses along the coast.

In 1867, Fr. Tom Mathews, who was then the parish priest of St. Mary's Drogheda, called a public meeting to discuss the possibility of building a new church in Laytown, and a fund for this new and exciting project was opened.

The site for the new church was given by Mrs Mary McDonough, Laytown.

In January 1876 the foundation stone was laid, (the church was built at a cost of about 1,800 pounds), and on the 25th June of the same year (The Feast of the Sacred Heart) Mass was celebrated for the first time.

On the 9th July the new church was solemnly dedicated to the Sacred Heart by Dr. Nulty, Bishop of Meath.

The architect was Mr. P. J. Dodd, and the contractors were Collins and Campbell, Drogheda.

The site of the new church was south of the parish boundary, and actually in the parish of Stamullen. This difficulty was overcome by the following arrangement, set out in a letter written by Dr. Nulty, Bishop of Meath, to Fr. Thomas Allen confirming the 'setting up' of the parish of the Sacred Heart as an independent entity, and Fr. Allen as its administrator. The new parish included only the actual site of the church and the surrounding ground, and must have been the smallest parish in Ireland.

This situation of the parish boundaries of Stamullen and St. Mary's was finally resolved in 1912.[16]

Church of the Sacred Heart, Laytown Co. Meath (1876-1979)

Description
"The building consists of a nave eighty feet long, by twenty feet wide, divided into bays by buttresses on the outside, and lighted by five lancet windows on each side, with cusped heads. The east end is terminated by chancel, in the form of an apse and is lighted by three two-light windows, with tracery heads, having high pointed gable over each. The roof of the nave was open timbered. The building was entered through the porch, on the south side, and by a large painted door in the east gable wall, over which there was a very fine three-light window. The building was faced externally with Allan and Manns' white facing bricks, and all the dressings....of chiselled limestone from Sheephouse quarries".

The church, which could accommodate five hundred to six hundred people was constructed from pale brickwork which resulted in it being referred to as the 'White church'.

During the construction in 1876, a severe gale damaged the chancel window, and the repairs to the window used up much of the money required to complete the building of the church. In 1878, there was a law suit between Fr. Allen and the contractor, although Fr. Allen won the law suit, these events placed a serious financial burden on the parish resources. It is not surprising, the completion of the church had to take place, without the erecting of the proposed spire.[17]

However, we owe a great debt of gratitude to the people of the 1870's. They certainly bequeathed to us a beautiful Church. If its size is now inadequate (a hundred years later), its appearance, atmosphere and setting are still superb. It really is a 'handsome edifice' as was reported of it, a hundred years ago.[18,19]

In the later part of the nineteenth century there was no road between the new Laytown church and Bettystown, so in those days the people went 'to Mass through the sands'.[20]

During November 1879, Dodd surveyed and prepared plans for a road between Bettystown and Laytown on behalf of local residents in the area. The locality was in bad need of a road, for general transportation, and access to the new Sacred Heart church. However, funds were not made available for this new road until 1885. The road was to cost only six hundred and twenty four pounds nineteen shillings, on the understanding that the landlord Mr. Wolfe who donated the land free of charge, should subscribe half the cost.[21]

Present Laytown Church (1979)
The present Sacred Heart church in Laytown was opened towards the end of 1979 a little over one hundred years after the first Sacred Heart church was built. Liam McCormack the architect said in his long career of being associated with the building of twenty one churches the building of the new Sacred Heart church in Laytown was somewhat different. For the first time, he was able to incorporate part of the existing edifice also it was the first church to include a stone blessed specially by Pope John Paul 11, on his historic visit to Ireland in October 1979.
But most significant of all, he brought in that dramatic new ingredient: the wild and blue Irish Sea. When deciding on a site for the new church, the spot on which the old church was built appealed very much to Liam McCormick, even though another site had been selected.
"It was a nice old Victorian church and I was enamoured with it", Liam McCormack said, and he liked the idea that it had been built from bricks landed many years before on the shore by sailing coasters. It was the front gable made from these same bricks that he retained. Also retained are portions of the old stained glass, some holy water fonts and two tablets commemorating the Rev. Thomas Ashe O'Connor, the first resident priest and Mrs Mary McDonough whose generosity was mainly responsible for the construction of the first building.
In the reredos area of other churches, the architect usually adorn this place with mosaics, carvings, oil paintings and gilded pillars, in this church Liam McCormack simply put a window on the superb view already there.

The new Sacred Heart church cost about 200,000 pounds, is built of steel and concrete and is whitewashed. Dr. John McCormack Bishop of Meath, was the main celebrant at the opening and consecration ceremony, he said to the vast congregation there present, amongst other things, "You must love it. You must visit it often and you must be close to it".[22]

Description:
A tall yellow brick gable, with a three-light lancet window and a two-centred arch, is all that remains of the mid-Victorian church. The architect has used this section of the old church as a historical frontispiece entrance to a short glass-covered tunnel leading to the new church, which is a low, white rough-cast building of an irregular circular shape.
The plan of the interior is like a fish, plaice-shaped, neatly arranged as a central nave with the confessionals, crying rooms and vestry, unobtrusively located in the crescents of accommodation at each side. Ronchamps-style punch-out doors and windows to the curving nave walls. Dramatic shafted lighting around the side walls is provided by a hidden slatted clerestory in the roof. The focus of the church lies in the altar and east window located directly opposite the entrance.
Here glass runs from floor to ceiling, with a rude cross placed centrally outside the building, and beyond is the sea and the sky. There is here a sense of quietude and spirituality that is sadly rare in modern Irish churches.[23]

CHAPTER 14
"Education and Care".

SCHOOLS:
Education through the years in the coastal villages of east Meath.
Little is known of education in the area before the nineteenth century. A writer (name unknown) travelling through the country around this time reported the following:
"In country villages I saw multitudes of children seated round the humble residence of their instructor with their books, pens and ink - where rocks took the place of desks".
These open-air classes were known as the 'hedge schools'. They were carried on in spring and summer, they broke up in the autumn, as the children were needed to help in the harvest, but lessons continued in the winter in outhouses lent by farmers. Such a school is very probably the one listed below in the Education Report of 1826.[1]
The 1826, Reports of the Commissioners of Education lists the following schools in the area:
At Donacarney a school was kept by Francis Kiernan in a thatched house. It had thirty eight pupils (this figure varies, as, some reports say there were forty eight pupils). A number of farmers promised the master a gratuity of eight or nine pounds annually, to enable him to keep his school going. The pupils paid one penny per week.[2]
At Mornington, eight children were taught free of charge by Elizabeth Brabazon in a mud-walled thatched house, built at her own expense, for the sole purpose of teaching the children[3]
At Colpe, eighteen children attended a school provided by George Richardson in a stone and lime thatched house.
In 1873, Donacarney N.S. was opened where the present Community Centre stands.
In 1831, the British Government set up a National School System, every child in the country was now entitled to free primary education at the public expense.
National schools were built everywhere, and teachers received special training. This was a very important development in education at the time, and most parents were very glad to avail of it, even though school attendance was not compulsory. There were many drawbacks in this so called Irish education, e.g. no Irish History could be taught, and no Irish language until 1913. However, it was a step in the right direction.[8]

Laytown
There is no record of a school in Laytown or Bettystown and the children from these areas either walked to Julianstown or Donacarney for an education.
The school masters at that time used text books such as the Rational Spelling Book, the Hibernian Preceptor and Vere Foster's arithmetic; Vere Foster, belonged to the Foster family from Collon, Co. Meath.

St. Mary's House.
There were three houses beside the church in Laytown, St. Mary's, St. Annes, and St. Josephs. The first two were built by Edward McDonagh, and the other by James McCullen, of Beamore, the houses were described as the 'Strand Houses'.
The Sisters of Mercy first purchased St. Mary's from the McQuillan family of West Street, Drogheda in 1913. In 1931, the McQuillan family offered St. Annes for sale, and the Rev. Mother of the Sisters of Mercy, Mother Magdalen Skelly bought it for 1,100 pounds.
The Department of Education was opposed to the idea of establishing a school in the area, saying that the number of prospective pupils did not warrant it. However, Fr. Nulty thought differently, and backed by the Bishop, Dr. D'alton (1942-1946), he decided to go ahead with the project independently, financing it from parochial funds. However, by October 1943 the Department did allow the foundation of a junior school at Laytown, on trial for one year.
The Sisters of Mercy were to staff the school in accordance with the wishes of Dr. D'Alton. They were to reside at St. Mary's Laytown, using St. Annes as a temporary school.
On January 6th, 1944, Fr. Nulty announced the long awaited news of the opening of a new school.

St. Mary's House School.
On Monday 10th January, 1944, Mass was celebrated at 10a.m., at which the nuns, parents and children assisted. Immediately after Mass, Fr. Nulty and twenty-five pupils proceeded to St. Annes where the roll was called for the first time.
The school was blessed and the picture of the Sacred Heart was enthroned.
January the 12th Most Rev. D'alton drove to Laytown to visit the new school.

Mount Carmel
The steadily increasing numbers attending the new Laytown School made it imperative that a proper building should be provided for the pupils. A committee was formed of Laytown/Bettystown residents by the priest of the parish, for the purpose of collecting funds for the building of the new school, and a considerable sum was raised.
On the feast of Our Lady of Mount Carmel (16th July 1946) the first sod was turned and building of the school started immediately.
Mount Carmel Junior School for boys and girls was in operation for the next twelve years Sr. Margaret Mary was the principal.

Scoil Mhuire
The population of Laytown was growing fast and Mount Carmel National School was not large enough to accommodate the numbers. The V. Rev. L. Lenehan, P.P. got in contact with the Department of Education with regard to this situation, and a new school for girls was set in motion. The Sisters of Mercy donated the site for the proposed new school in the field beside the church, and in 1958 construction commenced.
One year later the new three-roomed school was opened 'Scoil Mhuire, Port na Hinse 1959' can be seen on the wall plaque.
That same year Mount Carmel was handed over for the exclusive use of boys from 2nd class upward, Mr. Michael McEvoy was appointed principal.

Scoil an Spioraid Naoimh
Laytown and Bettystown continued to expand, many new housing schemes were underway. With the increased numbers of pupils more classrooms and space was needed. With the advice and influence of Mr. James Tully, a parishioner, and Minister for Local Government, the Department of Education sanctioned the building of an extension to Scoil Mhuire.
The site was again provided by the Sisters of Mercy. The architect was Mr. Edward Smith and the contractors were O'Reilly Bros., Dunboyne.
On the 25th June 1976, 'Scoil an Spioraid Naoimh', An Inse, was officially opened by Mr. James Tully, and the Department of Education was represented by Mr. John Bruton.
Scoil an Spioraid Naoimh contained sixteen large classrooms. Boys and girls had their own separate areas, while a spacious 'all purpose room' was common to both schools.
In 1974, Mr. Maurice Daly was appointed principal of Mount Carmel boys school. When the two schools amalgamated in September 1995, he was appointed as principal of Scoil an Spioraid Naoimh[4]

"The story of Scoil an Spioraid Naoimh is a story of endeavour and achievement, a story to be proud of, well worth celebrating. May it continue to flourish for many a future school year, to carry on its task of providing education for the children of Laytown and Bettystown. May it continue to guide our young people in their first steps in learning, helping to prepare them for a fruitful and fulfilling life, which in turn will lead them to the goal of all human living, the life that is for ever with God".
Monsignor John Hanly, P.P.[5]

Modern educational philosophy favoured the principle of co-education in mixed schools at primary level and more than seventy per cent of Irish primary children attend co-education schools. Co-education is not new to Laytown. Between 1944 and 1959, local children were educated in a mixed school 'Mount Carmel'. But between 1959 and 1976 the little boys and girls were educated in different schools, separated by about fifty metres. In 1976 when the new school building was opened the children were now being taught under the same roof, but the old system prevailed, and the boys and girls remained segregated. However, the wheels were being put firmly in motion for mixed primary school education.

By 4th Sept '95 it was 'back to the future' for the children of Laytown and Bettystown, under the more modern name of Co-Education (mixed school) at primary level.

The transition period is well documented by Maurice Daly himself, in Primary Education in Laytown (1944-1996), in the article Amalgamation 1995, the following, is the final passage in that article:

"We are very grateful to the parents, and teachers, the patron Bishop Michael Smith, the Dept. of Education and the O. P. W. and Mr. Gerry Watson for making the amalgamation of Laytown Boys' and Girls' schools a reality. Its much more than an amalgamation of two schools. It is the integration of pupils - boys and girls, of teachers - lay and religious and of ideas - traditional and modern. Our new school is both a memorial to the past fifty years of primary education in Laytown/Bettystown and a symbol of a progressive community with an eye to the future".

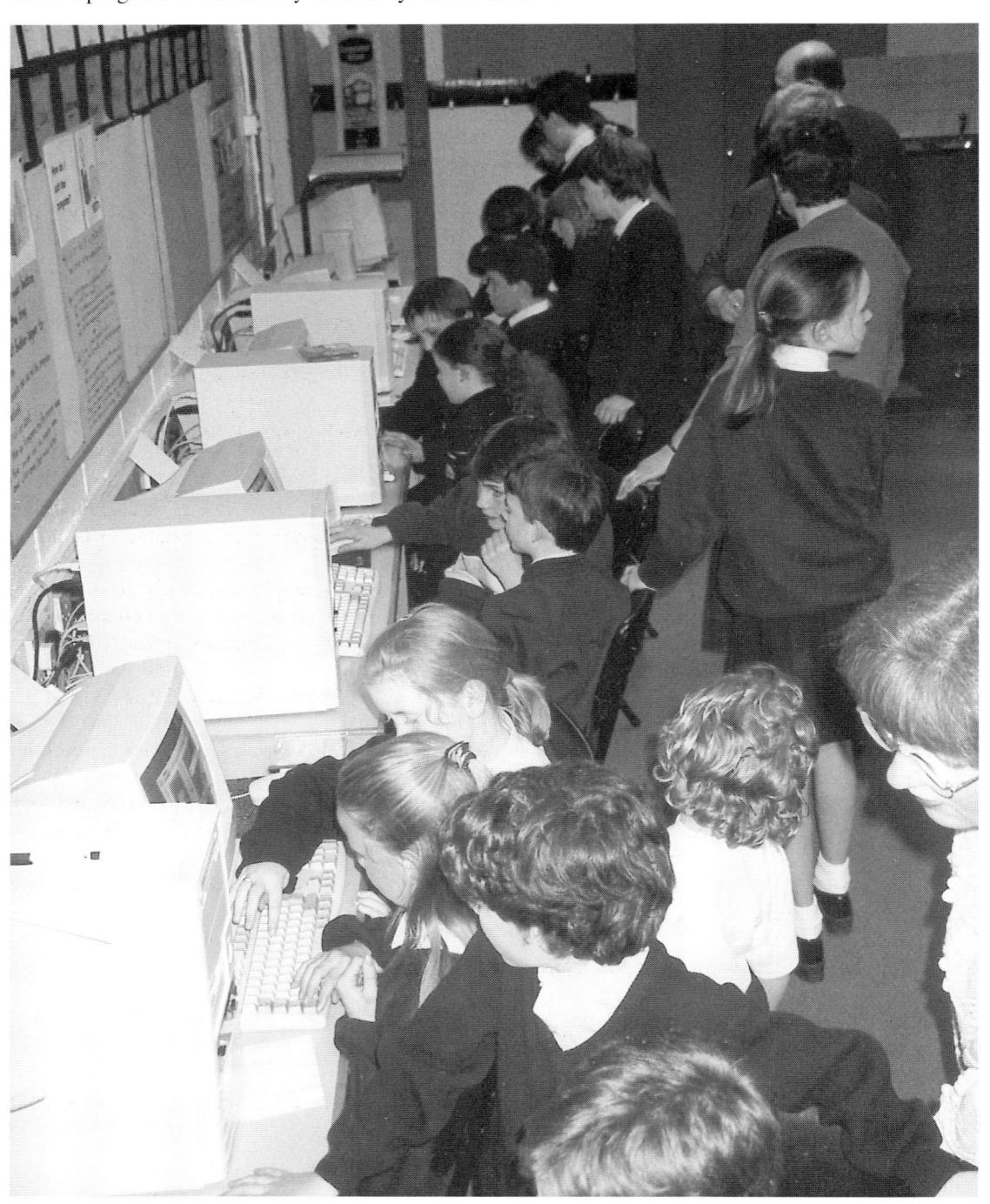

New computer room - Scoil an Spioraid Naoimh, Laytown/Bettystown, Co. Meath

Laytown National School joined the age of Information technology in May 1998, when Meath footballer, Trevor Giles opened the school's new computer room.

This progressive IT project will ensure that all children leaving Scoil an Spioraid Naoimh will be equipped in computer skills, to face their future with confidence.[6]

Donacarney School:

In 1835, the 'Report' states that a school was held in the chapel of Mornington.

In 1839, an application for recognition of the school at Doneycarney states that the building was established in March 1838.

In 1839, the school in Donacarney is described as follows: "It was erected by a private individual as a dwelling house. The farmers collect among themselves what pays the rent. There are two desks, at which sixteen children are seated, the master's chair is the only item in the school, deserving the name of seat". It is not known where this school was situated.[7]

In September 1872, the foundation stone of Donacarney School was laid. Miss Heeney of Mornington contributed one hundred pounds. By March 1873 the school was completed and opened to the pupils.

The school was designed by a Mr. P. J. Dodd, Fr. Allen was administrator in St. Mary's parish during the period when the school was being built.

1928, a new paling was built around the school, and, also a new cloakroom.

1929, a plot of land for the school playground was bought from the Land Commission for thirty two pounds fee simple - rent free.

1932, a new water-pump, septic tank and water-tank capable of holding one thousand gallons of water were added to the school.

The school catered for a wide area, not only for the Donacarney/Mornington district, but also for Bettystown/Laytown, Minnistown, Whitecross, Colpe, Beamore, Beabeg, Piltown and Painstown.[9]

Note: Donacarney boys' and girls' schools were among the very few rural schools, which never became amalgamated or mixed.

Miss Matilla (Tillie) Sheehy retired in 1962, after forty four years teaching in the boys school, 1918-1962.[9a]

New School Donacarney

By 1963, the old school, which had served the community of Donacarney and surrounding areas for ninety years was now inadequate for the growing numbers of pupils. The old system of heating by coal fires was unsatisfactory, also the sanitary arrangements were out of date.

The three acre site for the new school was acquired from the Drew family, Donacarney, situated about two hundred yards from the old school on the Bettystown road. Work on the new school commenced in the autumn of 1963, Messrs McDermott, Dundalk, were the main contractors, Messrs Power of Waterford were responsible for the landscaping.

On the 21st Feb. 1965, the school was formally opened and blessed by Fr. Johnson, P.P., St. Marys', in the unavoidable absence of Dr. Kyne, Bishop of Meath.

On its opening, the school was completely free of debt, thanks to the prompt and generous contribution of the parishioners, which was completely paid up by that date.[10]

A school extension to the existing four classrooms, became a necessity in the nineteen seventies. The extension consisted of five new classrooms, general purpose room, kitchen - library - staff room and office.

On the 15th March 1979 it was blessed by Bishop John McCormack. The pupils moved into the new classrooms on 4th Sept. 1978.

In 1996, two more classrooms were added to the school.

In 1998, with the ever increasing population, a further four new brick classrooms were added, and these new classrooms were occupied on 1st September 1998.

An interesting achievement worth recording, work commenced on the last extension (four brick classrooms) in July 1998, and was completed in August 1998.

Present situation:

Girls - Seven Teachers - 205 pupils.

Boys - Eight Teachers - 246 pupils. Total - 15 Teachers - 451 pupils.[11]

On the 4th November 1998, this new extension was blessed by Bishop Michael Smith.

Jenny Collier and Sarah McCarville pictured here with Bishop Michael Smith at the opening of the new extension at Donacarney National School.

Old Donacarney School (Community Centre).
In 1965 when the students were transferred to the new school, the old school was being used for various activities, club meetings etc. But the building was falling into disrepair, and this was a terrible shame, since this old building had served the parish as a school for over ninety years. The general feeling in the community was to preserve it.

A meeting was called on the 26th October 1971, it was then decided, to repair and renovate the building, which started immediately and was done mostly by local voluntary workers. At further meetings it was decided to build on an extension to facilitate other leisure activities, which were becoming increasingly popular in the area, like tennis and basketball.

By 1973 the Centenary of the old school after many years of dedicated local enthusiasm, partly by contract and partly by voluntary effort, had been transformed into the new Community Centre in Donacarney/Mornington.

It is the hope of all concerned, that the memory of the old school in the form of a flourishing Community Centre will be preserved as a happy and comfortable meeting place for all the people of the district.[12]

Father Bird and Father Johnson at the official opening of the new Community Centre, (1973) Donacarney/Mornington, Co. Meath. Terry Trench and his wife Bea Orpen standing on left, he was founder of "An Oige" and she was president of I.C.A. and a well known artist.

'Eden View House'/Grammar School:

The Grammar school is situated on the Marsh road about one mile from Drogheda.

Formerly known as 'Eden View' it was built sometime in the eighteenth century for the Chadwick family, who lived there for about a hundred years. In the mid nineteenth century it was sold to the Tighe family, Christopher and Jane who lived there for a considerable length of time, they had four children, Gertie, Jessie, Maggie and Paul, Paul died 1913, aged twenty eight years.

The Tighe family had twenty eight acres of land, and were involved in a bit of mixed farming on a small scale, consisting of cows, chickens, and a donkey! They grew their own vegetables, and made their own butter. Maggie married a Mr. O'Rourke, his people were bakers from Drogheda. Gertie and Jessie, remained unmarried and lived on in 'Eden View' until they died in the middle and late sixties and were buried with their family in St. Peter's cemetery, Drogheda.

These two ladies were very well liked by everybody in the area. They travelled extensively, and could speak several languages, except Irish!

Christie Doggett, was their chauffeur and handy-man, who originally came from Donore. He drove their 25 h.p. Vauxhall for many years, which was sold for seven hundred pounds, after their death.

Ms. Weir was the cook, who did her training in Stameen House, Mrs Farrell from Laytown was also employed at the Tighe's residence.

In 1968, 'Eden View House' a six bedroom Georgian house was sold to Drogheda Grammar/Quaker School for 16,050 pounds.

Drogheda Grammar/Quaker School:

In 1955, Drogheda Grammar School, which had been under the management of a local committee, since it ceased to be part of the Erasmus Smith Trust in 1937, and where Arnold Marsh had been head master for six years, was threatened with closure.

It had only thirty-five pupils, and could not continue to pay its way. Arnold Marsh decided to attend the yearly meeting of 'Friends' and appeal for some members to come forward and form a new committee. As a result of this appeal thirteen members of the society of 'Friends' joined Mr. Arnold Marsh in his endeavour to save the school from closure, form a new committee and took responsibility for the school and its outstanding debts.

The Grammar School was situated on Laurence Street, in Drogheda. It consisted of an 'old boys' building, and a Georgian townhouse, where the girls boarded, a garden and three classrooms. Arnold Marsh, wished to retire, after his long teaching career. The new committee appointed Eric Brockhouse a Quaker, to be the headmaster, his wife Kathleen, was to be the physical education teacher, and house mistress of the girls wing.

The school developed over the years under the guidance of the committee and the management of the Brockhouses. They were there for eighteen years, but by 1968 there were over one hundred pupils, and more classrooms were needed. A small playing field had been acquired, one and half miles away. It was decided to look for a new site, where school and playing fields could be together. The present site, Eden View House, a regency building and its lands, beside the Boyne river on the Mornington road were acquired, as the new site for the Grammar school.

It took seven years to plan for and eventually build the new school. This was financed by a large appeal and a Government grant. The grant paid for eighty per cent of the classrooms and the rest of the classrooms were financed from a very successful appeal. The sale of the old site in Drogheda financed the rest of the new school, including ten acres of playing field, the swimming pool and tennis courts. The Brockhouses were active with the committee in planning the new school but retired before it was opened. John Siberry was appointed new headmaster as the school moved to its new premises with one hundred and thirty pupils. The school continued to go from strength to strength.

One of the greatest benefactors to the present school was Basil Jacob, a 'Friend' and an accountant by profession. He was one of the original Quaker committee and acted as honorary treasurer until his death. As well as saving the school thousands of pounds, by his careful housekeeping of the school's finance, he managed the office work regarding the appeal, and finally left a substantial part of his will to the school as a gift.

During his eleven years as principal, John Siberry perceived the school needed to grow, and that need would be best filled by a new laboratory and an art/domestic economy block, which was built in 1986. Soon after this time John Siberry left the Grammar school.

The present principal is Mr. Richard Schmidt, formally of Sutton Park School joined Drogheda Grammar school in 1992. In recent years there has been a change in the pupil make-up in the school. There has been a steady increase of 'day' pupils as opposed to boarders.

When the Quakers founded the committee in 1955, the school was a boarding school, serving twenty-six counties. As a result of the above changes, it is rapidly becoming a multi-denominational, co-educational, boarding and day school for East-Meath and Louth. For two years now the board of management has been extended by inviting the teachers and parents group to appoint two members to the school committee.

The school is now becoming more established as a school for the children of the locality.

Drogheda Grammar School has been host to the Quaker meeting for the last fifteen years.[13]

Caring Institutions:

Creevelea Nursing Home:

The site in Laytown was bequeath to the Dublin Central Mission, (the Methodist Church). In 1948, a holiday home (for the less well off families from Dublin's inner city and surroundings areas) was completed by Mr. Joe Healy, a well known building contractor from Drogheda. Its original name was 'Somerholm', and the total cost for building it, came to 18,000 pounds.

The primary function of 'Somerholm' in Laytown was to provide a holiday home for many disadvantaged families for the period between Easter to September/October. For the remainder of the time, Somerholm was used as a conference centre by the Methodist Clergy. The caretaker of the home at that time was a Mr. George Kells, and one of his many duties was to 'keep the home fires burning', Mrs Kells, was the housekeeper.

In 1973, Somerholm came on the market, it was bought by Malachy and Margaret Gordon, with two things in mind; a hotel, or a nursing home.

After a certain amount of research the Gordons found the greatest need was for a nursing home for a section of the community not catered for, the middle-class to upper. After major internal renovations to convert the premises into a nursing home, it opened in June 1974, as the Creevelea Nursing Home. The first patients to the new Home for a short convalescent stay was a gentleman from Kilkenny, and a lady from Northern Ireland.

Mrs Margaret Gordon was the matron/registered nurse and manager of the nursing home.

Over the next couple of years the nursing home gradually grew to a capacity of twenty four residents, all of which were long-term stays. The following are names of some of the residents who spent time in the comfortable caring surroundings of the Creevelea Nursing Home: Miss Elizabeth McCann from 'The Bawn', Laytown; Francie Stafford, Laytown; Henry Jones, known as 'Colonel' Jones, who after his wife died, emigrated to New Zealand, to be with his son-in-law. The renowned Monsignor McCullen, whose family came from Beamore, was also a resident there. In 1985/6, the Gordons sold the nursing home to a Mr. Gerry Murphy. Mr. Murphy died in October 1992 but his family have continued to run the Creevelea Nursing/Rest Home very successfully to this day.[14]

St. Ursula's Nursing Home in Bettystown was built in the 1950's by 'the Bard' William Walshe, as a summer holiday house originally for his staff, and later his family used it. Towards the end of the sixties it was sold to the Medical Missionaries of Mary sisters, who continued to use it as a holiday/rest home for the sisters returning from the missions. In 1979/80, St. Ursulas' came on the market, and, Eileen Harmon from Saulterstown (near Togher) bought it for her sister Dolores, and her sister's friend Anna Deignan from Leitrim both of whom were in the States and wished to return to Ireland, to start a Convalescent/ Nursing home here. Major renovations were necessary, as St. Ursula's had not been used by the M.M.M. for some time. The upstairs part of the house was used as accommodation for the resident nursing staff. The eight single rooms on the ground floor were for the resident patients.

Dolores Harmon and Ann Deignan through dedication and very hard work turned St. Ursula's into a comfortable and successfully convalescent/nursing home. In 1987, Jim and Eileen Castle bought St. Ursulas it was then catering for eight elderly people.

In 1990, they carried out major improvements and extended the premises, in order to meet the demand for more beds, and to comply with new regulations. They now look after twelve elderly people in comfortable pleasant surroundings.[15]

The Ozanam Home, the site at Mornington was presented to the Society of St. Vincent de Paul in 1962, by an anonymous donor, for the purpose of building a holiday home for children from families living in the inner cities and towns in the surrounding areas.

Cardinal Conway, Archbishop of Armagh, and Bishop John Kyne, Bishop of Meath, gave the funding committee of the project their full Episcopal backing. On 26th July 1964, Bishop Kyne opened and blessed the building.[16] It has grown and developed over the years and now caters in a much wider area of assistance.

In 1975, with the introduction of the Sunshine homes the St. Vincent de Paul society, decided to reconstruct the building from the open plan dormitory style accommodation, to a more private twin bedroom accommodation, endeavouring to cater for couples in the senior citizen's bracket.

Today, Ozanam House is available to the elderly and handicapped as a holiday home by the sea from May to September, providing twin bedroom accommodation for thirty two couples (senior citizens) per week. According to Kathleen O'Neill (president) the holiday home has been very successful and the senior citizens who have enjoyed a break at the Ozanam House come from all parts of Ireland and England. At the end of their holiday, they usually leave well rested, refreshed and happy, hoping to return again one day.

Since 1975, it also has worked in conjunction with the north-eastern Health Board in providing an all-year round Day Care Centre for senior citizens, who are collected from their homes and transported to the Centre by ambulance.[17]

1975

Back row, *Left to right: Anne Clinton, Geraldine Daly, Elaine Daly, Angela Holohan, Maureen Watters, Grainne Ward, Eleanor Hussey, Catriona Dunne, Evelyn Nally, Louise O'Neill, Caroline Regan, Patricia Flynn.*

Fourth row, *Left to right: Bernie Reilly, Rose Hannon, Susanne Hannon, Annette Lynch, Cathern Gogarty, Ann Coyle, Louise Donoughue, Ann McManus, Valerie Reilly, Kathleen Bulger, Chrissie Ferris.*

Third row, *Left to right: Anne Healy, Patricia Ryan, Brenda Ryan, Sandra Dillon, Shirley Scanlon.*

Second row, *Left to right: Veronica O'Reilly, Elaine Cooke, Helen Downey, Aideen Traynor, Fiona Kerbey, Grainne Collins, Orla McManus, Sandra Lynch, Yvonne Traynor.*

Front row, *Left to right: Marie Hussey, Anne Marie McDonough, Fiona Murray, Karen Durnin, Brenda Kerby, Elizabeth Ferris, Karen McDonough, Joan Reilly.*

CHAPTER 15
"The Stormy Sea".

A Storm overland can cause great damage as the following report shows:
On Epiphany Night, 1839, the worst recorded storm to hit Ireland left two hundred and ninety one people dead and did incalculable damage to houses, agriculture and woods. So thorough was the damage, and vivid the folk memory, that a key test for those applying for the first old age pension, in 1911 was, "what do you remember of the Night of the Big Wind?"
Snow fell on the 5th January, seasonable weather one might say. The following day 'Little Christmas' as it was popularly known in those days, the children were out playing in the snow. By 3 p.m, it began to get unusually warm as the temperature rose to a sickly heat and an unnatural calm descended, so calm that voices floated between farmhouses more than a mile apart. Everyone realised that something strange was about to happen but no one knew exactly what. The storm erupted about 9pm and raged in some places until 5am. The gale-force winds were accompanied by lightning and torrential rain. Tension mounted by the hour.
Impact:
Meath felt its impact and Trim was 'a mass of slates, tiles and bricks'. The church, Grant Charter School, the military and police barracks were 'truly pitiable spectacles'. A writer noted 'the awful scene at the dead of night.....the shouts of men, the piercing cries of women and children......their lives in imminent danger from flying slates and bricks.' Two young men were found dead in Riverstown's ruins.
The big houses in Navan were badly damaged. Barely a tree still stood in the demesnes of Arch Hall, Mountainview, Gibbstown. The Bishop of Meath's Ardbraccan estate lost two thousand trees. The Boyne river became so thick with hay and oats one observer wrote, it seemed it could be walked across. At Duleek the Catholic Church bell was blown down, but the old Abbey miraculously escaped damage. Behan's steam mill and his own home were burned, while a fire at Balrath Mill was quickly put out.
A 'great fire' destroyed much of Kells, 'it started in a bakery, where a man under the influence of alcohol was burnt to death', said one account. There was money lying around everywhere on the streets, obviously blown from burnt-out houses!
At Julianstown, Ballygarth Castle had its dome destroyed, and nearby Barmeath was also badly damaged. Virtually every tree on the demesne at Slane and Beauparc fell. The Marquis' permission to locals to remove the brush was much praised.
Collon lost rare pines, ilex, black larch, magnolias and cedars on Lord Ferrard's estate.
Ardee's 'almost incalculable damage' included the complete destruction of Mulkittrick's mill and Charlestown Church, many of the 'big' houses were un-roofed. Kingscourt suffered a 'bombardment', with its church totally shattered. Kilmainhamwood and Nobber were also badly ravaged. Drogheda's Windmill Lane had thirty two houses un-roofed.
The pre-industrial Irish society of the time equated the storm with some divine or diabolical intervention. More recent weather frights, even 'Hurricane Charlie' pale by comparison.[1]

Mornington Lifeboat Station (1872-1926)
For centuries, the effects of a storm on the sea along the coast of East Meath, has been to throw up victims in their ships, and often the local people could only watch helplessly as the sailors and their ships was battered and swallowed up by the angry waves. Many stories are recorded:
In a severe gale storm the brig Manly was driven onto the sands at Bettystown. The lifeboat was immediately on its way but it was not able to reach the Manly due to the hazardous weather. A Miss Campbell from Bettystown helped by a Mrs Fox from Kells made a very brave attempt in saving some of the crew, Miss Campbell was later awarded the RNLI silver medal, and Mrs Fox was accorded the thanks of the Institution, inscribed on vellum.
Following the loss of the brig Manly of Whitehaven, at Bettystown on 27th September 1871, the RNLI records state that:
"After mature consideration, the Institution decided to form a lifeboat establishment at Mornington, on the south side of the mouth of the Boyne, in addition to the original station on the north side". "A new ten-oared boat, 32feet in length by 7.5 feet breadth, was sent there, with a transporting carriage, in April last, and placed in a commodious boathouse built for them on a suitable site. The expense of the lifeboat was met by legacy bequeathed to the Institution by the late Mr. Henry Fothergill Chorley, of Eaton Place,

with the view to a lifeboat name 'John Rutter Chorley' being placed on the coast. The boat and carriage were granted a free conveyance from London to Dublin on one of the steamers of the British and Irish Steam Packet Company".

"On 7th August, the assistant Inspector of Lifeboats, had the boat conveyed in its carriage from the boathouse to Bettystown Strand, a distance of nearly three miles to show those who had been of the opinion that it was not possible to transport the lifeboat there in time to be of any service, in the event of a wreck on that direction, that it could be done. The boat was then launched, close to the place where the ill-fated Manly took place and the crew put through the usual exercises...."

Mornington's first call was 28th January 1873, and the 'John Rutter Chorley' lifeboat, started its journey of heroic work, saving lives from the raging sea. The Mornington lifeboat service lasted fifty three years, many lives were saved and we salute those brave men of yesteryear. The last lifeboat at Mornington was the 'John Dunn', from a legacy of Miss Jane Dunn, from Belfast, in memory of her father. She was only called once and made no rescues. When the Mornington station closed down in 1926, the 'John Dunn' was transferred to Clogherhead where she remained until 1931.

Mornington Lifeboat..Coxswains:
John Garvey   1872-1877
Laurence Garvey   1877-1913
Patrick Byrne   1913-1922

Mornington Lifeboats
John Rutter Chorley   1872-1885
Charity   1885-1901
Rose Baddington   1902-1914
John Dunn   1914-1926

Mornington Lifeboat..Hon. Secretaries:-
James Brabazon   1872-1873
W. H. Brabazon   1877-1880
Thomas Gilroy   1888-1895
R. O. Hill   1917-1922

John McNamara   1873-1876
James McCartain   1880-1888
Thomas Connolly R.N. 1896-1916

38 lives were saved during the period 1872-1885.[2]

****

Shipwrecks of the Eastcoast (17th, 18th and 19th Centuries)
Name unknown:
On 9/4/1749 an unknown vessel captained by Mr. Albo was stranded and lost near Drogheda. The cargo of 20,000 travelling from Drunton for Dublin were saved.
On 26/1/1796, a large rigged ship (name unknown) was lost a short distance north of Drogheda bar. The same day a brig was lost on the Nanny River at Laytown.
Swedish Barque:
On 17/11/1852 a three masted Barque was wrecked in the bay between Bettystown and Clogherhead. All were lost except the captain and cabin boy. The Swedish Barque carried sugar rum and tobacco for Liverpool.
Agnes:
On 19/12/1853 a fine brig went ashore between Laytown and Gormanston Co. Meath. Seven of the crew climbed the rigging but three were washed away. Rockets were fired but could not reach the wreck. The local gentry assembled to render assistance. One man went to Dublin to obtain a lifeboat in Dublin Docks. A boat was obtained at Kingstown and transported to Laytown. Three men were saved after sixty two hours in the rigging. The brig was the Agnes of Whitehaven bound for Dublin with iron ore.
Canada:
On 14/12/1868, the 281 ton Barque Canada was wrecked a mile from Bettystown Co. Meath. The voyage was from Liverpool to West Africa, with general cargo.
Manly:
On 27/9/1871, the 165 ton brig Manly of Whitehaven was driven ashore at Bettystown Beach, Co.Meath. Some of the crew were rescued by Miss Campbell from Bettystown and Mrs Fox from Kells. The Manly cargo, coal from Newport bound for Dublin.
Williamson:
On 27/1/1873, the 126 ton Williamson was wrecked at Bettystown, Co. Meath.
The cargo, coal from Whitehaven to Cardiff.
On 5/12/1873, a large schooner was wrecked at Laytown.

Sisters:
On 11/1/1877 the 354 ton Barque Sisters was wrecked a mile and a half Southeast of Drogheda bar. The cargo was maize from Baltimore bound for Drogheda. The crew of eleven survived.
Delight:
On 5/12/1877 the 119 ton brig Delight was wrecked at the North Bull, Drogheda. The cargo was coal from Workington for Dublin. The crew of four were saved.
Eilean Glas:
On 2/5/1980 the Scottish motor vessel Eilean Glas was driven ashore at Bettystown Beach, Co. Meath, near the golf club. The tug Carmelhead of the Holyhead towing company had tried to tow the vessel but was prevented by strong easterly gales. The cargo was 450 tons of salt from Belfast bound for Devon. Captain Reilly and his crew of three were safe.[3]

Jaws.....the doomed shark

On the 1st June 1984 a very large fish was washed up on Laytown beach after being dead about three days. The fish which local people identified as a whale, but Dublin Zoo said was a shark, was about fifteen feet long, black and blue in colour with a white underside. No one knows exactly how the fish died, but it is generally believed that it was hit by a ship and drifted helplessly for some days, but died before it reached the shore at Laytown.

As the locals waited for the Co. Council workers to arrive to bury the fish, some of the local school children were brought down to see the very large animal from the deep even though it was dead. When Dublin Zoo was contacted with regard to the identity of the fish, they said that although they couldn't be certain without actually seeing it, it very probably was a basking shark. Basking sharks are quite common in Irish waters, they do not eat humans, but rather, like the whales they live on tiny microscopic fish called plankton.[4]

Nanny Water Coastguard:

The Coastguard Service in Ireland and Britain was formally established in 1822, when the Preventive Water Guard, the Revenue Cruisers and the Riding were united following the recommendation of a committee set up one year earlier, to bring all the preventive services under a single authority. In 1856 control of the service was transferred to the Admiralty. The Coastguard Service Act of that year laid down its main responsibilities; along with those of Coastguarding the Service had a variety of other functions to carry out in the years that followed, ranging from assisting ships in distress and taking charge of wrecks, to the recording of wild birds and rare fish washed ashore, and many more worthy services at sea.

In the eighteenth and nineteenth century, smuggling in the Irish Sea was becoming a very lucrative business and growing rapidly. With a ready market in Dublin, the smugglers and sailors of Rush Co. Dublin had developed their own operational strategy and were experts in illegal trafficking. A chain of Coastguard stations set up at strategic points along the east coast was designed to curb this flourishing illegal trade.

Eight of these stations in the district were at Balbriggan, Skerries, Rush, Malahide, Portmarnock, Donabate, Howth and Baldoyle. In the Topographical Dictionary of 1837, Samuel Lewis noted under Ballygarth: "At the mouth of the Nanny Water is a Coastguard station, which is one of the nine that constitute the district of Swords".

Nanny Water Station was housed in Nanny Water Cottage in the townland of Corballis and leased from the local landlord Robert Taylor of Corballis House. Cottages were also leased to accommodate the Coastguard staff and their families.

The Nanny Water Coastguard station was in operation from early eighteenth century to early twentieth century. A series of letter books relating to Coastguard stations for the periods 1847-1849, and 1866-1873, can be found in the National Archives, Bishop Street, Dublin. These letters make interesting reading, and give an insight into some of the serious difficulties the Board was confronted with, in their dealings with two landlords, Robert Taylor of Corballis House and later Robert J. Kennedy of Drogheda. The proprietor of the Alverno Hotel in Laytown was also an owner of six cottages there.

The Nanny Water Coastguard Station was housed in three different houses, during its operational period. All three houses were in close proximity to each other.

The little school house at Corballis, overlooking the Nanny River, was built in the mid nineteenth century, but, over the years the school house fell into disrepair. In 1911 Mrs Smyth, of Cooper Hill,

Julianstown, had it renovated at her own expense.
It was in this school, the children of the Coastguard staff, received their early education until 1915. It was sold in 1981, the bell which hung on the west gable now stands in the porch of St. Mary's Church, Julianstown.

Robert Taylor of Corballis was born 1818, and educated in T. C. D. where he received a BA in 1844 and LL.D. in 1859. Called to the Irish Bar in 1844 he was a magistrate for Meath. The Taylor family arrived in Ireland around the same time as Oliver Cromwell, the family grave can be found in Julianstown graveyard.[5]

Corballis:
Corballis, at the mouth of the Nanny river was once a fishing village, a community consisting of about one hundred and twenty seven people around one hundred years ago.
With mussel beds at the mouth of the Nanny River, mussel fishing was the main source of livelihood within this small fishing community. However, the mussel beds did not survive the Laytown Sewage Scheme of 1937. This Sewage Scheme also brought to an end another way of life, willow and sally trees which grew around the river at Corballis were uprooted, all in the name of progress! These lovely trees had been used to make potato baskets and mats.[6]
The Delaney family have been associated with Corballis House from the beginning of this century, to the present day. Niall and Elma Delaney and their family (third generation) are the present owner/occupiers.

Elma tells an interesting story of when a member of the Taylor family returned to Corballis House to see the home of her ancestors who had lived at Corballis for most of the nineteenth century.
Last November, Elma was in her kitchen preparing the dinner and happened to look out the window only to see a quaint old lady wandering about the garden. She appeared to be very much at home in the surroundings. Surprised, Elma immediately went out to inquire from the lady who she was, and what her business was. It appears she was a fine gentle lady, and introduced herself as Mary Cametoa and proceeded to tell Elma that the Taylor family who were once the landlords of Corballis House and estate, were her ancestors.
Elma became very interested and invited the lady in for a cup of tea, as she also very much wanted to note down what this lady was telling her. When she was sitting comfortably in the kitchen, she produced a letter, which had been obviously given to her by her mother who was a member of the Taylor family.

This letter was written in 1939, and some of the contents are as follows:
John Taylor, originally came from Waterford, but he had been living in Dublin for some time. A gentleman of means, he was a 'sleeping-partner' with a Dublin forestry firm (name unknown). He met a beautiful London lady called Ellen at the Embassy Ball in Dublin, and was totally smitten. Shortly after that first meeting John proposed to Ellen, she accepted, and so the lovely romantic story begins: In 1840, he purchased Corballis (pronounced Corbliss) 'a beautiful house and estate near Julianstown, in Co. Meath' They had a very happy married life at Corballis, and had thirteen children, six girls and seven boys. The eldest son Robert inherited Corballis House and the estate. The children of this happy union went on to make very successful lives for themselves. The eldest daughter Ellen (called after her Mother) had nineteen children, Luisa the grandmother of the writer of this letter, became Luisa Taylor Allman, and died young at the age of thirty two years, in 1862. Even though her life was cut short by illness, she was a very talented and gifted lady in many areas; painting, music and an excellent needleworker, she was also a skilled linguist. Luisa would have been the great-grandmother to Mary, who was revisiting the home of her ancestors.[7]

Just to conclude this story, there is a tomb in St. Mary's, Church of Ireland cemetery, Julianstown, where members of the Taylor family are buried, the inscription on the tomb, goes as follows:

JOANNES SMITH TAYLOR.

MORTALITATEM INIIT IN URBE WATERFORD.

OCTAVO IDUUM SEXTALIS MDCCLXXIX. (1774)

IMMORTALITATEM INDUITI

IN COMITATE MEATH APUD CORBALLIS

OCTAVO IDUUM JANUDRII MDCCCXLVIII (1848)

OMNIBUS AMATUS VIXIT.

NEMINI INFLECTUS OBIIT.

CHAPTER 16
"A Threat from the Sky".

Arthur Griffith died on 12th August 1922. Michael Collins was killed in an ambush on 22nd August 1922. The bitter civil war ended in May 1923.

William T. Cosgrave succeeded Arthur Griffith, and remained head of the Free State government until his party was defeated in a general election in 1932.

The Fianna Fail party lead by Eamon de Valera came into power in 1932, with the support of the Labour party. This new government proceeded to make changes in the Free State constitution by removing the oath of allegiance to the British crown which was followed by a decision to withhold from Britain the land annuities along with other payments, amounting in all to about five million pounds a year. The annuities were twice-yearly instalments payable by farmers in respect of the capital cost of buying out the landlords.

Britain retaliated by taxing imports of Irish cattle into Britain, the Free State counter-reacted by placing a levy on British imports. And so began the 'Economic War' which lasted for over six years. This dispute was brought to an end in 1938, by the payment to Britain of a capital sum of ten million pounds, and the treaty ports were handed over to the Irish Government.

In 1937, de Valera introduced a new constitution to replace the one he regarded as imposed with the Treaty. This, declared Ireland to be a 'sovereign, independent, democratic state'.[1]

During this time of an emerging new State, life in East Meath went on, and one of the most exciting developments, was the presence in the skies of aeroplanes. These often came from the Aerodrome at Gormanston, and also on special occasions from further afield providing the people of these parts with magnificent aerobatics displays. These occasions were very special, and attracted huge crowds. Unfortunately, in some cases serious tragedies marred the excitement of this new spectacle of the flying machines.

Pilot Killed:...Drogheda Couple's miraculous escape.

It was a beautiful Indian Summer's afternoon on Sunday October 1st 1933 at the big field near the railway bridge known as Colpe Farm. An estimated two thousand people had come to see Sir Alan Cobham's Air Circus. Suddenly there was a gasp of horror from the huge crowd as they heard a little biplane splutter and then come twisting down from about 800ft and crashed beside them into bits. There were three people in the plane, Canadian pilot Captain Rose who was killed and Paddy and Rose Hoey who suffered fractured skulls and other injuries. Paddy and Rose were rushed to hospital. It was a tragic climax to what was reckoned at that time to be an historic day in aviation locally. Ironic indeed was the fact that the ill-fated incident was the last scheduled flight of the day. Paddy Hoey a well-known Drogheda builder with a great love for flying, had earlier the same day gone up thousands of feet in a special acrobatic flight. It was also the only disaster, which the highly distinguished Sir Alan Cobham had in the course of his numerous air displays throughout several countries.

Feeling very distressed the world-renowned flier who bore the title of K.B.E. and A.F.C. was unable to see the Hoeys before his departure. He wrote them a long letter expressing his grief at the unfortunate mishap and best wishes for their full recovery. The pilot's body was taken to St. Marys and his remains were taken away by his brother, a clergyman from Canada.[2]

Paddy and Rose Hoey lived through their spine-chilling experience and went on to enjoy a long and happy life.

Paddy Hoey died, 8th June 1983, and Rose died 18th February 1994. May they rest in Peace.

Airliner brought Passengers over Drogheda.

The Air-Display at Colpe was held under the auspices of The Irish Aero Club and was known as Sir Alan Cobham's Air Circus. Admission was 1s. 3d. (6p.) and flights 5/- (25p.) per head.

During the morning prior to the display an 'airliner', which carried about a dozen passengers made several trips over and around Drogheda. For many local people this was their first experience of air travel. One of Alan Cobham's pilots, Captain Rose, (who was the pilot killed later the same day) was an aerial photographer, which was a very uncommon occupation in those days.

Some weeks prior to the display at Colpe, Alan Cobham had held similar aerobatic shows in Co. Louth. One of these was in a field adjacent to Beaulieu House near Baltray and those who took to the air (including Paddy Hoey) were flown over the Boyne estuary, Baltray golf course, and other well-known landmarks. Another display was held at North Marsh, Dundalk.
Sir Alan Cobham had a splendid record for safety and in his letter to the Hoeys he stated:
"The whole occurrence was most unfortunate and I think it should never have happened at all".

Sir Alan Cobham, K. B. E., A. F. C., was born on the 6th of May 1894, London - died October 21st. 1973, Bournemouth, Dorset. A British aviator and pioneer of long distance flight he promoted 'air-mindedness' in the British public.
He entered the Royal Flying Corps in 1917, and in 1921 joined Geoffrey de Havilland's new aircraft company for which he undertook a succession of long distance flights, 5,000 miles around Europe; 8,000 miles across Europe and north Africa; 12,000 miles through Europe to Palestine, Egypt, along the North African coast and back through Spain; to the Cape of Good Hope and back; to Australia and back. From 1926, the year in which he was knighted, he operated his own firm. For Imperial Airways he flew 23,000 miles around Africa in 1927, and in 1931 he made a survey flight up the Nile River and across the Belgian Congo (now Zaire) for the Air Ministry. During the next four year, his flying circus team of pilots toured Britian and gave many, their first thrills of aerial display.
He wrote a number of books about his activities, including My Flight to the Cape and back (1926) and Twenty Thousand Miles in a Flying Boat (1930). His memoirs, A Time to Fly, were edited by C. Derrick and published in 1978.[3]

Picture shows Gardai Hanley and Maguire, standing at the crashed aeroplane.

World War 11 (1939-1945)
Even though the 'Free State' stayed out of the war, the people of Ireland endured grave difficulties, with hardships of unemployment, emigration and rationed supplies, as a small price to pay for neutrality. During this period, east Meath and along the east coast also witnessed serious tragedies on land.
The following are some brief accounts of such tragedies:

The German Airmen:
During the War (1939-45) a number of German Airmen were washed ashore on the east coast. One of these was found on the strand at Mosney, 26th October, 1940.
At the inquest in Julianstown he was identified, from his belongings, as **Horst Felber of Poumern, Germany,** aged twenty years. There was also found on his body, French and German banknotes, some francs, photographs, and a watch. On the breast of his flying jacket, an Iron Cross dated 1939, his identity number was 73712/49. Horst Felber was interred in Mornington graveyard.
During the same week another airman was found washed ashore at Clogherhead. He was **Walter Hoppmann of Tilberg,** also, aged twenty years. His belongings consisted of, a penknife, cigarette lighter, a nailfile, an identity card, a disc with the number 73712/48. He also had an Iron Cross. Both he and Horst Felber were wearing an airfield life-saving jacket with compressed air pump and mouth piece attached.
Walter Hoppmann was interred in the Co.Board of Health graveyard at St.Mary's, Drogheda, which really means he was buried in 'Bully's Acre'.
The German Minister to Ireland attended both funerals and laid wreaths on the graves. These were bound with red sashes, bearing the German Swastika.

In March 1941, the German Legation sought permission from Meath Co. Council for exhumation of Horst Felber. This was not granted, probably, because the war was still going on.
During the years 1959 to 1961, Germany with the support of the Irish Government, built a special cemetery at Glencree, Co.Wicklow, for the German War Dead buried in Ireland. In 1960, Horst Felber was exhumed at Mornington and Walter Hoppmann was exhumed from 'Bully's Acre' and both remains re-interred in Glencree.
The site of the German Airman's grave in Mornington, is a single grave kerbed in cement, next to the path, beside the railed in Sherlock grave.[4]

Holiday Makers Witness Air-smash.
People on holiday at Laytown were eyewitnesses of a terrible tragedy, when an Irish Army Air Corps plane crashed on the strand. The pilot Lieut Michael Ryan (nineteen) and the gunner Private Patrick Power (twenty) were killed. The machine was one of three army planes on tactical exercises in North Co. Dublin. The plane approached Laytown from the Gormanston direction and flew over the strand. The pilot seemed in difficulty and appeared to be trying to land on the strand on which there were many people including children. The pilot was waving his hand, as if to get a space cleared, he turned back towards Gormanston.

Tried to avoid children
He changed his course again and flew in the direction of Bettystown strand, the plane coming lower and lower, narrowly missing some houses on the roadside.
The women and children ran off the strand, and the pilot attempted to land, but the plane seemed to nose-dive on first hitting the ground then bounced again splitting in two. The engine was found thirty yards from the body of the aeroplane. The pilot was found dead under the fuselage, and the gunner died soon afterwards.

Rev. J. White C.C. St. Mary's Drogheda, who was in Bettystown at the time rushed to the spot immediately after the crash, as did doctors who were holidaying at Bettystown. Army doctors and ambulances arrived later.
The tragedy was a painful shock to the residents and holiday makers in the area at the time. Some men when they realised the plane was in serious difficulty did everything possible to clear the strand but for the presence of mind of those men, the tragedy might have been much worse.
Owing to the beach being so crowded the pilot delayed too long in coming down, so that the machine lost all its speed and crashed. The crew did have enough height to use their parachutes. The bodies of the two young men killed in the crash were taken to Drogheda District Hospital and later removed to St. Bricin's Military Hospital, Dublin. The wrecked plane was taken away by the military.

The victims
Lieutenant Ryan was a son of Mr. and Mrs W.P. Ryan, Central Hotel, Cashel, Co. Tipperary, aged nineteen years. Private Patrick Power, Tramore, Co. Waterford, was aged twenty years.

Impressive Funeral Tribute
Draped in the tricolour and bourne on the shoulders of their comrades of the Army Air Corps, from the Mortuary at St. Bricin's Military Hospital to the waiting motor Hearses. The remains of Leiutenant Ryan and Private Patrick Power were taken to Cashel and Tramore respectively. Beautiful wreaths were laid upon the coffins.
An Taoiseach, Mr. E. DeValera and Mr. Oscar Traynor, Minister for Defence, were present. Mass for the two young Airmen was celebrated at 9 am in the Arbour Hill Church by Rev. W. M. O' Riordain C. F. Baldonnell.[5]

Laytown Plane Crash: Popular old Showman killed.
At approximately 6.45pm on Wednesday 1st. July 1942 a two seater army aeroplane crashed at Laytown, Co. Meath. Samuel Farrell aged seventy seven years, proprietor of a travelling show was tragically killed. Lieutenant M. T. O' Callaghan of Kimmage, Dublin, and Corporal Peter McEvoy of Cloneydown, Portarlington, the occupants of the aeroplane were seriously injured. The plane from Gormanston got into difficulties, it came down suddenly at a very steep angle with smoke pouring from the engine and crashed into a group of Caravans killing Samuel Farrell instantly. Mr. William J. Guiler who was talking to Samuel a short while earlier narrowly escaped. The engine of the plane immediately caught fire. Joe Guiler, son of William, with the help of Mr. N. Traynor, Mr. T. Monk and Garda Sergeant Loughran succeeded in rescuing the injured airmen from the blazing wreckage. Despite all efforts from Laytown section of the L.D.F. the plane and caravans were burnt to ashes. Mr. Fred Hoey of Ratholland made desperate attempts to save Samuel from the burning caravan as it was not known at the time he was already dead.
The injured airmen were brought to the Levin's family home and from there later removed to St. Bricin's Military Hospital. Lieutenant O' Callaghan suffered serious injuries Corporal McEvoy's injuries were less serious.
The actual scene of the fatal crash is known as St. James's Park. It has been occupied for many years by the late Mr. Farrell and his travelling show. He was a great favourite in the locality and very popular with the children whom he loved very much. His sudden and tragic death came as a great loss and sadness to all who knew him.
The Laytown L.D.F. who acted so promptly in the crisis were led by the section leader Mr. Dick Carter, other locals included S. Matthew, Ted Ferris, and J. Mooney, Corballis who were also very active in keeping the fire under control. The crash occurred only a quarter of a mile from the scene of the tragedy where two young Irish Air Corps personal were killed two years earlier. Amongst those early on the scene were Dr. Hardy, of Drogheda, Dr. P.P. McNamara, Drumconrath, and Major Dr. C. Stuart A. M. C. who rendered medical aid to the injured airmen.[6]

The following are accounts of tragedies of a different nature:
Bombs dropped near Drogheda, at Stagreenan and Duleek, more bombs dropped in Carlow, three people killed.
In 1941, during the 2nd World War, it was reported that seven bombs were dropped at Stagreenan. The area where the bombs were dropped belonged to Colonel Cairnes of Stameen, just behind Balmarino House on the road from Drogheda to Mornington. The bomb holes or craters varied in size from twelve feet wide by six feet deep to four feet wide to one foot deep.
It was considered at the time that the immense cement factory situated only a few hundred yards away on the north bank of the Boyne River was the possible target of the unknown airmen. That is if they had an object at all, or were merely unloading their bombs harmlessly on finding themselves over neutral country! Unidentified planes dropped both high explosive and incendiary bombs in a number of places along the east coast of Ireland. The first attack was in the Drogheda area (Stagreenan).
Borris, Co. Carlow, suffered the most severe effects where three members of one family were killed, and two others seriously injured.
The only casualties reported from the Drogheda area were two rabbits who found dead near one of the craters. Miss Agnes Johnston, who lived in a cottage at Colpe, told a reporter, the explosions seemed to

be happening just outside the door and gave both herself and her sister a terrible shock, "for a moment" she said "I thought I was dead".

Mr. Gerald Daly from Julianstown told a reporter he had seen an aeroplane flying at normal height shortly before the explosions. Mrs O'Rourke (wife of Thos O'Rourke, caretaker of Bettystown Golf Club) was wheeling her bicycle across the railway bridge at Colpe at the time when the bombs were dropped. She said "the bicycle was wrenched from my grasp and thrown against the wall of the bridge".

Windows in Mr. V. Smith's house at Colpe were damaged by the blast. Another house, fortunately unoccupied at the time of the explosions was very seriously damaged. The craters in front of this house were about nine feet in diameter and about three feet deep. Other explosions were reported from the Duleek area, the station-house and the Parochial house had suffered damage with broken windows and severely shaken foundations but no one was reported hurt or killed.[7]

Bombing in Bettystown:
During the late Autumn or early Winter of 1943 another bomb was dropped in Bettystown, close to the Village Hotel. Col. Henry Jones, who was living in Bettystown House owned a black hunter, this beautiful horse dropped dead from the noise of the explosion near by. Colonel Jones's father was Colonel Ludlow Mainwaring Jones.[8]

In 1949, a small aircraft made a successful bellyland in a field belonging to Sean Lynch, whose farm bordered Mosney Holiday Centre. This aircraft was endeavouring to land at Gormanston Military Camp, when it got into difficulties. The two pilots on board miraculously escaped injury. The aircraft was taken to the Gormanston aerodrome by road. The back road to the military camp was very narrow and not suitable for anything the size of even a small aeroplane. The wings were raised over the body of the aircraft and after it was carefully manoeuvred through narrow farm gates away it went with a military and garda escort some spectacle, all of fifty years ago.

The above picture shows Sean and Margaret Lynch standing by the aircraft in 1949.

CHAPTER 17
"Modern Times"

James Tully.
Jimmy Tully was born in 1915 at Carlanstown, Kells, Co. Meath. He was educated in St. Patrick's Academy school in Navan. He worked in a variety of jobs until he joined the army in 1941. He served as a corporal in the eighteenth Battalion in Dublin and Gormanstown during the second World War. In 1946, he left the army and shortly afterwards he joined the Federation of Rural Workers, in 1947, he became its organising secretary in Co. Meath, remaining with (FRW) for twenth six years, until his appointment as a Minister.
Jimmy Tully became Labour TD for Meath in 1954-serving until 1982 except for a four-year interruption. A Minister for Local Government from 1973-1977. He is best remembered for initiating an extensive programme of local authority house building, which saw record levels of house completions.
On his first trip abroad as Minister for Defence in the short-lived Coalition Government of 1981-1982, he escaped death when he was on the reviewing stand in Cairo during the assassination of President Anwar Sadat of Egypt, and was injured by part of the shell intended for the President.[1] The following tributes were paid to James Tully who died suddenly at his home in Minnistown, Laytown, Co.Meath in May 1992 by his friends and colleagues. Practical, thorough, humorous, energetic are all adjectives that have been used to describe former Government Party Minister and Dail Deputy James Tully.
Monsignor Hanly said: "There was no hypocrisy about him, no lies, no deceit. He always brought with him the gift of charity, he always did what he could, he listened to peoples' needs".[2]

The following tribute was made by the Union General Secretary, Tom Garry.
"Jim Tully demonstrated an exemplary commitment to the men and women of no property in this country - in his Union work and in his Minsterial career. He will be remembered with affection by the many whose lives were substantially improved by his practical concern".
The Fine Gael leader John Bruton said, in his view Jimmy Tully was one of the best, if not the best Minister for Local Government the country ever had.[3]
Former Taoiseach Liam Cosgrave, also paying tribute to Mr. Tully said: "He was a most honourable man of integrity, worked hard and achieved, while Minister for Local Government (now Environment) a record number of houses built - over 100,000 in four years".
Senator Jack Harte, said that Mr. Tully, as Minister for Local Government had set up An Bord Pleanala, 'in the belief it would take the argument about corruption in planning away from local level'.
The number of local authority houses he had built still stand as a record above anybody who had served in that ministry. He also brought in a Bill, which allowed local authorities to buy houses for the first time.

Gaelic Football in the area:

Gaelic Football was well established in east Meath, before the turn of the century.
Bettystown G. F. Team were the winners of the Meath Junior Cup in 1907, and winners of the Meath Junior Championship in 1908.

Back row - left to right: Pack Mc Donough, Jim Smith, Patsie Grogan, Willie Drew, Tom McEvoy, M. McDonagh, Willie Sheehy, Fan Wade, Tom Carry (Sub), Pat Purfield, James McCann (James Deery Sec.).
Front row - left to right: Tom Mc Donagh, Tom Sheehy, Ben Cabe, Paddy Sheehy (Capt.) James 'Quick' McQuillan, Vin Smith and Jemser Walker.

But according to the following article taken from - Gaelic Football, by Carbery, football was played and enjoyed on the banks of the Boyne as far back as the seventeenth century.
Seventeenth Century Football in Ireland:
A well-known Gaelic Poet of North Leinster-one Seamas Dall Mac Courta, who was born in 1647, has left us a very fine poem, "Imirt-na-Boinne", descriptive of a game played on the Banks of the Boyne in his young days, over three hundred and fifty years ago. Twelve verses have been preserved. This match was played in the townland of Fennor, on the south side of the Boyne, not far from historic Slane. The parish of Mornington mentioned in the poem is close to the mouth of the Boyne. It is Seamus Mac Courta that tells us of the popularity of football from the Erne to the Sea-or rather that the fame of the rival players stretched amongst footballers that far. The men from the Nanny river Watershed played the Men of the Boyne Valley, and it is clear that the poet favoured the victors-his Boyneside neighbours, with their stalwart Captain-Seoirse O'Clerigh. Mac Courta's praise of the Boyne men is fulsome; each player's qualities are extolled.[4]

Note: Hurling and Football Teams up to and including 1891 consisted of twenty one players. From 1892 to 1912 inclusive, a team was reduced to seventeen players. From 1913 onwards, a team was reduced to the present fifteen players.

A goal up to 1891 outweighed any number of points. From 1892 to 1894 a goal equalled five points, and from 1895 onward, a goal equals three points. The team was called 'Donacarney Parnells', which was beginning to show signs of greatness, in the early twentieth century, with players like James (Red) McCann (an uncle of Frank Mc Cann, Julianstown). In the early days James played for the local team, he also played for Meath, and he was considered to have the longest kick in Ireland at that time!

The football team was re-organised in the 1920's and the name changed to 'The Star of the Sea'. This team it appears included Bettystown, Laytown, Mornington and Donacarney, their colours were black and white, even the goal posts in the football field were black and white. The field was at the cross-roads below McDonough's Pub in Bettystown. Travel became very difficult before and during the war years, and the team did not play competitively until around 1944. The name of the team changed to St. Mary's. During this period St. Mary's trained and practised a great deal, this was serious business, and as a result, they became very skilled on the football field.
In 1945, a neighbouring team called Parnell's, from the Marsh Road, won the Junior Championship. This team was considered excellent at the time, and because both teams came from the same parish, there was great rivalry when the two teams met in the Feis na Boinne Cup final the same year. Although Parnell's were the Louth Junior Champions, St. Mary's won that match by 6 points.

This result caused an uproar as the team from the Marsh Road could not believe they had been beaten by St. Mary's. There was even dissension in the Parish House as the priests were on different sides. In 1946, St. Mary's got to the final of the Meath Junior Championship, having beaten Rathmolyon by 5 points. In the semi-final Jimmy Tully T.D. was the captain. The final was set for late autumn of that year but it snowed heavily for several weeks, and the final was postponed until the end of February 1947.

St. Mary's trained hard during the months leading up to the 'big day' and they were in excellent form for the final. Their many supporters travelled from Laytown to Navan, there was great excitement, and the place was packed. Alas, St. Mary's lost the final to a team from Nobber in north Meath. This was a very sad day for the team from east Meath, and an even sadder day for their loyal supporters. However, St. Mary's played a good game, and that help to ease their great disappointment. In the following years St. Mary's continued to play well, but alas, with no major successes until 1958 when they won the Intermediate championship.

During the early sixties football in the area went through a very low patch.
In 1964, two separate clubs were formed within the parish, Star of the Sea, from the east of the parish, and St. Columcilles from the west of the parish. Star of the Sea reached the Junior A final in 1969. St. Columcilles Shallon, reached the Junior B.final, also in 1969. In 1971, both clubs amalgamated, and, the new club was called St.Columcille's G.F.C. East Meath. In 1984, the club purchased a new playing field at Piltown from the Christian Brothers and a new club house was later erected.

The club has had many successes at Juvenile, Minor, Junior and Intermediate level since its formation. In the early years, McDonough's pub in Bettystown, was a focal point for all the activities in the area. It was here in McDonough's that Gaelic football was re-started after a lapse of nearly twenty years. It flourished under the leadership of Eamon Delany, taking in parishes of Donacarney/Mornington and Bettystown/Laytown. In those days they may not have had huge success on the field, but at least it worked well for the community spirit in the area, and, this community spirit is still very much alive today, and long may it continue.[5]

St Mary's Gaelic Football Team 1945/46
Back row, Left to right: Bill Dolan, Des Taaffe, Mick Lyons, Gerry Monahan, Ned Ferris, Patrick Taaffe and Dessie Smith.
Second row, Left to right: Paddy Monahan, Jimmy Tully, Paddy Byrne, Joe Hinchey, Jimmy Black and Paddy Collier.
Front row, Left to right: D. Wheerty, Paddy Reynolds, Christy Collier and Sean Lynch.

Major Historical finds in recent years:
The following is an article written by Eamonn P.Kelly for the Irish Times 4th Nov. 1983.

In 1979 two new brooches were found at Bettystown in close proximity to the find place of the 'Tara Brooch'. The train of events leading to their discovery began in 1977 during the building of the Brookside estate. During the excavation of a foundation trench a grave built of stone slabs was found by Mr. James Gaffney, Lusk, Co. Dublin. The burial, which was roofed with a large slab, contained a crouched skeleton of a young male and a pottery vessel. The find was dated by Carbon 14 method, to the early Bronze Age, around 1800 BC.

In August 1979, Mr. John Gaffney, 70, Brookside Estate, who is a cousin of the man who found the Bronze Age grave decided to erect a washing-line in his garden. His activities resulted in the discovery of another grave, and with Mr. Gaffney's consent the National Museum conducted an archaeological excavation of the garden. This uncovered a cemetery containing at least sixteen graves and although these were different in form to the grave found in 1977, it was at first assumed that the new finds also dated to the Bronze Age.

This belief was soon altered by the discovery of a burial containing a number of objects which showed that the cemetery dated to a period during the Iron Age, perhaps between the second and fourth centuries AD.

The grave in question was a pit burial containing a skeleton, presumed to be of a woman. She had been buried in her finery of which a pair of iron brooches, a buckle, a bronze hair ornament and an axe-shaped pendant remained. Traces of two types of textile and of a hair net were also present. The brooches were simple penannular forms with rolled back terminals, and they are believed to be the earliest type used in Ireland. They were probably inspired by the Roman types, which were in use in northern Britain.

Simple and unimpressive though the early type may have been, it quickly evolved and developed in complexity until in the eight century the zenith of artistic achievement was reached by Irish brooch-makers, in that other Bettystown brooch——the 'Tara Brooch'.[6]

The following extract is taken from:-**EXCAVATIONS 1988**

Colpe West
Early Christian enclosure, cemetery.
The site in a field adjacent to the 'Mill Road' some 500m to the north-west of the well known medieval foundation of Colpe, with its nearby fort and castle. It is situated on a gentle north-facing slope at the summit of the long rise in ground from the southern bank of the River Boyne southwards, just below 100ft O.D.

The site was discovered when removal of topsoil revealed a concentration of articulated and disarticulated human remains, some of which were placed in stone graves.

The Gas pipeline corridor crosses the east-north-eastern quadrant of a large enclosure within which a Christian cemetery was found.

The Cemetery:
The remains of over one hundred individuals were exposed, excavated and retrieved for study. All the burials were aligned east-west, many placed on top of earlier burials and fourteen were placed in stone-lined graves. The stone-lined graves were not lintel-graves in the strict sense of the term, as none were actually covered with lintel-type stone. The graves were roughly stone lined, sometimes with flat slabs, but also with rounded boulders, only some were roughly covered with flattish slabs which didn't cover the complete grave. The burial activity appears to have been carried out over a long period of time, with no great consideration for pre-existing interments. There were several levels of burials, the deepest occurring at the west of the area excavated under the gas way.

All the bodies were laid out carefully, with the hands at either side. In some cases the hands, joined, were placed low in the pelvic area. Occasionally, one hand was placed across the midriff. Only one example displayed the medieval 'prayer-pose'. Almost all the skeletons retrieved appeared to be those of adults. There were a few obvious adolescents but no children. All the skeletons, with the exception of one were placed inside the line of the ditch, the one exception was revealed within the ditch fill.

It appears there is some documentary evidence, which may indicate that this historical find of stone lined Christian burials, with the presence of E-ware and B-ware on this site, dates back to the fifth and sixth century. But further documentary research is required before a more definite outline can be established.[7]

On a visit to the site of the most recent historical find in the Bettystown area, the site was still in the process of being excavated. Actually getting an opportunity to view the exposed graves was very rewarding. However, as one stood there staring, thoughts and feelings flooded into the mind, as to- *who were these people, who lived, and died here thousands of years ago?* One could not help feeling a deep sense of sadness at this primitive final resting place being disturbed. It was very interesting talking to James Eogan, archaeologist from Dublin, who was the director of the excavations in Bettystown, and it appears that this particular burial ground, could go as far back as the Early Bronze Age. It was also consoling to hear that these grounds would be considered 'sacred ground'.

Bronze age burial ground found in Bettystown dig.

Extensive archaeological excavations at Bettystown have unearthed burial grounds dating back to Early Bronze Age, almost four thousand years ago.

The remains of a Late Neolithic timber structure over four thousand years old has also been discovered at the site.

The excavations are being carried out by Archaeological Development Services Ltd. Under the conditions of the planning permission, Meath County Council required the developer the O'Connor Group to facilitate and pay for an archaeological investigation on the site opposite the Neptune Hotel, Bettystown, in advance of the construction of a residential estate.

In this interview with the Drogheda Independent, Archaeological Development Services Director James Eogan, pointed out that this is a unique site in terms of the richness of the discoveries, which date from late Neolithic age right through to the fifth and sixth century AD.

The Late Neolithic timber structure discovered on the site is approximately 7.5 metres in diameter and is defined by eighteen large post-holes. A similar type timber structure has been discovered at Knowth, and a number located in England.

Excavations at the site commenced at the end of May and was completed by mid-September.

Ten of the skeletons were recovered from an Early Bronze Age Cemetery, (3,500 years old) at the southern end of the site.

Mr. Eogan, also said that four of the inhumations were accompanied by beautifully decorated bowls, food vessels. Three of these vessels were found with children, and one with a teenage girl.

Other burials, were three children, a middle aged female and two adult males in the same grave, one of whom had been cremated.

Thirty seven burials have been excavated, the majority of which are contained within stone lined graves. Two lintel graves and two slab lined graves have also been found.

A total of forty six skeletons have been removed from the site to date for examination by Drogheda Doctor Laureen Buckley, who has also worked on the site.[8]

CHAPTER 18
"Precious memories and Changing times".

Our past has been meticulously and passionately recorded by the many archaeologists and historians local and national, who have gone before us. They have left behind a legacy of important information, an ocean of recorded knowledge of our origins, from which we gain the knowledge, of who we are, how it was, and when it all began. The recording of history is never ending, the present, is a continuation of the past, recorded and updated with the same enthusiasm and skill, as those that went before. But for some local historians it can be a labour of love as well, getting to the heart of the matter, with the invaluable assistance of the local storyteller. And so, it goes on and on tirelessly, from one generation to the next.

The following are stories told by local people, who can remember back sixty and seventy years, and also have the added ability of being able to remember stories told to them by their parents and peers. These stories are the light-hearted but none the less important side and are the real gems of our local history. To keep the scale balanced between the strict recording of the facts, and the human existence in it all, told in simple language by ordinary people, we won't ever hear the likes of them again. When these people leave us, it will be the end of an era.

Local Storytellers:
Willow Keneghan is a well known local man from Bettystown, who has lived here all his life. He has a wide and varied knowledge of his beloved Bettystown and the surrounding areas. We were surprised and delighted at our good fortune at being able to spend a few hours talking and listening to this fine man. He related stories about times past, in his quiet unassuming way, many interesting anecdotes about local characters and strange happenings in the area that has been long since forgotten.

The following are some of these very interesting tales:
Delaney a well known local family, along with Captain Lyons of Mornington, bought or leased the ground where the Golf-links are to-day, from Mr. J. Brabazon. The land at the time was a mass of rabbit burrows, (if anyone wanted to catch these rabbits, they had to pay a fee to a man by the name of Andrew Murphy, who set the traps). However, in time the land was sorted out and the golf course was laid out, and opened to the public, which is still going strong. Mr. Delaney sold his share to the present owner Mrs Lyons, which she leases to the Golf Club. Her property stretches from the back of Pat Boshell's Supermarket in Bettystown, to the Maiden Tower in Mornington.[1]

In 1972/73, **Tara Mines** (John Tully) considered shipping their 'ore' from Mornington. In order to enable them to do this, they had to buy the lease from the Golf Club, and then purchased the lands from Mrs Lyons, they also bought more land from Harry's Supermarket, all the way down to the sea. However, the fishermen from Mornington objected to this project, on the grounds, that it would ruin their own livelihood, which is fishing.[2]

In those days all the fishermen and their families owned a donkey. The donkey was used to cart water from the pump. Every Saturday the donkeys were given a 'day off' and let out to graze the grass where the golf course is today. The young boys from the locality would line up the donkeys in the field, which is now Bettystown's Caravan park (the property of Dessie Lynch) and have a rodeo.

One Saturday, Willow was riding one of these donkeys, and the donkey raced after a dog, Willow fell off and broke his arm. He had to spend seven weeks in Navan Hospital, this was in the year 1932 when he was only ten years old. A Taxi driver in the neighbourhood called Casey drove him to the hospital.

Nanny Bolger was a local character, her father came from Wexford, and her mother had relatives in Drogheda, people by the name of McGinns, who lived in Mell. Her parents emigrated to America and we believe Nanny was born on the boat, when they were returning to Ireland, she used to say she was American. This lady was a woman of means, but she never married. She owned three thatched houses in Bettystown. Even though she used to say that she was an American, she was also proud to be from Wexford. Her father worked as a butler in Piltown House for Colonel Brodigan and his daughter Nellie, who became Mrs McClintock. During the war, Nanny spent most of her time in Piltown House, knitting socks and gloves for the forces. One of her cottages was situated where St. Ursula's private nursing home is now. She used to rent it out for the summer months.

One summer this lovely cottage was burned to the ground in a fire, and all that was left standing was the chimney! Nanny had three other houses in Bettystown square. One very stormy night with a serious gale force wind blowing in from the sea, low and behold, another of Nanny's cottages was burned to the ground. It appears that this lady was a real character from the past. She had many cats and hens and looked after them all very well in her home!

Little Jack (another local character) got his name because he was under five feet tall. His real name was Jack Fitzsimons, who originally came from Duleek. He was known in those days as a 'journey man',and eighty years old, he used to do odd jobs around the country. A family by the name of Menzies owned a summer house in Bettystown, (the house today is called 'Rannock' and is run as a Bed and Breakfast) they hired little Jack as the caretaker for all the year round. During the summer months when the house was let out to holiday makers, Jack used a shed close by as his place for sleeping. Every night he'd walk down the strand to McLoughlins 'The Beach Inn' for his bottle of porter.

There used to be a shop beside McLoughlin's Pub (The Beach Inn) called the Cosy Corner. This was a confectionery shop, and during the summer months the Keneghans used to make ice-cream in their home that was sold in the Cosy Corner. Also during those same months Willow used to caddie for people playing golf. He was kept very busy, his pay was 1s 3p for every three hours work.

There was also a shop attached to the Neptune Hotel and another one at the Bawn.

Piccadilly were a group of houses in the vicinity of the Neptune Hotel, these were only rented out during the summer months. One house could cost as much as four pounds for the season. May Murphy, who was well past her prime, used to rent one of the Piccadilly houses regularly. In those days, you had to rent a house for at least one month. Bettystown was a very popular seaside resort, with holiday makers coming from different parts of Ireland. The residents who owned a summer house started in May to get their houses in order for the holiday season. This work involved airing the mattresses, scrubbing out the floors and white washing the walls inside as well as outside.

Bettystown gardens on the Eastham road was owned by a family called Comiskey. The father and son in this family grew their own fresh fruit and vegetables, and ran a very successful garden centre and shop. Every Saturday they sold their own fresh fruit and vegetables in the shop. The Comiskeys didn't have the facility of 'credit', and to remind their customers of this, they had hanging on the door, a clock, and written on its face in large print the words 'no tick'.

Before the Meath Co. Council built the golflink's road in the 1950s there was a path called the sandy path or sandy track.

When the **Burrows hall** was built it was known as the 'blue shirts' hall. The 'blue shirts' were a political organisation, and they wore blue shirts and black berets. They used this hall for their meetings. A local building contractor bought the hall and then sold it to the Medical Missionaries of Mary. The nuns ran it as a Bingo hall to make money for the Missions and the Hospital.

*Bingo in the Burrows Hall 1960/61 - Top Prize, a trip to Lourdes.
Right to left - Sean Taylor; Maureen taylor; Kevin McAlister and Maureen McAlister;
main man - Pat Moylan (organiser)*

Right to left - Patsy Stack, Mrs. Bennett, Moria McGuirk, Peggie Kerbey, Tilly Noone and Sean Taylor.

During the war years coal became very scarce as the ships at sea were run on coal like the steam trains. Quite often coal would be washed up on the beach. The local people went down to the strand daily, in the hope of finding some coal in order to keep their own home fires burning.

Most foods were rationed during the war. People were allowed half an ounce of tea per person per week. There was no sugar or jam, and because of the shortage of coal, fires in homes were kept going on damp turf during the cold winter months. All households had ration books, and nothing could be bought without these books. There was plenty of meat and potatoes around, and tea was sometimes made from dandelion roots and scraped potatoes, which helped as a substitute during the tough war years and for many years after.

When the parish of Laytown was very small, the Catholic Church used to close during the winter months. Later when the community grew in numbers, it was decided to leave the church open all the time. Laytown and Mornington were the one parish and it was agreed that each church would take its turn having the early and late masses, and so it was.
The sacristan, Jenny Mulligan, lived near the church. Every Sunday after Mass, the priest had his breakfast in her home. Jenny considered this a great privilege, and the water used during the Mass and also for the breakfast had to be especially drawn from the well.

Willow remembers hearing about the 'bathing boxes' that were lined all along the beach. These boxes had wheels on them and the story goes like this; the ladies would assemble on the beach, step into these boxes, fully clothed in all their finery, change into their bathing costumes, and when they were ready to plunge into the foamy sea, they'd call to the men who were ready, willing and waiting outside for the signal, then two or three would push them down (in the box) to the water edge. When the ladies were finished bathing, they would get back into the boxes, and the men would push them back to the dry sand. The ladies would change back into their finery, and step 'gracefully' out of the box.

In the old days, it was common practice for the farmers to use seaweed to fertilise their land with it. The farmers living around Bettystown and Laytown were no exception to the rule. The seaweed was piled up in banks of 12ft high on the beach, the farmers used to load it up on their carts and take it to their farms.

Most of the children in Bettystown attended Donacarney school and to get there they used to walk through the fields in their bare feet. This was not unusual as most young children went barefooted in those days. There was only one car in the area, and if they were very lucky, they might get a lift to school. Mrs Sheehy was the head school mistress at the time. The children did not use pen and paper for writing purposes, instead, they wrote on slates with special slate pencils.

There was a small shop business run by the Keneghan family situated where 'The Cottage Inn'- Lounge/Bar and Off Licence is now, and owned by John and Emer Gilna of Laytown.

There was a building opposite O'Reilly's supermarket and this was the local dance-hall. Years later this building was bought by Paddy Traynor. He used the premises for making machinery and maintaining it, he also sectioned-off part of the building and used it as a shop for selling his machinery. Not a trace of it can be seen today.

When Willow was about thirty years of age, which would be well over forty years ago, he was digging for gravel in the local gravel pit in the centre of Bettystown, he unearthed a skeleton! Asked, what he had done about it? he replied, "I didn't do anything about it at the time, and, there was no archaeologists notified". Considering the major activities going on there at present, with the discovery of several burial places including a pregnant woman, this particular site which is at present being excavated for the construction of a new housing development cannot be very far from where Willow was digging all those years ago![3]

Sean Faulkner, another local man from Bettystown, with whom we spent many hours. Sean was like a local encyclopaedia with an unbelievable amount of knowledge of the area, covering a period of more than a hundred years.

He knew something about everything, with a memory as clear as spring water, he was indeed very helpful to us and imparted his knowledge with patience and generosity. He also had a collection of funny stories and memorabilia relating to events that may have slipped through the passage of time unrecorded, and 'local characters' of the old days.

In the early 1920's the I.R.A. blew up the railway bridge on the Piltown road because they believed a train travelling from Northern Ireland to Dublin was carrying British soldiers. A man called John Smith, who lived in the bridge house heard the explosion and knew what had happened. As the train approached the bridge, John Smith ran up and down the track waving a red petticoat and demanding the train to stop. He succeeded in bringing the train to a halt, thus, saving the lives of the soldiers. John Smith was awarded a gold watch for doing this. After blowing up the bridge, the culprits went into hiding.

There was always great rivalry between the local football teams, Bettystown and Julianstown. 'Bulky' Barret a local character, played for Bettystown and a man nicknamed the 'Bird' from Ballygarth, played for Julianstown. There are many 'colourful words' put to rhyme, that describe these mighty footballers in action very well, which can be obtained from Sean Faulkner.

At Bettystown Cross, there used to be a forge owned by a Frank Soraghan, who was another local character. This man was big and burly, he used to make up stories for the local children, the stories were about 'Judy Gluepot' and 'Biddy Muck a Pussy'.
Frank Soraghan used to take firewood from Bettystown wood, without permission. At that time, this wood was the property of Colonel Henry Jones. It was clear that no friendship existed between these two men, Frank didn't like Col. Jones, because he never frequented his forge.
One day, Colonel Jones arrived at the forge on horseback, demanding to know if Frank was stealing his wood. Frank being the character that he was, wanted to know where he heard such a story, the Colonel said, it was Mrs. Percy his housekeeper, to which Frank replied," Did she whisper it to ya on the pillow".

Joe McCann ran a soda fountain business just across from the Neptune Hotel, before it was converted into a laundrette, it is still in the hands of the Trustees for the McCann family.[4]

Dessie Lynch
Dessie was delighted to tell us about his family history, which went back to the late nineteenth century. In the 1930s, the Lynch family were well established in Bettystown. Dessie's grandfather accumulated a lot of property, primarily summer houses in and around Bettystown village, some of these we have referred to as 'Piccadilly'.
Grandfather Lynch was the father of four children, two sons and two daughters, Peter one of the two sons was Dessie's father (the other son Andy died at an early age of an unknown illness). While they lived in 'Strandview', his wife became seriously ill and the grandfather brought a housekeeper called 'Cissy' down from Dublin to care for his sick wife.
After Mrs Lynch's death in the 1920s, Cissy remained on as housekeeper. This created much gossip among the people of Bettystown. In an effort to put an end to the vicious gossip that ravaged the village, one Sunday morning Cissy and Dessie's grandfather eloped to Laytown, she, by the beach, and he, by the road.
The priest arrived on horseback from Drogheda and they were married that Sunday morning in Laytown Church. Grandfather Lynch was in his seventies when he married Cissy. They had only three years together, when he died in 1928.
Cissy inherited some of the summer houses for her own use for the remainder of her life. She died in the 1960s.
Peter was around fifty years old when his father re-married. Peter being the only son left, inherited the bakery in Drogheda. He didn't want this responsibility. He loved singing and won medals at the Feis Ceoil, which he took very seriously, and all he wanted to do with his life was to become a professional singer and travel around the country.
In 1954, the new road from Bettystown village to Mornington opened to the public. Before the new road was put in place, there was only a little gate on a dirt track between two sheds (which is now the local hair dressing salon) and the Beach Inn. The two sheds were removed by the Local County Council to make way for the new road.
That same year Dessie and Betty Lynch were married.[5]

Leo Boyle
Leo, a local mussel fisherman, who needs no introduction, has lived in Mornington all his life. However, it was a great pleasure and a unique opportunity for me who doesn't live in Mornington, to spend several hours listening to Leo relating stories of the life and times of this fishing community from when he was a boy.

The following are just two of these fascinating stories:
Mr. and Mrs Kealy lived in comparative comfort in a big house on the High Road in Mornington. Their family was reared and had gone their separate ways to make their fortune.
Mr. Kealy was a solicitor by profession, and employed a butler and housemaid. Mrs Kealy wanted for nothing, she was waited on hand and foot and had enough jewellery to make the Queen of Sheba envious.
Everything was running very smoothly in the Kealy household, until one day when Mrs Kealy died. It was just before the turn of the century, in the 1890's, she was in her early sixties and in very good health, and her sudden death came as a great shock to her family and friends, Mr. Kealy was devastated. Before her final journey she was laid out in the house, and friends came from near and far to pay her their last respects. They marvelled at how lovely she looked even in death. Her beauty was enhanced by some very fine pieces of jewellery, with which she was bedecked.
A large crowd attended the removal and burial, after the ceremony some people went back to the house on the High Road to spend a little time with Mr. Kealy and his family.
Eventually all the neighbours and friends left. Around 2 am, Mr. Kealy was sitting alone in front of the fire, when a knock came to the door, 'that's odd', he thought, 'that sounds exactly like the mistress's (Mrs Kealy) knock'.
As he walked down the hallway towards the front door, he pulled himself together and decided that it must be one of the sympathisers returning for something they left behind. He opened the door and there standing before his eyes was his wife, who was only interred some twelve hours earlier, her hands were bleeding very badly.
Mr. Kealy was obviously in great shock, and in his bewilderment he managed to get her inside and sat her down on a chair, then the mystery unfolded.
The butler who worked for the Kealys had seen the 'corpse' laid out in magnificent jewellery, and thought, 'what a terrible waste of wealth!'.
He decided there and then, when all had quietened down, he would dig up the 'corpse' and remove the jewellery.
At midnight he started digging, it was hard work, but eventually the shovel hit the top of the coffin. He opened the lid and started to strip the body of its valuables, a beautiful necklace worth a fortune, the necklace alone would come to more than his annual wage. There was a brooch, and bracelets all worth a lot of money. He then attempted to remove the rings off the fingers, but with no success. There was only one solution, he thought and took from his pocket a penknife, which he normally used to cut tobacco, and proceeded to cut the ringed finger.
As soon as the knife penetrated the skin of the finger, blood appeared, and Mrs Kealy sat straight up in the coffin. The butler, even though he was a heavy smoker, and in his late fifties, would have broken the world sprint record in his haste to get away.
Mrs Kealy climbed out of the coffin and up the side of the grave and made her way home.
The reality of the situation was - Mrs Kealy had not died, she was in a 'trance', and an air pocket in the coffin kept her alive.
The butler was sought far and wide by the Kealy family, they wanted to reward him for saving the mistress's life, but alas, he was never seen again.

"When I was a kid (Leo) I knew an old lady, who lived adjacent to where the tenth tee is located on the Bettystown golf course. She would have been in her eighties then, her name was Katie Reynolds, but she was more commonly known as Katie the Block.
She was born around 1850, an unmarried lady, Katie lived with her brother Peter, I also remember Peter. Peter and Katie probably had other brothers and sisters, as in those days it was very normal to be part of a large family.
I'm sure times were tough for them all, as Ireland was only coming out of the famine holocaust. The reason why I remember Katie so well is to do with a story my granny told many years ago.

Apparently Katie always had a couple of goats and a few hens, which helped to make ends meet. I'm sure that on many occasions there would be a gap, with the ends not quite meeting.

However, the day dawned when Katie decided to sell the two goats to a local farmer. The goats were great milkers and in the best of condition, and being a very saleable commodity fetched a good price. Katie was delighted with the sale, and the farmer was very happy with the purchase. Nature being sometimes unpredictable, it was not long until the farmer was very unhappy. Whether it was the change of land, or the new ownership, the goats were not giving any milk to the farmer. People at the time were saying, it was hardly the land, as their new home was only two fields away.

The goats became a great talking point at the cross-roads, all sorts of opinions were given, maybe the goats were not happy, maybe they are like some people who find themselves thrust into a new environment and go into a shell.

A couple of months passed and nothing had changed, the mystery continued. Then one morning the farmer got up a little earlier, he headed out to the field, where the goats were. When he came in view of the animals he was rooted to the ground in astonishment at the sight he beheld, there was Katie the Block milking the goats, as she had been doing since the sale, some months ago, as it later transpired".[5a]

Kevin Somers

Kevin was born and raised in Bettystown, he joined the local storytellers with the same enthusiasm and interest to share some of his memories of Bettystown as it was, in the sixties and seventies. For history and posterity, it seems so important to recall and record the life and times of yesteryear, who knows what to-morrow will bring, with the rapid and radical changing face of these fishing villages on the east coast of Ireland.

During World War 11 there were 'war exercises' conducted between the army in Gormanston military camp and the (local) navy reserves, which had their headquarters on the Bettystown/Laytown beach. The nature of the 'exercise' was the local navy reserves had to attack Gormanston camp and the army had to defend it. Well it appears, or so the story goes, the army were out in full strength guarding the roads and beaches, the 'naval reserves' made their way through the fields rivers and marshes, and walked straight into the military camp.

In the early 50's Kevin McAllister introduced the first television to Drogheda, but in order to receive the BBC signal 'it' had to be taken to Bettystown. The T.V. signal from Bettystown, was considered then to be one of the best in the country and has continued so, to this day.

In 1980, there was a national general E.S.B. strike, and the whole country almost without exception was thrown into darkness.

Piltown House was using up to eight cylinder's of gas to heat the house, during this period. At that time Kevin was working in Somers shop in Bettystown. An order for eight cylinders of gas for Piltown House came in. Kevin was assigned to do the delivery. On his way he noticed how dark it was everywhere, with the odd candle flickering in the windows. There was a touch of Christmas in the air, however, when he arrived at the driveway up to Piltown house he was very surprised to see the house lit up. The owner of Piltown House, a Mr. Nevins, endeavoured to explain how he became an exception to the rule and was considered a 'special case', and as young Kevin was unloading the gas Mr. Nevins told him this fascinating story that went as follows:

His beloved faithful dog had died some time earlier, unable to part with the dog, he decided to get the dog stuffed. The only suitable place to have this job done was in England, so he stored the dead dog in his freezer until such time when he could take the animal there. This was his story 'special case' indeed, needless to remark Kevin didn't believe a word of it, but he was very curious as to how this man managed to have the electricity connected in his house, when everyone else was without.

Mr. Nevins invited Kevin to come along and see for himself, and lo, and behold, there was the dead dog (a very large Alsatian) wrapped in a plastic bag in the freezer.[6]

Post Office in Bettystown

Owen Somers, Maureen Taylor's father worked in the Post Office in Drogheda, he married one of the Clinton ladies from Bettystown, and we are told the first Post Office in Bettystown was run from Maureen Taylor's present home, early this century. When Owen's wife died, he married a second time to Jane Keneghan, Maureen's mother.

In the 1930's the office was moved next door and run from a small galvanise shop attached to the main house (on top of the hill) Maureen's mother was the then the post mistress.

In 1945/46, Denis (Den) Somers a brother of Maureen"s took over the post office from their mother, and ran it from a two storey house, called 'the redbricked house' (where Pat's Supermarket is now situated) in Bettystown square. It then had the telephone exchange with about ten subscribers.

In 1964, the Post Office returned to Maureen Taylor's house, its original place, and Maureen became the post mistress. When Maureen retired in 1987, she handed the business over to Nellie Ryan, who ran the Post Office from the Narroway, until it was moved again to its present address Strand View. Sinead Hampshire, daughter of Nellie Ryan, manages the Post Office in Bettystown today.[7]

Owen Somers and the Miss Clintons outside the original Post Office in Bettystown. Maureen Taylor's present home - nearly a hundred years ago

Considering the radical changes already underway, the old images of the fishing villages and seaside resorts, have almost disappeared, and, are now rapidly becoming memories of times past, taking their rightful place in the history books, and making way for progress and the unknown.

Since this compilation of our history is very much the local people's book, the following, gives a very small example of how some of these people, whose families have lived here for generations, feel about the many changes that are taking place all around them.

Tillie Faulkner:
"Bettystown's village has changed greatly since I grew up there in the 1940's. When I go into Bettystown today, I cannot say I feel much enthusiasm for the future of the village. The development which is taking place in the area at present is mainly a concentration of buildings so tall they block out much of the coastal view, and the skyline. I also feel this development will cause massive traffic congestion especially during the summer season, resulting in visitors visiting the resort, seeking relaxation and enjoyment on our lovely beach, will be forced to go elsewhere. I feel relieved, I do not live in the village now".[8]

Anne Somers:
"Bettystown is like a building site at the present. I walk by it all every day and watch the progress, and I am looking forward to the new scene, the new hotel, new shops, new people. But I can always look back and remember Bettystown as it was, with its friendly local small community, sadly, many of whom have since passed away. They will be cherished memories for me, and I can at least reminisce".[9]

Pat Rooney:
"I have lived in Bettystown/Laytown all my life, and now sometimes I find it difficult to grasp all the major changes that are taking place. On the one hand it is bringing fresh new life into the area, and hopefully posterity, but on the other hand I feel we will lose the close community spirit, where the families all knew each other well".[10]

Sean Faulkner:
"Bettystown in 1930, was a very different place from the Bettystown of to-day. Take the area from the Golf Club house to the stream at Brookside, and from McDonough's Pub to the village square, there was a total of sixteen families in permanent residence, some of whom were there over a hundred years. However, the number of houses in the same area exceeded seventy, most of which were owned by the residents in the area. In the Spring the big push got underway, to have the village looking its best for the visitors, during the Summer months. The vacant houses were scrubbed from top to bottom, and mostly let out on a monthly basis.

Coal, paraffin oil and candles were top of the list, when the visitors left their orders in the local shops. There was no electricity in Bettystown during the 1930's. There was a lovely unspoiled beach with no pollution, no cars, motorbikes or even horses. The cars usually parked on the Burrows, as it was very difficult to drive onto the beach, with no solid surface, only loose soft sand, it was an ideal place for a family holiday. However, during the war years and after, holiday bookings were down, and the best of the holiday houses were rented out to business and professional people. When the coast road was constructed in the 1950's, between Bettystown and Mornington, and with car ownership soaring in the sixties the day trippers began to replace the long stay visitors, and a period of decay set in. Some of the holiday houses, through a form of neglect, fell down and became eyesores.

In the 1970's, new houses were built, with the result, it brought new people into the area, and life was returning to the community.

In 1999, the village as we knew it has almost disappeared, on any given day during the Summer months, when the weather is reasonably good, the beautiful beach is almost covered with cars, bikers and horses tearing the dunes to bits. In the evenings, groups of strangers congregate in the square, and the chances of seeing a familiar face when I take a walk in the village, are very slight indeed".[11]

Jim McDonough:
"I have been a resident of the Laytown/Bettystown area for all of my sixty six years - living roughly half of my life in each village. Throughout this time I have seen many changes take place in the twin villages, and, in my opinion, most of these have been positive improvements.

When I lived originally on the Eastham road, I witnessed the arrival of electricity, running water, and a sewerage system - young people today would find it difficult to imagine life without these basic necessities.

When I was young, only a few hundred people lived in the area, and while some may regret the passing of village life as we knew it then, I for one welcome most of the changes that have taken place.

These changes all seemed to start with the opening of the new road from Bettystown to Mornington in the fifties, followed by new housing schemes, first in Laytown and later in Bettystown. Since then the villages have developed rapidly including the building of new schools, a new church and Garda station. All these developments resulted in major improvements in the infrastructure, such as new shops and services, improved transport and communication systems. With the arrival of the 'Celtic Tiger' in the nineties, signs are that, with more and more developers building new houses, apartments and shops, also a new hotel and leisure centre, the area is set to expand more rapidly than ever, during the next few years. I find all this new development in the area very exciting, and please God I will be around a while longer to witness the further expansion of Laytown and Bettystown".[12]

Maureen Taylor:
"I live in one of the three oldest houses left in the village. In the thirties and forties, the main means of earnings was from renting houses to holiday makers during the summer period, which caused an explosion in the population especially during the months June, July and August. May and September were also busy months but not to the same extent.

We had the run of the village to play in and had plenty of entertainment on Sundays watching some cars who risked going onto the beach, getting stuck in the sand. On many of these occasions we would offer our assistance in pushing some of the cars on to more solid ground.

Since there was no proper transport service, most of the children in the area had to walk to Donacarney school. Public transport in the Bettystown area consisted of one bus each way to Drogheda on a Saturday, which improved considerably during the holiday season, mostly for the benefit of the holiday makers.

We did a lot of beach combing, and had many a great haul. For instance, in 1939, the beginning of World War 11, there were shoals of herrings, washed up alive on the beach at Bettystown, and were hopping around on the sand. We gathered them into buckets, and, had salted herrings for a year after that.

Many homes were kept warm, with the coal collected from the beach, before the ships changed over to oil.

I am sad that none of these activities exists today. The strand is littered with plastic bags, bottles, cans and many other unpleasant things. I can no longer see the sea from my home, with all the high rise buildings around me - not a green field in sight.

Where we used to run the area in our bare feet and play ball in the square, it is no longer safe you have to hold a child by the hand".[13]

Vincent McDonough
"I wish to compliment everybody who helped to compile this book. It is of great interest to somebody like me who lived in the district and knew so many locals and holiday makers from both the nineteenth and twentieth centuries. I wish it every success".[14]

References

Maps
1. Cover: extract from William Larkin's Map of 1812.
2. Extract from Map of the Lands of Mornington, Donneygarney, Betagh'stown, Minitstown, and Ninch. by Samuel Bowe, (March 1771).

Chapter 1
1. The Kingdom and County of Meath : *by Rev. John Brady, Diocesan Historian* Riocht na Midhe. (1956) Vol 1. No 2,
1a. Prehistoric Ireland: *by...G.F. Mitchell.* Course of Irish History (1994)
2. Tara, The European Background (The Celts-Iron Age): *by...Rev. R.R. Callary P.P.,V.F., M.R.S: AI:,* Riocht na Midhe, Vol 1. No.1. 1955.
3. Prehistoric Ireland: *by...G. F. Mitchell.* Course of Irish History (1994)
4. The Territory of Ancient Meath: *by...Rev. R.R. Callary M.R.S.A.I.* Riocht na Midhe, (Vol 1. No 1. 1955).
5. History of Ireland: *by. .E.A. D'Alton (1845)*
6. Heroes and Warriors - Fionn Mac Cumhail: *by...John Matthew (1988)*
7. Poem : *by...Standish O'Grady (Heroes and Warriors by John Matthew, 1988)*
8. Heroes and Warriors - Fionn Mac Cumhail: *by...John Matthew (1988)*
9. Cuchulain - The Champion of Ulster: *by...Kevin McCaffrey. (1989)*
10. A History of Julianstown: *by...Julianstown Guild I.C.A.(1985)*
11. Poem, The Death of Laogh, Cuchulain's Charioteer: *by...Francis Ledwidge*
12. Iron Age, Burial Mound: *by...David Sweetman M.A.* Riocht na Midhe 1982/83.
13. Julianstown: *by...Michael Ward, M.R.S.A.I.* Riocht na Midhe (1967) Vol 4. No. 1.
14. Poem, The Nanny Water Stream: *by...James McCullen (1848)*
15. A Social History of Ancient Ireland : *by...P.W. Joyce Vol 1. Published Longmans - Green & Co., London 1903.*
16. Our Ancient Heritage: *by...Edward James Published in 1977, by...The Educational Co. Ireland.*
17. History of Ireland : *by...Richard English, (Gill & Macmillon, 1991)*
18. Patrick, In His Own Words: *by...Joseph Duffy(1972)*
19. Patrick, In His Own Words: *by...Joseph Duffy (1972)*
20. Ancient Meath: *by Dean Anthony Cogan, 3 Vols. (1862, 1867 and 1870.)*
21. Patrick, In His Own Words; *by...Joseph Duffy(1972)*
22. A History of Julianstown: *by...Julianstown Guild I.C.A.(1985)*
23. The Life of St. Columba: *by...St. Adamnan- translated by Wentworth Hushe. Education Co. of Ireland 1905.*
24. A History of Julianstown: *by...Julianstown Guild I.C.A.(1985)*
25. The First Christian Kings: *by...E.A. D'Alton* History of Ireland (1845)
26. Song/Poem, The Harp that Once Through Tara's Halls: *by...Thomas Moore*
27. Ancient Meath (Diocese of Duleek) : *by..Dean Anthony Cogan. (1862,1867&1870)*
28 The Beginnings of Christianity 5th/6th Centuries: *by...Thomas Cardinal O'Fiaich* The Course of Irish History.(1994)

Chapter 2.
1. The age of the Viking Wars: *by...Liam de Paor* The Course of Irish History.(1994)
2. Ancient Meath (Annals of Duleek): *by...Dean Anthony Cogan. (1862,1867&1870)*
3. History of Drogheda: *by E. A. D'Alton (1844)*

4. History of Duleek - Chaos A.D. 1000 - 1169 *by...Rev. Philip Cuffe, C.C.*
    Riocht na Midhe. (1964) Vol.3. No. 2.
5. The Age of Viking Wars: *by...Liam de Paor*
    The Course of Irish History.(1994)
6. 11th and 12th Century: *by...Brien O'Cuiv*
    The Course of Irish History.(1994)
7. The Normans: Arrival and Settlement (1169-c 1300) *By... F. X. Martin*
    The Course of Irish History.(1994)
8. Medieval Settlements in Co. Meath: *by...Brian Grahan*
    Riocht na Midhe, (1974) Vol. 5. No. 4.
9. Settlement and Society in Medieval Ireland: *to...F. X. Martin o.s.a.*
    Edited by...John Bradley (Boethius Press, Kilkenny 1988)
10. Unpublished notes: *Kieran Campbell (Archaeologist), Laytown, Co. Meath.(1992)*
11. A History of Julianstown: *Compiled by Julianstown Guild I.C.A. (1985)*
12. Gormanston Register (1175-1397) Royal Society of Antiquaries of Ireland.(1916)
13. The Civil Survey (1654-56) The Barony of Duleek' In the County of East-Meath.
    by...R.C. Simington (1940)
14. Griffith's Valuation (1856).
15. East Meath Dovecot: *by Michael Ward.*
    Riocht na Midhe V. No. 3, 1973.
16. Ref. from Property Deeds: *Luke Van Doorslaer,-Owner of Ninch farm.(1998)*
17. Notes-Sonairte Ecology Centre: *Trevor Sargent.(*
    Published by..W.P.Kelly, of Grafton Street and Lower Ormond Quay, Dublin.(1873)
3. History of Drogheda: *by...E A. D'Alton (1844)*
4. Draycotts of Mornington: *by...Stephen B. Barnwall F.I.G.R.S.*
    Riocht na Midhe (1977). 1992)
17a.The Nanny : *by... Tom Wiseman ——A History of Julianstown (1985).*
18. History of Julianstown (1985): *Compiled by Julianstown Guild I.C.A.*
19. Unpublished notes, from the Mosney Holiday Centre File .
20. Summer Guide to Inis-na-Righ (1987): *by Joe Downey.*
21. Medieval Settlements in Co. Meath: *By... Brian Grahan*
    Riocht na Midhe.(1974) Vol. 5. No. 4.
22. The Normans: Arrival and Settlement (1169-c. 1300) *by...F. X. Martin*
    The Course of Irish History.(1994)
23. Mornington, Alias Marinerstown: *by...Michael Ward*
    Journal of the Old Drogheda Society. No 6.(1989)
24. Diocese of Meath, Ancient and Modern: *by...Dean Anthony Cogan*
    Riocht na Midhe. (Vols.1, 2,3, 1862, 1867, 1870)
25. High Crosses of Ireland (1992): *by...Peter Harbison*
26. Small sandstone - High Cross and base Colp, Co. Meath.(1981)
    Kieran Campbell, (Archaeologist), Laytown, Co. Meath. (In reference 25)
27. Colpe an East Meath Parish: *by Micheal Mac an Bhaird*
    Dinnsean Chas, (1964).
28. Some Notes on Rath Colpa: *by...Ormonde D. Waters,*
    Riocht na Midhe, (1965) Vol.3 No.3.
29. Notes on the Rise and Fall of a Great Meath Estate: *by...Rev. C.C. Ellison M.A.*
    Riocht na Midhe.(1966) Vol 3.
30. Wellington, His Irish Connections: Published by...Meath Heritage Centre, Trim, Co. Meath. (1992).
31. Notes on the Rise and Fall of a Great Meath Estate: *by...Rev. C.C. Ellison M.A.*
    Riocht na Midhe. (1966) Vol.3.

Chapter 3.
1. Draycott of Mornington: *by...Stephen B. Barnwall F.I.G.R.S.*
    Riocht na Midhe (1977)
2. Monastic Hibernicum: *by...Mervyn Archdall*
5. The Death of Alice Draycott: *by...E. St. John Brooks, Ltt. D., M.R.I.A.*
    Co. Louth Archaeological Journal.(1954)

6. Donacarney School Centenary (1873-1973).
7. Draycotts of Mornington: *by Stephen B. Barnwall F.I.G.R.S.*
   Riocht na Midhe (1977).

Chapter 4.

1. The Rebellion of 1641: *by Aiden Clarke*
   The Course of Irish History.(1994)
2. History of Drogheda: *by E.A. D'Alton(1844)*
3. Unpublished notes *by Mary F. McCullen (1884-1970)*
4. Draycott Castle: *by...Mr. O'Donohoe*
   I.T.A. General Survey (19/9/42).
5. The Tichborne Acquisition of the Plunkett Estate of Beaulieu:
   By... Harold O'Sullivan, Journal of the Old Drogheda Society, No. 7.(1990)
6. 1603-1660: *by...Aiden Clarke*
   The Course of Irish History.(1994)
7. Cromwell at Drogheda: *by...Tom Reilly (1993)*
8. Cromwell at Drogheda: *by...Tom Reilly (1993)*
9. Cromwell at Drogheda: *by...Tom Reilly (1993)*
10. The Black Curse of Cromwell (Ireland 1649-1650): *by...Denis Esson (1971)*
11. Drogheda Library File on 'Battle of the Boyne'.
12. Battle of the Boyne: *by...Enda O'Boyle. (1990)*
13. Duleek: *by...Enda O'Boyle. (1990)*
14. Battle of the Boyne, symbol past and present: *by...Interchurch Group for Faith and Politics*—— The Irish Times, 30th June 1990.

Chapter 5.

1. Penal Laws: *by...Maureen Wall*
   The Course of Irish History.(1994)
2. Part 1. The years before, Tyrant and Slave: *by...Seamus O'Loinsigh*
   Riocht na Midhe.(1966) Vol.3. No.4.
   Poem '98. (Source unknown)
3. Bi-centenary of 1798 in Meath: Comaradh,
   Riocht na Midhe (1998).
4. Poem - Paud O'Donohoe: *by...Patrick Archer*
   The 1798 Rebellion in Meath...*by Seamus O'Loinsigh.*
   Riocht na Midhe (1997)
5. 1798 Bi-centenary celebrations: Meath Chronicle (23rd May 1998)
6. Beaulieu House: *by...James Garry*
   Co. Louth Archaeological and Historical Society. (1990)
7. Burke's Peerage, London. (Brabazon Family)
8. Monumental Inscriptions from Termonfectin Cemetery, Co. Louth: *by...James Garry* and Donald Murphy. The Irish Genealogist (1991/2).
9. Mornington Graveyard Inscriptions: *by...James Garry*
   Journal of the Old Drogheda Society, (1989) No.6.
10. Notes on the Rise and Fall of a Great Meath Estate: *by...Rev. C.C. Ellison M.A.*
    Riocht na Midhe. (1966) Vol 3. No. 4. and (1967) Vol. 4. No 1.
11. Burke's Peerage, London. (Brabazon Family)
12. The Building's of Ireland-North Leinster: *by..Christine Casey and Allister Rowan.*
    Penguin (1993)
13. Life and Correspondence (1914) - Martin M. Wellesley papers.
14. Mrs Bawn Drew, Mornington. (Oral and notes,1999)

15. Mornington Graveyard Inscriptions: *by...James Garry*
    Journal of the Old Drogheda Society, No.6. (1989)
16. Colpe Graveyard Inscriptions: *by...James Garry,*
    Riocht na Midhe. (1992/3)
17. Mrs Bawn Drew, Mornington. (Notes,1999)
18. Letter (dated, 17th. March, 1978): *from Dennis Betagh, Wellington, New Zealand.*

19. The Drogheda Argus, 6th Feb. 1847.
20. Sean Faulkner, The Narroways, Bettystown. (Oral 1998)
21. The Story of the Irish Race: *by...Seamus MacManus*
    Third Edition - New York and Irish Publishing Co. (1922)
22. Letter (dated,17th. March,1978): *from Dennis Betagh, Wellington, New Zealand.*
23. More Irish Families: *by...Edward McLysaght/ Lieutenant. (O'Gorman Ltd.,1960)*
24. Agrarian violence in Meath 1835-44: *by...Desmond Mooney*
    Riocht na Midhe (1990-91).

Chapter 6.
1. The age of Daniel O'Connell (1800-47): *by...J.H. Whyte*
   The Course of Irish History.(1994)
2. Donacarney School Centenary (1873-1973).
3. Topographical Dictionary of Ireland *by.. Samuel. Lewis (1837)*
4. A celebration of Drogheda's 800: *by...Drogheda Independent.(1994)*
5. Frank Johnson, Colpe/Donacarney. (local storyteller,1998)
6. The Buildings of Ireland - North Leinster: *by Christine Casey and Allister Rowan.* - Penguin (1993).
7. Sean Faulkner, The Narroways, Bettystown. unpublished notes. (1998)
8. Willow Keneghan, Bettystown. unpublished.(1996)
9. A celebration of Drogheda's 800: *by...Drogheda Independent.(1994)*
10. Sean Faulkner, The Narroways, Bettystown. Oral and unpublished notes (1998)
11. Peter McEvoy, The Uncrowned King of Drogheda.
    Published by Wilson &McBrinn Ltd. (1926-1986).
12. The Building's of Ireland - North Leinster: *by ...Christine Casey and Allister Rowan.* - Penguin (1993)
13. Cairnes of Stameen: *by...John McCullen*
    Journal of the Old Drogheda Society, No.7. (1990)
14. St. Mary's Church of Ireland, Drogheda. Graveyard Inscriptions: *by..James Garry*
    Journal of the Old Drogheda Society, No.5. (1986)
15. Sean Faulkner,The Narroways, Bettystown. Oral and unpublished notes. (1998)
16. 'The Threshing' ....*by... Patrick Kavanagh.*
17. Sean Faulkner, The Narroways, Bettystown. Oral and unpublished notes (1998)
18. St. Mary's Church of Ireland, Julianstown, Graveyard Inscriptions: *by Jim Garry*
    (Not published yet)

Chapter 7.
1. Cholera: *by...Maureen Wilson*
   Journal of the Old Drogheda Society. 1986, No. 5, page 27.
2. Famine and the Local Economy, Co. Meath. 1845-55: *by...Peter Connell*
   Riocht na Midhe (1963).
3. The Famine Story: Millmount Museum, *150th Anniversary Commemoration.(1995)*
4. The Great Famine in Co. Meath. *150th Anniversary Commemoration (1845-1995)*
5. Famine and the Local Economy, Co. Meath. 1845-55: *by...Peter Connell*
   Riocht na Midhe (1963).
6. The Famine Story: Millmount Museum, *150th Anniversary Commemoration.(1995)*
7. Famine and the Local Economy, Co. Meath. 1845-55: *by...Peter Connell*
   Riocht na Midhe (1963).
8. Summer Guide to Inis-na-Righ. *(1987)*
9. A History of Duleek: *by...Enda O'Boyle. (1990)*
10. The Tara (Bettystown) Brooch: *Drogheda Independent 29th December 1967.*
11. Summer Guide to Inis-na-Righ. *(1987)*
12. History of Ireland: *by...E. A. D'Alton. (1845)*
13. Griffith Valuation (1856).

Chapter 8.
1. Fenianism, Home rule and the Land War (1850-91): *by...Dr. T. W. Moody*
   The Course of Irish History.(1994)
1a. Salmon Fishing: Oral and unpublished notes, *by..Christy Reynolds (1998)*

2. Mussel Fishing: *by...Leo Boyle, Mornington, Co. Meath. (Unpublished notes, 1996)*
   Song: 'Red Sails in the Sunset': *by immy Kennedy and Hugh Williams.*
3. "My Life at Sea": *by...Captain Denis Lyons - Privately Published*
4. Poem: Wooden Ships and Iron Men *by...Frederick W. Wallace*
   "My Life at Sea": *by...Captain Denis Lyons*
5. A Tribute to Captain Denis Lyons: Drogheda Independent 18th June 1938.
6. Celtic songs of the Sea ' The Water is Wide' Dolphin Records, Great Ship Street, Dublin (1998).
7. Frances Moran, Mornington,
   Resident at St. Ursula's Nursing Home, Bettystown, Co. Meath. (Oral,1996)
8. Tragic death of Mr. Nicholas Moran, Julianstown:
   Drogheda Argus, 27th Nov. 1909.
9. Visit Mornington, with Jim Garry: The Local News 12th June 1987.
10. Death of the Rev. Druitt, Vicar of Colpe:
    The Drogheda Argus, 30th Oct. 1869.
11. The Yacht Club...*by...Dorothy McQuillan (Oral and notes,1998)*
12/13. Visit Mornington, with Jim Garry: The Local News, 12th June 1987.
14. I.T.A. Topographical and General Survey, 19th Sept 1942.
15. The Woman who lived in Maiden Tower: *by...the late Dr. George A.Little.*
16. and - The Dublin Penny Journal Vol 11, page 74.
17. Sean Faulkner, The Narroways, Bettystown. (Oral 1998)
18. I.T.A. Topographical and General Survey. 19th Sept. 1942.

Chapter 9.
1. Neptune Hotel, Bettystown: Drogheda Independent (1884-1984)
2. Griffith's Valuation (1856).
3. Louth County Guide and Directory: *by...G. H. Bassets (1886).*
4. Leinster Journal (25th June 1870).
5. The Drogheda Independent (25th June 1887)
6. Willow Keneghan, Bettystown.(Oral,1996)
7. Paddy Monahan, Baltray. (Oral and notes, 1998)
8. Sean Faulkner, The Narroways, Bettystown. (Oral,1996)
9. Paddy Monahan, Baltray. (Oral and notes, 1998)
10 Sean Faulkner,The Narroways,Bettystown. (Oral, 1996)
11 Terry and Michael Keogh, Bettystown. (Oral,1998)
12 Paddy Monahan, Baltray, Co. Louth. (Oral and notes,1998)
13. Deeds: part of lands at Laytown, Co. Meath. 1852, 1864 and 1897.
    John McCullen, Beamore, Co. Meath.
13a. Paddy Monahan, Baltray, Co. Louth. (Oral and notes, 1996)
14. Bassetts Louth (1886): Drogheda Independent (22nd July 1885)
15. Paddy Monahan, Baltray, Co. Louth. (Oral and notes, 1998)
16. Margaret O'Donaghue, Alverno (House) Hotel, Laytown. (1999)
17. Dubliner's Diary: *by Terry O'Sullivan*
    Evening Press, 12th May 1973.
18. Marie Callan (nee Stafford) Donacarney. (Oral, and notes,1998)
19. Dubliner's Diary or Drogheda Independent (March 1976).
20. Drogheda Independent

Chapter 10.
1. The Old House by the Boyne: *by...Mrs J. Sadlier (Gill &Co. 1904)*
2. Visit Mornington, with Jim Garry - The Local News, 5th June 1987.
3. Scotland's gift to Ireland - Part 2 - Consolidation 1886 - 1889:
    Tom Gilroy and Mornington Golf Course 1886.
4. Centenary of Baltray Golf Club..*by...Steve Mulqueen, researched by Jim Garry(1992)*
5. Laytown and Bettystown Golf Club (1996): *by...O.T. Somers (unpublished)*
5a Pauline Lally - sister of Paddy Farrell.
6. Drogheda Independent (19th August 1901).
7. Dubliner's Diary: *by...Terry O'Sullivan,*
    Evening Press, 11th June 1973.

8. Drogheda Independent (12th August 1983).
9. Drogheda Independent (13th August 1993).
10. Drogheda Independent (12th August 1994).

Chapter 11.
1. When Bettystown had a railway station: *Researched by Jim Garry*
    The Local News, 26th June 1987.
2. Dublin/Drogheda railway line: *by...Elcock Delaney (1901)*
3. When Bettystown had a railway station: *Researched by Jim Garry(1987)*
4. Drogheda Merchants of the 18th century: *by...John Fitzgerald M.A.*
    Journal of the Old Drogheda Society, No.5. (1986)
5. The Whitworths and Drogheda in the 19th century: *by...Jane M. Renfrew*
    Journal of the Old Drogheda Society, No 6. (1989)
6. Colpe church of Ireland Graveyard Inscriptions: *by...James Garry*
    Riocht na Midhe 1992/3.
7. Christian Brothers (Piltown House): Brother Aodh P. Caomhanach, Dublin.(1996)
8. Monsignor John Hanly, P.P. Laytown, Co. Meath. (Oral 1999)
9. The Building's of Ireland - North Leinster: *by...Christine Casey and Allister Rowan.*
    Penguin (1993)
10. I.T.A. Survey 19-9-42—O'Donaghue
11. Some notes on the Ogham Stone at Piltown: *by Ormonde D.P. Waters*
    Riocht na Midhe.(1969) Vol.4. No. 3.
12. Ted McCormack, Piltown Rd., Piltown. Local storyteller (Oral,1996/98)
13. Auction at Piltown House: Hamilton and Hamilton (Estate) Ltd. Auctioneers.
    (Catalogue,1960)

Chapter 12.
1 Drogheda Argus: 10th and 17th January, and 6th March (1880)
2. Grangegorman Prison records/ Mountjoy Prison records.(1890)
3 Grangegorman Prison records/ Mountjoy Prison records.(1890)
4. 1938 - Archives of Folklore Department, University College, Dublin.
5. Christina Bowden, Chord Rd., Drogheda/ Mrs Smyth, Chord Rd. Drogheda.(1938)
6. Anthony McDonnell,/Mr. Peter McDonnell, 42,John Street, Drogheda.(1938)
7. Mathew Reilly, 11, Old Hill, Drogheda/Mary Meehan, Sampson's Lane,
    Drogheda.1938)
8. Grangegorman Prison records/Mountjoy Prison records.(1890)
9. Sean Faulkner,The Narroways, Bettystown, (Oral, 1996)
10. Vincie Mullen, Mornington.(Oral, 1996)

Chapter 13.
1 1891 - 1921 *by...Donal McCartney*
    The Course of Irish History.(1994)
2. Willow Keneghan., Bettystown, (Oral, 1996)
3. Events of Easter 1916 in Drogheda: *by John McCullen,*
    Journal of the Old Drogheda Society, No.8. (1992)
4. National Gallery: Adrien Leharivel (Oral,1998)
5. Mornington, alias Marinerstown: *by Michael Ward,*
    Journal of the Old Drogheda Society. No 6 (1989)
6. The Call of St. Mary's: *by... John McCullen. (1984)*
7. Colpe Church of Ireland Graveyard Inscriptions: *by...James Garry*
    Riocht na Midhe 1992/3.
8. Henry Draycott and the Draycotts of Mornington, Co. Meath:
    by... Stephen B.arnwall F.I.G.R.S. Riocht na Midhe (1977).
9. History of Drogheda: *by...E.A. D'Alton. (1844)*
10. Donacarney School Centenary (1873-1973).
11. Visit Mornington, with Jim Garry: The Local News, 5th June 1987.
12. The Call of St. Mary's: *by...John McCullen (1984).*

13. The Building's of Ireland - North Leinster: *by...Christine Casey and Allister Rowan.*
    Penguin (1993)
14. History of the Diocese of Meath 1860-1993: *by...Olive C. Curran. (1995)*
15. Mornington Graveyard Inscriptions: *by...James Garry.*
    Journal of the Old Drogheda Society No 6. (1989).
16. Sacred Heart Church, Laytown, Centenary 1876-1976: *by... Michael Ward.*
17. P.J. Dodd, Drogheda, Architect and Civil Engineer:
    by... P.J. Geraghty BSc., DIS., MCD., MRTPI.
    Journal of the Old Drogheda Society, No. 9. (1994)
18. Sacred Heart Church, Laytown, Centenary 1876-1976: *by...Michael Ward.*
19. Sacred Heart Church, Laytown, Centenary 1876-1976: *by...Michael Ward.*
    (A Final Word. *by...Fr. P. Fallon.*)
20. The Tale of two 'Towns': *by... O.T. Somers (1995)*
    Published as a supplement to Laytown/Bettystown Golf Club Newsletter.
21. P.J. Dodd, Drogheda, Architect and Civil Engineer:
    by...P.J. Geraghty BSc.,DIS.,MCD.,MRTPI.
    Journal of the Old Drogheda Society, No. 9. (1994)
22. Irish Times (22nd October 1979). Caroline Walshe.
23. Irish Times (22nd October 1979) Liam Mc Cormack.

Chapter 14.
1. Donacarney School Centenary (1873-1973).
2. Donacarney School Centenary (1873-1973).
3. School and Schoolmasters: *by...Michael Ward,*
    Journal of the Old Drogheda Society No 7. (1990)
4. Primary Education, Laytown (1944-1996):
    Education through the years, Laytown/Bettystown area.
5. Primary Education, Laytown (1944-1996):
    Foreward, *by Monsignor John Hanly P.P.*
6. Primary Education, Laytown (1944-1996):
    Amalgamation 1996, *by Maurice Daly.*
7. History of the Diocese of Meath 1860 -1993 *by...Olive C. Curran, (1995)*
8. History of Drogheda: *by...E. A. D'Alton.(1844)*
9. Brigid Weir, Donacarney School, Donacarney. (Oral and notes1998)
9a. Tillie Faulkner, The Narroways, Bettystown. (Oral 1999)
10. Donacarney School Centenary (1873-1973).
11. Brigid Weir, Donacarney School.(Oral and notes,1998)
12. Donacarney School Centenary (1873-1973)
13. Christie Doggett, St.Mary's Dublin Rd.,Drogheda. (Notes,1996)
14. Malcolm Gordon, Bettystown.(Oral,1998)
15. Jim and Eileen Castle, St. Ursula's Nursing Home, also, Eileen Harmon, Salterstown (Oral 1998)
16. History of the Diocese of Meath (1869-1993): *by...Olive Curran (1995)*
17 Kathleen O'Neill, Ozanam House, (Oral 1998)

Chapter 15.
1. The Night of the Big Wind: *By...Peter Carr, (1991)*
2. Lifeboats on the Boyne (1856-1926): *by Patsy McKenna,*
    Journal of the Old Drogheda Society. No.8. (1992)
3. Shipwreaks of the Irish Coast (1105-1993) *by...Edward J. Bourke.*
4. Drogheda Independent Centenary, 1st June 1984.
5. Nanny Water Coastguard: *by...Michael Ward.*
    Journal of the Old Drogheda Society, 1996, page 112.
6. St. Mary's Church, Julianstown (1995): *by...Bernie Daly.*
7. Elma Delany, Corballis, (Oral 1998)

Chapter 16.
1. Ireland 1921-1966: *by...Patrick Lynch.*
    The Course of Irish History. (1994)
2. Pilot Killed, Drogheda Couple's Miraculous Escape:
    Spectrum Magazine November, 1980.
3. Encyelopedia Britannica, 15th Edition.
4. Mornington Graveyard Inscriptions: *by...James Garry*
    Journal of the Old Drogheda Society. No. 6. (1989)
5. Drogheda Independent, 3rd August 1940.
6. Drogheda Argus, 4th July 1942.
7. Bombs dropped near Drogheda..........*Drogheda Independent 4th Jan. 1941*
8. Sean Faulkner,The Narroways, Bettystown. (1996)

Chapter 17.
1. Death of James Tully: S.I.P.T.U., Vol 3, page 1.
2. Drogheda Independent, 29th May 1992.
3. Irish Press, May, 1992.
4. Gaelic Football: *by...Carbery, Published by Gaelic Publicity Services July 1941.*
5. Oral and written notes: *by..Sean Faulkner, Bettystown, Patrick Reynolds, Mornington, Des Taaffe, Dublin, Paddy Monahan, Baltray and Tommy Weir, Mornington (1998)*
6. Irish Times, 4th Nov. 1983. *Eamonn P.Kelly (Archaeologist)*
7. Colp, Co. Meath. *by...Margaret Gowen,*
    Excavations 1988, Summary Accounts of Archaeological, Excavations in Ireland.
8. Drogheda Independent, 4th Sept. 1998.

Chapter 18.
1. Willow Keneghan, Bettystown, Co. Meath. (Oral, 1996)
2. John Tully, Painstown, Drogheda.(Oral, 1998)
3. Willow Kenaghan, Bettystown, Co. Meath. (Oral, 1996)
4. Sean Faulkner,The Narroways, Bettystown. Co. Meath. (Oral and notes,1996)
5. Dessie Lynch, Bettystown, Co. Meath. (Oral,1996)
6. Leo Boyle, Mornington, Co. Meath. (Oral and notes, 1999)
7. Kevin Somers, Bettystown, Co. Meath. (Oral,1998)
8. Maureen Taylor, Bettystown, Co. Meath (Oral,1999)
9. Tilly Faulkner, The Narroways, Bettystown, Co. Meath. (Unpublished notes,1999)
10. Anne Somers, Bettystown, Co. Meath. (Unpublished notes,1999)
11. Pat Rooney, Laytown/Bettystown, Co. Meath. (Unpublished notes,1999)
12. Sean Faulkner, The Narroways, Bettystown, Co. Meath (Unpublished notes,1999)
13. Jim McDonough, Laytown/Bettystown, Co. Meath. (Unpublished notes,1999)
14. Maureen Taylor, Bettystown, Co. Meath. (Unpublished notes,1999)
15. Vincent McDonough, Bettystown, Co. Meath. (Unpublished notes,1999)

SPONSORS

We would like to gratefully acknowledge our Sponsors for their great support.

Frank Flynn, R. B. Daly Auctioneers, Laurence Street, Drogheda.
Tom Kelly, Inse Pharmacy, Laytown & The Anchorage Pharmacy, Bettystown.
Laytown & Bettystown Golf Club, Bettystown, Co. Meath.
East Meath Credit Union, Laytown, Co. Meath.
Phelim McCloskey, Mosney Holiday Centre, Mosney, Co. Meath.
Halco (Plant) Ltd., Halco Hire Centre, Mell Industrial Centre, Drogheda.
Chris Hampshire, Blue Line Transport Ltd., Tubberfin, Donore, Co. Meath.
McCormack's Amusements, Bettystown, Co. Meath.
Donal Black, Black's Garden Centre, Smithstown, Co. Meath.
John McGrane, Welding Company, Mornington, Co. Meath.
Tony Stafford, Solid Fuel & Gas Supplier, Donacarney, Co. Meath.
Paul Berrill, Lawnmowers & Bicycle Sales & Repairs, Mornington, Co. Meath.
William Murtagh, Suppliers of Wallpaper, Paint, Hardware, Fair Green, Drogheda.
Vincent Black, Builder, Mornington Road, Drogheda.
Gormanstown Service Station, Gormanstown, Co. Meath.
Murphy's Concrete, Balbriggan, Co. Meath.
Sandra"s Quick Shop, Keenogue, Jullianstown, Co. Meath.
John McGrane, Antiques, Delvin Bridge, Gormanstown, Co. Meath.
Tony Stafford, The Cock Tavern, Gormanstown, Co. Meath.
Tom Woods, Pine & Cane Furniture, Moorechurch, Julianstown, Co. Meath.
O'Reilly Bros., Narrow West Street, Drogheda.
Sean McManus Tyres Ltd., Balmarino, Marsh Road, Drogheda.
Glenside Hotel, Dublin Road, Drogheda.
Sinead Hampshire, Bettystown Post Office, Bettystown, Co. Meath.
Ellen Ryan, The Narroway, Bettystown, Co. Meath.
Boyne Valley Hotel, Dublin Road, Drogheda, Co. Meath.
Boyne Valley Foods, Platin, Drogheda.
Jimmy Gilna, The Cottage Inn, Laytown, Co. Meath.
John O'Callaghan, Butchers, Ballsgrove, Drogheda.
Pat Boshell, Centra Supermarket, Bettystown, Pat's Foodmarket, Laytown.

Supported by FAS
****

The aerial photographs on the opposite page were taken in July '99 by David Smith, Prefton, Minnistown, Laytown, Co. Meath.